Expatriate

Manchester University Press

Expatriate

Following a migration category

Sarah Kunz

MANCHESTER UNIVERSITY PRESS

The right of Sarah Kunz to be identified as the author of this work has been asserted by them in accordance with the Copyright, Designs and Patents Act 1988.

Published by Manchester University Press
Oxford Road, Manchester M13 9PL

www.manchesteruniversitypress.co.uk

British Library Cataloguing-in-Publication Data
A catalogue record for this book is available from the British Library

ISBN   978 1 5261 5429 3   hardback
ISBN   978 1 5261 8257 9   paperback

First published 2023
Paperback published 2025

The publisher has no responsibility for the persistence or accuracy of URLs for any external or third-party internet websites referred to in this book, and does not guarantee that any content on such websites is, or will remain, accurate or appropriate.

Typeset
by New Best-set Typesetters Ltd

Contents

Acknowledgements

In researching and writing this book, I have experienced great generosity, helpfulness and support from many people, some of them literal strangers. This has been inspirational and important, and I would like to thank all these people for their support. I am especially grateful to everyone who allowed me to learn about their life, who shared feelings, thoughts and ideas. I am also grateful to the many wonderful family, friends, teachers and colleagues who have accompanied and supported me in writing this book. Tariq Jazeel has been incredibly supportive throughout the project, and I thank him for his always sharp and generous engagement with my work. I am also thankful to Claire Dwyer for sharing her kindness and insight and for supporting the project throughout. Ben Page and Parvati Raghuram provided engaged feedback and stimulating suggestions as examiners of the thesis. Jason Dittmer provided helpful feedback on the book proposal and told me to get on with it when I much needed the encouragement.

Research depends on countless acts of support, small and large, and from London to The Hague and Nairobi, the kindness and generosity of many people has been indispensable. I thank everyone at the Expatriate Archive Centre, particularly Kristine Racina and Eva Barbisch, for their warm welcome and committed assistance with this research. I fondly remember my time with the many women and some men at the East Africa Women's League in Nairobi, who let me join them for a while and shared their personal and organisational stories. I thank especially former League President Clare Jethwa. Kuda, Sarah and Akinyi shaped my research in Nairobi in crucial ways and I remain grateful for their kindness and support. I also thank the staff at University College London, the British Institute in

Eastern Africa in Nairobi, the various archives I consulted, and at Manchester University Press who so competently supported my work.

I am grateful to those who provided feedback on chapters, thoughts and inspiration: Bridget Anderson, Emily Miller, Erika Polson, Kristine Racina, Meghann Ormond, Saskia Bonjour and Rutvica Andrijasevic. I also thank Aidan Mosselson, Amir Tehrani, Andrea Lagna, Joel Beresford, Judit Kuschnitzki, Katie Higgins, Philip Chikwiramakomo, Lien Rakuscek, Lioba Hirsch, María José Oomen Liebers, Murray Mackenzie, Nabeela Ahmed, Rachel Seoighe, Rafaella Lima, Richard Boreham, Soledad Martinez and Srilata Sircar, for reading draft chapters of the book, or the thesis that preceded it, for helping with technical questions or sticky points, for providing vital encouragement and inspiration, nourishing friendship and care. The doctoral research that this book has grown out of would have been a much less enjoyable, and a much more challenging, experience without the community of doctoral researchers I was lucky to be part of at UCL Geography. Two anonymous reviewers read the proposal and manuscript and provided important comments and encouragement. Without the generous funding of the UK Economic and Social Research Council, I would not have been able to do this research.

Finally, Mama, Papa, Barbara and Ness, thank you for your love, support and appreciation, always.

Introduction

In August 1961, at the eve of Kenyan independence, two colonial civil servants, B. D. Pinto and A. J. D'Cunha, wrote in protest to the Chief Secretary of the Colony and Protectorate of Kenya. They decried years of discriminatory treatment of 'Asian' civil servants at the hands of the colonial government, which now culminated in being denied the status of expatriate.[1] As they wrote,

> And now to crown it all the term 'Expatriate' has been twisted and turned to mean something other than it is. If certain officers recruited to the service locally in Kenya have been granted expatriate status, together with all that it implies, we feel that we have a much stronger claim to the misnomer 'expatriate'.[2]

The British Empire was fast unravelling, and across Britain's African territories colonial administrations were hastily transformed into national civil services, and colonial civil servants reclassified into either 'local' or 'expatriate' staff. While expatriate staff were eventually to be replaced by local staff, they received a greatly enhanced salary, generous compensation on leaving and a guaranteed pension. Such privileges meant that the struggle over who was an expatriate was fierce. While 'European' staff serving in Kenya – including many born and recruited in Kenya – were largely reclassified as expatriate, 'Asian' and 'African' civil servants – whether born and recruited in Kenya or not – became generally reclassified as local staff. As Pinto and D'Cunha learned, the undoing of the empire was as steeped in racialised inequality as the empire had been.

Fast forward to 2015 when my inbox filled with messages from friends and colleagues who sent me a *Guardian* article that struck a chord with many. 'Why are white people expats when the rest of us are immigrants?' Mawuna Remarque Koutonin asked provocatively in the piece, which was widely shared online and mentioned frequently during the research for this book. Koutonin (2015) goes on to write that 'Africans are immigrants. Arabs are immigrants. Asians are immigrants. However, Europeans are expats because they can't be at the same level as other ethnicities. They are superior. Immigrants is a term set aside for "inferior races".' Evidently, the question of who is an expatriate was as hotly debated in 2015 as it was in 1961. Now, as then, the making of the category is entangled with the making of racialised, classed and gendered social inequality. And now, as then, the category is enlisted in state and corporate struggles for economic gain and geopolitical influence – struggles fought also on the grounds of migration and mobility.

This book is about the category 'expatriate'. Who are expatriates? What does expatriate mean? (How) do they differ from other categories of migrants? And why should we care about such distinctions? This book engages such questions as it follows the expatriate through three sites to tell situated stories of the category's history and politics, its making and remaking, contestation and lived experience. Drawing on ethnographic and archival research, the book offers a critical reading of *international human resource management* literature, explores the work and institutional history of the *Expatriate Archive Centre* in The Hague, and studies the historical and contemporary making of expatriates in *Nairobi, Kenya*. In doing so, it traces the category's postcolonial history and presence from mid-twentieth-century political decolonisation to today's politics of migration.[3] The book shows the expatriate to be a malleable and mobile category, of shifting meaning and changing membership. It is also a contested category, as passionately embraced by some as it is rejected by others. Finally, it can be a surprising category, doing unexpected work, effective in ways that are not determined. Yet, throughout its conceptual meanderings and the disputes over its meaning, the expatriate proves consistently central to struggles over inequality, power and social justice.

The book works on the premise that as categories travel and change, their journeys and transformations offer useful analytical gateways to examine broader social changes and shifting power geometries. If migration categories are socially produced and productive, then following the expatriate is a fruitful research strategy to explore not only the category itself but also the social processes it intervenes in, to appreciate the social histories the term condenses and its political mobilisation and effects. Thus, following the expatriate allows an investigation of both the category itself and its role in the postcolonial politics of migration and mobility. The book does so in two parts.

Part I charts a history of the category expatriate from the mid-twentieth-century anti-colonial moment to the peak of the neoliberal counterrevolution in the early twenty-first century. Each chapter unearths a critical moment of the category's transformation that reflects the postcolonial politics of the time. This genealogy of the expatriate is by no means linear or exhaustive, but offers snapshots of significant moments of the reformulation and contestation of social inequalities and power relations in and through the category expatriate. Specifically, the chapters address the mid-twentieth-century transition from formal colonial administration to postcolonial nation-state building and development, the contemporaneous rise of corporate-driven US dominance and the neoliberal individualisation and diversification of work and migration from the later twentieth century. Part II focuses on the discursive and material making of the expatriate today, and its role as a lynchpin structuring individual migrant subjectivities and broader migration debates. Each chapter discusses a central definitional element of the category expatriate, now commonly understood to denote an international, temporary, highly skilled migrant subject. Throughout, the book also offers a set of observations on the politics of migration categories more generally, and on migration as a site of postcolonial 'worldmaking' (Walters 2015).

The expatriate is a relatively young social category, but one that has had a rich career. The Merriam-Webster Dictionary tells us that the first known use of the verb 'to expatriate' was in 1768, with the noun 'the expatriate' first used in 1818. Indeed, an analysis of Google's corpus of digitalised books suggests that in nineteenth-century anglophone writing, expatriate was used predominantly as a verb, rather than as an adjective or noun.[4] The popularity of the verb 'to expatriate' reached its peak in the mid-nineteenth century, then declined by the turn of the century, and has remained more or less steady since. In contrast, usage of 'the expatriate' as a noun, i.e. to describe a type of person, rose steadily from the turn of the twentieth century, and first overtook the term's use as a verb in the 1930s. Its rise in usage then really took off from the 1950s.[5] The ascent of the expatriate as a social category thus coincided with the mid-twentieth-century era of worldwide political decolonisation and capitalist economic expansion, which saw the end of European colonial empires and the rise of the US to economic and military dominance – geopolitical changes that also implied new forms, political uses and discourses of international migration. The popularity of the category 'expatriate' seems to have reached its peak around 2005, with usage in decline since. Instead, the shortened form 'expat' has gained ground since the 1990s, also suggesting that expatriate has become such a common nomenclature that it has inspired a colloquially used abbreviation, primarily deployed as an informal marker of identity. This brief sketch reveals key coordinates of the trajectory of the expatriate's use as a social category. However, it cannot offer insights into the category's changing meaning and membership, its practical uses and political implications. Inquiring into these matters is what this book sets out to do. To situate this study, the following will briefly relay some common uses of 'the expatriate' today.

But first a note on language and translation. This book attends to the anglophone expatriate. This is partly because the globalised expatriate is an English term – which is itself evidence of ongoing Anglo-American global influence. Yet other languages too know the expatriate or other equally significant figures of migration and mobility – figures that condense different histories and struggles. For example, romance languages have literal counterparts to 'expatriate', like the French verb 'expatrier' and noun 'l'expatrié(e)'. In other languages, expatriate does not necessarily translate easily. In any case, as I discuss in Chapter 6, what is at stake is more than the literal transla-tion of a term. The development of different languages is tied up with different historical experiences. In any language, the available labels and cultural tropes of mobility differ also because of different histories of migration and, closely related, different positions in international economic, political and sociocultural hierarchies. This book thus ultimately studies *a*, not *the*, expatriate.

The expatriate emerges as a polysemic and protean category that historically evolved to hold multiple, and at times contradictory meanings. It is also a contested term that stirs passions and inspires heated debates. The Cambridge Dictionary defines an expatriate as 'someone who does not live in their own country' and the Merriam-Webster Dictionary lists synonyms for the expatriate – including 'deportee' and 'refugee' – that show its now largely displaced associations with expulsion and forced exile. More recently, many proudly self-identify as expatriates, or expats, as evidenced by the vast fictional, autobiographical and self-help literatures assembled under these headings. Anglophone institutions and media alike have deployed the label to denote citizens abroad, for instance when the UK government announces its pledge 'to give back expats the right to vote' or the *Telegraph* newspaper features an 'online periodical for expatriates'.[6] Similarly, the organisation *American Citizens Abroad* (ACA) produces a podcast to help 'Americans residing abroad' with 'managing expat life'.[7] The US government, in turn, retains the term's legal meaning, as defined under the Internal Revenue Code, for 'US citizens who have renounced their citizenship and long-term residents … who have ended their US resident status for federal tax purposes' (IRS 2022). As this shows, the legal meaning of the expatriate in the US has become increasingly incongruent with the term's sociocultural uses. Multinational corporations (MNCs) have used expatriate as a supposedly technical term for their internationally relocated staff. Finally, expatriates are also targeted by a plethora of online forums and service providers including relocation firms, tax advisers and the social and professional networking platform *InterNations*. These mobilisations generally assume that expatriate is a self-evident category and that, regardless of the targeted audience, they will *want* to be addressed as expatriates.

However, not everyone enthusiastically embraces the label, as evidenced by Koutonin's (2015) article cited above, and the many people who pointed me to it to articulate their discomfort with the racialised uses of expatriate. Critical scholarship on privileged migration, as well as heated debates waged in news and social media, have addressed the racialised and classed politics of the category expatriate, and might be partly responsible for its decreased use and replacement with alternative labels such as 'internationals' (Chapter 5). However, while highlighting the category's ongoing enlistment in the reproduction of racialised inequality, including in international mobility, this book also shows that it has never been only white people who have claimed the label expatriate or been identified as such by others. Indeed, assuming as much takes part in the occlusion of historical struggles over the term, and, by extension, over social inequality. Examples range from 'Asian expatriates' in Kenya's colonial civil service (Chapter 2) to international human resources management's (IHRM) Zimbabwean inpatriates (Chapter 7) and many interlocutors I met in The Hague and Nairobi (Chapters 5 and 6). This does not mean that the category expatriate is 'racially undiscerning' but that its work in racial politics is not best understood by presuming that it maps easily and exactly onto the racial category of whiteness. Categories like the expatriate are central to the racialised politics of migration and mobility, and thereby to broader social and political struggles, precisely through their conceptual multiplicity and malleability (Kunz 2020a). The polysemy of the expatriate is entangled with power, and as such is politically useful and used.

Attending to the expatriate's polysemy is also analytically fruitful because the category's transformations speak about reconfigurations of racialised, gendered and classed power that reveal the indebtedness of current migration regimes to Euro-American-dominated imperial formations which have been challenged and destabilised, translated and adapted, but not fully dismantled. The changing category reveals precisely *how* present inequalities are related to past ones, how 'the longstanding patterns of power that emerged from colonialism' (Ndlovu-Gatsheni 2013:16) – and, one should add, imperialism – continue to fundamentally shape the way migration and mobility is imagined, experienced and governed today. Importantly, the category expatriate is not only a product of this social history, but has been mobilised to actively intervene in its making. Not only do migrants commonly called expatriates take part in constructing, and sometimes challenging, uneven economic, political and social relations, but the transmuting category expatriate has itself been enlisted in fashioning these inequalities. As the book shows, migration categories are at the heart of the insidious ways that intersecting material and symbolic inequalities are enacted today, both within and across borders, and any project for social justice thus needs to dissect and dismantle them.

Migration has been a key discursive and material site of what Walters (2015) calls 'worldmaking': a site where social difference is articulated, social inequality generated and power relations negotiated. Following the contestations and transformations of the expatriate and associated categories like 'international' or 'migrant' leads to the heart of some of today's most heated debates about migration and mobility. This includes the often implicit – but therefore all the more essential – debate about what migration is and who is a migrant. Interrogating the expatriate in this context reveals that not only are mobility and border regimes deeply unequal today, but so is the very way we imagine, label and study mobility. It suggests that the everyday, legal and analytical categories we use to understand and thus help invent migration have to be further examined as a key terrain on which the coloniality of power is reproduced, reworked and translated.

The book hopes to offer innovative methodological and analytical strategies to study and thus challenge these processes by following the expatriate to three sites of its articulation. In each site, ethnographic and archival research are combined to explore the past and present constitution, contestation and lived experience of the expatriate. The three research sites, while disparate, share their reliance on the expatriate as a central organising category, and in turn they give actuality and relevance to the category. First, the book follows the category expatriate to Nairobi, Kenya, an important regional political and economic node since the time of the British Empire and a thriving 'expat hub'. Second, the book offers a critical reading of scholarship of international human resource management (IHRM), the main academic field to have studied 'expatriates' since at least the 1960s. Third, the book visits the Expatriate Archive Centre (EAC) in The Hague, which began as a project by 'Shell wives' to document their lives on the move with Shell and now collects expatriate social history worldwide. Writing from each site, the book tells situated stories about the category's making and remaking. In this way, the three sites are approached in their 'incomparable singularity' (Jazeel 2019a). But the chapters also offer *combined* insights into the history and politics of the expatriate. By putting the different sites in conversation, the book builds a constellation that illuminates consistencies and ruptures in the meaning of the category expatriate, and its associated social and political processes. Adopting Walter Benjamin's approach of 'bricolage' (Ladwig et al. 2012), the book's method of putting the three sites into conversation thus resembles a conscious and constructive assemblage of fragments in the hope of shedding light on a contested category, rather than the recovery of any true meaning or the reconstruction of a whole.

Expatriate: following a migration category – an outline

Following this introduction, Chapter 1 introduces the scholarship that this book centrally engages with, and which have helped me think about the 'categorical' ordering of movement and belonging as a site where power is negotiated. The chapter first situates this study of the category expatriate within migration research on expatriates and privileged migration, before discussing scholarship on the coloniality of migration and mobility and interdisciplinary perspectives on social categories. The chapter then outlines my research strategy of following the expatriate and introduces the three sites visited for this research.

Part I of the book, Chapters 2, 3 and 4, traces a postcolonial genealogy of the expatriate. Chapter 2 discusses the use and contestation of the category expatriate in the archive of Kenyan independence. Specifically, it looks at the transformation of the colonial civil service into a national Kenyan civil service and the associated transformation of colonial civil servants into either 'local' or 'expatriate' officers. The chapter traces how, in the 1961 Overseas Service Aid Scheme (OSAS) and associated measures, the term expatriate was used to reproduce the privileges of European (i.e. white) officers and, closely related, British regional influence for the post-colonial period. The newly conceived 'expatriate' OSAS officer was key to British international development assistance, which was understood as a tool to retain global influence in a Cold War world. In Kenya, the institution of greatly privileged 'expatriate' civil servants had the indirect but significant effect of entrenching socio-economic inequality in the Kenyan civil service and Kenyan society more broadly. Yet, if the category expatriate was used to translate colonial into postcolonial racialised inequality, it did so without relying explicitly on 'race', as racism was increasingly enunciated through a lexicon of culture and economic 'logic' and 'common sense'.

Chapter 3 traces the emergence of the category expatriate in 1960s and 1970s anglophone IHRM literature, a new and fast-growing field that accompanied the US ascendancy of its day. IHRM scholarship recognised the seminal challenge (and opportunity) of decolonisation for US business and geopolitical interests abroad and, the chapter argues, academics self-consciously carved out their role and relevance in the post-war US imperial project by positioning the expatriate as a vital yet troublesome figure of multinational business that needed to be carefully selected, thoroughly trained, cautiously positioned, appropriately compensated and successfully repatriated – all requiring the support of specialist scholarship. This process of building an academic field of study around the category expatriate also involved translating discourses of white supremacy and the immature native into management knowledge, to establish the importance of US expatriate management and sanctify the asymmetrical power relations characterising multinational business. This history is rendered invisible by more recent IHRM literature that largely ignores the imperial roots of its research object and of its own role as knowledge producer.

Chapter 4 traces the transformation of Royal Dutch Shell's expatriate at the turn of the twenty-first century. In the mid-1990s, in the context of a broader corporate restructure and, centrally, in response to gendered challenges to its management model, Shell enacted a neoliberal reform of its system of expatriation and introduced a diversity agenda. It transformed its expatriates, Shell's elite cadre of staff, from loyal 'Shell men' who migrated with 'Shell families' within the 'Shell world' into individualised and flexible mobile workers circulating within a global labour market. This reform, however, did not fundamentally change the patriarchal constitution of the Shell expatriate, or decolonise this managerial institution. Meanwhile, a group of 'Shell wives' seized this moment of change and founded the Shell Ladies' Project (SLP) to collect and publish their own memories in two anthologies and thereby position themselves as expatriates in their own right. The Shell Ladies' Project and its subsequent development into an independent archive of expatriate social history mirrors organisational and societal trends – it reflects the gradual transmutation of women's *self-identification* from company-rooted 'Shell wives' into 'global expats', a subject seen to sit at the heart of globalisation. Chapter 4 thus traces, through the transforming Shell expatriate, the fashioning of neoliberal forms of elite migration and its ideological ideal-type: the transnational professional, commanding a global consciousness and skill set, moving self-directed and flexibly, at home in the world.

Part II of the book, Chapters 5, 6 and 7, explores how the category expatriate is articulated and experienced today, and with what effects. The expatriate emerges as a polysemic category that cannot easily be fixed onto a particular type of migrant. Among the various readings of the expatriate today, a key one is that of the 'international', a term often used synonymously with expatriate. Chapter 5 traces the production of this 'international' expatriate and its 'international community' as assembled and narrated in Nairobi by the expat service provider InterNations. The chapter discusses how an individual in Nairobi becomes international performatively, through the consumption of casual cross-border mobility, which in the context of uneven border regimes involves the reinterpretation of privilege as achievement. The chapter then examines the unevenly valued labour that socially reproduces the InterNations community, and discusses how the international community is produced through the everyday racialised, gendered and classed arrangement of bodies in Nairobi's expat spaces. The expatriate's international emerges as an imaginary that idealises flux and mobility across a space that remains intensely bordered and ordered along ascribed characteristics. Although the category is diversified in line with broader shifts in local and global power relations, the normative ideal at the heart of the international expat remains whiteness, spatialised as 'Western'.

Chapter 6 examines the definition of the expatriate as a temporary migrant through the work of the Expatriate Archive Centre. The EAC defines the expatriate as anyone who lives abroad temporarily. The chapter explores how the category is constituted and negotiated in the archival space, and what readings of migration, the city and the nation the temporary expatriate helps produce. It finds that the expatriate at work in the archival space does not abide by the category's designation as a temporary migrant. Temporality emerges as key to the politics of the expatriate in more subversive ways, and the temporary expatriate introduces both archival dilemmas and progressive potential. On the one hand, it achieves the discursive occlusion of past and present structural inequalities that centrally shape the migrations documented by the archive. On the other hand, it facilitates the collection and public availability of documents that aid our understanding of the workings of power and privilege, and release migration from its association with marginality which renders it a fertile proxy ground for racist politics.

Chapter 7 discusses recent debates in IHRM literature on alternatives to the 'traditional expatriate', including debates on 'self-initiated expatriates', 'inpatriates' and 'migrants'. The chapter interrogates these new categories of IHRM literature and notes a 'selective flexibility' that stretches the category expatriate in ways that often reproduce the inequalities that already underwrote the 'traditional expatriate'. Power and inequality are still frequently evaded in seemingly technical debates about the proper boundaries of analytical categories. The chapter then traces how migration studies turned to studying expatriates as high-powered corporate migrants within a framework of (highly) skilled migration. This expatriate, the chapter argues, stands in marked contrast to the usual migrant considered in migration studies, a field that has collectively, if inadvertently, helped to reproduce popular imaginations of migrants as the global racialised poor, and thereby enabled postcolonial racialised governance through migration. From this vantage point, the field's much-critiqued methodological nationalism can be understood as a racialised technology of governance with an imperial genealogy. Finally, the chapter examines the relationship between IHRM and migration studies, their mutual disregard and shared silences. It argues that colonial aphasia not only shapes their ultimately quite closely aligned categories, their 'typical' expatriate and migrant, but underwrites their academic disconnect and division of labour – i.e. colonial aphasia is at work in the very constitution of the two fields as *separate fields*.

Throughout, the book documents how the category expatriate has become ensnared in the politicisation of migration. The very fact that the expatriate is now understood as a *migration* category evidences the possibly increasing use of migration as a discursive and material site of articulating social subjects and producing social inequality, a site of 'worldmaking' (Walters 2015). At the current conjuncture, increasingly bifurcated migration regimes demonise some movements while glorifying others. Such differentiated (im)mobilisation as a technology of governance depends centrally on ostensibly innocuous and technical categories. Migration categories are thus at the heart of the insidious ways that intersecting material and symbolic inequalities are enacted today, and any project for social justice thus needs to dissect and dismantle them. The book's conclusion further elaborates this argument.

Notes

1 British colonialism in Kenya, as elsewhere, relied on the racial categories 'Asian', African' and 'European', hence in this book I refer to these historical categories where necessary.
2 Memorandum attached to a letter to the Provincial Commissioner, Rift Valley Province, 30 August 1961; KNADS Folder C5/5362.
3 The 'postcolonial' here refers to a social reality that continues to be shaped by the social structures and institutions, epistemologies and discourses of the colonial era. See Chapter 1 for details on my use of 'postcolonialism'.
4 'Google Ngram Viewer' is a tool that can be used to chart the frequency of words in Google's digitalised books, and while not a precise scholarly tool, it can indicate historical trends in language use (Michel et al. 2011).
5 See Green (2009) for a history of the earlier category expatriate in the US context, including its transformation from positively to negatively connoted term and back again.
6 See www.telegraph.co.uk/expat/news/ and www.gov.uk/government/news/government-delivers-on-pledge-to-give-back-british-expats-the-right-to-vote [Accessed 27 January 2022].
7 See www.americansabroad.org/aca-podcast/ [Accessed 27 January 2022].

1

Following the expatriate: theoretical and methodological starting points

From studying expatriates to studying the category expatriate

Expatriates are primarily researched in international human resource management (IHRM) literature and migration studies, two well-established and diverse yet largely separate academic fields. IHRM literature has studied organisational migrants under the rubric of the expatriate since at least the 1960s. Given this historical depth and its volume of publications, IHRM can be seen as the main academic field producing knowledge on expatriates. The principal focus is on staff migrating in the service of MNCs, which have used the label expatriate to denote often high-ranking employees who they dispatch abroad for a number of years, often on an enhanced salary and with a generous benefits package. Yet, as discussed in Chapters 3 and 7, the meaning and membership of IHRM literature's category expatriate has not been straightforward. The potent inequalities and power asymmetries structuring international business also shape its category expatriate. Academic IHRM literature, in its adherence to a supposedly technical definition of the expatriate and its commitment to do research in support rather than critique of corporate practice, has actively participated in these 'definitional politics', not least by depoliticising international business.

Engagement with expatriates in migration studies is a more recent affair and can be traced to British geographers working on skilled international migration from the late 1980s (Findlay and Gould 1989). Scholars of migration initially followed IHRM's lead by primarily studying, as expatriates, migrants moving in higher-echelon professional and managerial roles for multinational business. As

Beaverstock (2005:712) writes: 'The term "expatriation" is more often than not associated with the labelling of highly skilled individuals sent by their employers to work outside their home countries in a subsidiary or private entity for a contracted period of time.' Hindman (2013:12) similarly conceptualises 'Expatria' as 'a community defined by a unique labour structure', centrally including frequent rotation and generous compensation packages. Like IHRM, early migration literature identified the growth of MNCs and associated recruitment agencies as key for creating the globalised labour markets within which expatriates moved (Salt and Findlay 1988). However, unlike the largely uncritical and corporate-centric IHRM literature, the emerging migration literature situated its enquiries within literatures on the 'new international division of labour' and linked expatriate migration to the global expansion of capitalism and the growth of global cities. Expatriates were found to create 'spaces of flows' through building transnational networks that connected globalising cities and deepened and expanded global capitalist integration, while they themselves often remained disembedded from local spheres (Beaverstock 2002). Moreover, mechanisms of social and professional reproduction were found to be intertwined with private members' clubs and social lives recognised as key spheres where power in the global economy is negotiated and reproduced (Beaverstock 2002, 2011; Meier 2016). While expatriates were said to hold transnationally valid knowledge and skills, research also noted the cultural construction of skill (Findlay et al. 1996) and inquired into how multinational employers and the growing 'global mobility industry' shaped the sociocultural norms governing corporate work and produced idealised performances of being an expatriate (Cranston 2014, 2016; Findlay and Cranston 2015).

This early research on corporate migrant elites has provided important correctives to a field shaped by a prevailing 'marginality bias' that means much scholarship implicitly treats migration as the movement of the global racialised poor (Chapter 7). However, it has proved limiting in its rather unquestioning reproduction of IHRM's understandings of who expatriates are – namely (Western, white, male) corporate elites – in its own conceptualisation, and at times conflation, of the expatriate with the highly skilled migrant, and its silence on the imperial origins and ongoing racialised and gendered construction of expatriate migration and skill (although see Salt 1988). For example, Findlay's (1988:401) article 'From settlers to skilled transients: The changing structure of British international migration' finds that 'reflecting Britain's changing position in the world economy', 'the well-established process of "settler" emigration' was by the 1980s largely 'replaced by temporary emigration of skilled workers'. The article names empire only once, and in rather depoliticised terms, noting that 'The decline of the empire and the increasing interaction of British capital and labour flows in a hierarchically organised global system of production has reduced the need and the opportunities for settler emigration and has promoted new forms of international labour transfers' (Findlay 1988:408). Similarly, writing on Hong Kong, still a British colony at the time, Findlay et al. (1996:60) observe that 'while many of the functions fulfilled by expatriates could have been achieved by locally trained professionals', expatriates' 'internationality' and 'cultural origins' often explained their employment in preference to local skilled staff. The racialised nature of colonial capitalism and colonial labour hierarchies is critical for understanding this finding, but instead of being named in the analysis, coloniality shapes the analytical naming. The authors write that 'the term "expatriate" is used in this article to refer to non-Chinese … people holding foreign passports', yet they diverge from their definition instantly when distinguishing between 'expatriates from advanced industrial nations' and 'low-wage immigrant groups such as Filipinos' (Findlay et al. 1996:51). The authors' differentiation between 'expatriate' and 'immigrant' is ultimately based on migrants' origin. In the remainder of the article, 'expatriate' remains tied to 'skilled migration' and associated specifically with engineers employed in managerial roles in the private sector. Such associations of origin and category linger, origin and skill become tethered together and the directionality of causality becomes easily blurred. Suddenly, in the reader's mind, those from 'advanced industrial nations' are not expatriates because they are skilled, but they are skilled because they are expatriates because they are from 'advanced industrial nations'.

From the early 2000s, a new wave of research on expatriates addressed the earlier silence on gender and sexuality, by examining the gendered production of 'expatriates' and 'trailing spouses' (Yeoh and Khoo 1998; Yeoh and Willis 2005; Kofman and Raghuram 2006; Walsh 2006, 2011, 2012; Coles and Fechter 2008; Fechter

2007; Spiegel and Mense-Petermann 2016; Kunz 2020b). This literature demonstrated that gendered work and migration trajectories are produced by interlocking heteronormative and patriarchal norms and practices that operate within families, organisations, immigration legislation and society more generally. In MNCs, men still fill the majority of expatriate assignments, and corporate actors reproduce gendered inequality in the workplace and, indirectly, in the families of expatriated employees. In professional heterosexual families, men's careers are frequently prioritised over those of their female partners, which are put on hold or discontinued altogether. Professional women in expatriate families thus often experience the devalorisation of their productive capabilities and a redomestication. Yet, contrary to dominant imaginations, spouses' newly foregrounded emotional and social labour is often essential to the migratory project and for advancing their partners' careers (Beaverstock 2002; Fechter 2007, 2010).

This second wave of expatriate research also showed how 'race' and racism structure expatriate roles and identities, in work and social contexts, and uncovered the imperial and colonial genealogies and functions of expatriate migration. Leonard (2010ab) discusses for post-colonial Hong Kong how the term 'expatriate' as often used in work contexts ties together Western whiteness and middle-class privilege, and normalises their association. 'Western' is here taken to denote not an innocuous geographical category, but a powerful cultural one that, while fungible and fuzzy, has been, as Stuart Hall (1993) writes, historically constituted in imperial inequality vis-à-vis the global 'Rest'. Lopez (2005:17) accordingly suggests that 'Western' has 'less to do with where one sits on the map than with one's relation to an imperial and colonial history, in which "Western-ness" is bound up with both colonial dominance and whiteness' (see Chapter 5). That those migrating for multinational business are frequently white, Western and privileged attests to the imperial roots of our 'global economy', and the ongoing privileging of white Westernness for which work contexts emerge as crucial spaces (Leonard 2010ab; Kunz 2020b). Accordingly, Leggett (2010) shows how colonial imaginations and race-based hierarchies remain inscribed in the organisational structures and hiring practices of expatriate corporate workplaces in Jakarta, and Redfield (2012:359) examines the 'micropolitics of national origin amid global circulation' in the NGO (non-governmental organisation) Doctors Without Borders (MSF). Research such as this also broadened the types of labour migration studied under the heading of expatriate to include development and humanitarian workers alongside corporate employees, which further points to the shared imperial genealogies of staffing practices in development and humanitarian organisations and multinational business (see Chapters 2–4). Although no longer assured, or as easily conferrable and defendable as in the past, this scholarship on expatriates shows that Western whiteness and masculinity continue to be highly valued attributes in global labour markets, and normatively associated with the 'skilled migrant' (Leonard 2010ab; Le Renard 2021).

Further evidencing the inequalities structuring labour migration is the fact that not all skilled migrants are labelled expatriates and not all those called expatriates are skilled. Specifically, the label expatriate is often applied to white Western migrants regardless of whether they are skilled, unskilled, retired or migrating for non-professional reasons altogether. Already in 1977, Cohen observed that Western expatriates who perform lower echelon jobs enjoy elevated social status in many formerly colonised contexts. More recently, Hayes (2014, 2018) noted that many so-called expatriates are 'economic migrants', partly driven by financial duress and practising a form of 'geographic arbitrage' by using international differences in living costs. Similarly, Farrer (2010:1225) encountered 'perhaps as many "refugees" from global capitalism as elite "talents"' in Shanghai, and noted pronounced class boundaries within the 'expat community'. The label expatriate not only *results from* but *bestows* skilled status and symbolic capital to the migrants that can claim it, often due to racialisation and nationality as much as individual qualifications. Such observations feed into broader critiques of the concept of skill and its measurement, which are far from straightforward or coherent (Koser and Salt 1997; Findlay and Gould 1989; Kofman and Raghuram 2006; Raghuram 2009; Leinonen 2012; Le Renard 2021). As Liu-Farrer et al. (2021:1) discusses, 'the interpretation of migrants' skill is frequently distorted by their ascriptive characteristics such as race, ethnicity, gender and nationality, reflecting the influence of colonial legacy, global inequality as well as social stratification'. Who gets to utilise their skill on migration is not always representative of who is skilled, as also amply demonstrated by research on deskilling, labour market exclusion and discrimination experienced by professionals moving from poorer to richer countries (Yeoh and Willis 2005; Parutis 2014; Meier 2016). Research findings on expatriates thus only apply to a small subset of skilled migrants and they do not even apply to all intracompany assignees, as work on 'inpatriates' suggests (Chapter 7). In other words, the expatriate and the skilled migrant do not comfortably map onto each other, either in policymaking and corporate practice, or in academic usage. Migration scholarship participates in the production of migrants and their differentiation into more or less valuable forms of mobility, and the continued framing and sometimes casual conflation of the expatriate with the (highly) skilled migrant risks reinforcing the prevalent tethering of skill and white Western masculinity.

Ethnographic research over the last two decades has also expanded the previous focus on corporate work contexts by examining the expatriate as an identity category that is embodied and performed in everyday life and mobilised to create community in diaspora space. The expatriate emerges as an especially potent sociocultural identity category in previously colonised countries of the Global South, where it circumscribes self-consciously segregated and socioeconomically privileged 'expat communities' and narrates everyday enactments of foreignness that frequently remain grounded in inherited assumptions of cultural superiority versus the local Other. For example, Fechter's (2007) research in Indonesia, Walsh's (2010, 2012) work in Dubai, Leonard's (2010abc) and Knowles and Harper's (2009) research in Hong Kong and Lundström's (2014) work in the US, Singapore and Spain all address the privileged features and often carefully maintained borders of white Western migrants' transnational lifestyles, and show them to be enabled by colonially rooted inequalities and power relations. Here, everyday racism couched in discourses of cultural difference, hygiene and safety prescribe a broad range of strategies to 'manage' the local in daily life (Fechter 2007, 2010; Leonard 2008, 2010a; Armbruster 2010; Coles and Walsh 2010; Smiley 2010; Walsh 2012). Yet, privileged migrants also rework and sometimes challenge rather than simply accept what they inherit from the past (Leonard 2008; Lester 2012). Some vehemently reject the label expatriate as part of a broader effort to not lead lives reminiscent of the colonial past, while others aim to resignify it, often by associating it with a globally oriented cosmopolitanism (that often remains steeped in similar power asymmetries) as Hindmann (2013) shows. While cautioning against homogenising stereotypes that downplay historical change, Fechter (2007:28) thus notes 'substantial and meaningful continuities between colonial and contemporary expatriate contexts' and highlights that 'there is certainly a case to be made for regarding corporate expatriates as neo-colonials given their involvement in, and their benefitting from, global capitalism which is arguably based on the exploitation of the developing countries that expatriates are posted to'. Hayes (2018:92) similarly notes that white North Americans' migratory 'geoarbitrage' includes the 'reclamation of hegemonic and privileged forms of whiteness' through participation in racial projects in their Ecuadorian host context that unwittingly reproduces white supremacy and the exploitation of non-white Ecuadorians.

While critical migration scholarship has thus shown that the label expatriate is frequently conflated with Western whiteness, research has arguably reconstituted its subject by employing the category primarily to frame examinations of precisely these migrations. Scholarship thus participates in constructing the category expatriate as normally white and Western, and more often than not as skilled and moving temporarily within the overlapping labour markets of international business, development and governance (Chapter 7). Given this research focus, it remains largely unknown how migrants that do not hail from the West and/or are not racialised as white relate to the category expatriate. This includes migrations labelled expatriate in *organisational practice*, or demanding to be labelled as such, like the 'Asian colonial civil servants' of Chapter 2, some 'third country nationals' in Chapter 3, Shell's 'expatriated regional staff' in Chapter 4 and IHRM's 'inpatriates' in Chapter 7. Also largely invisible in scholarship are the negotiations of a more precarious and ambivalent *expatriate identity*, as narrated by some of my interlocutors from, for example, India, Turkey and Zimbabwe (Chapters 5 and 6). Another example of people called expatriate in *political practice* (Parween 2013; Al Mukrashi 2016), while often grouped under other categories in scholarship, are the North African, Arab and South Asian workers in the Gulf states, including both the highly compensated and the harshly exploited, who share an imposed temporary status (although see Pagès-El Karoui 2016; Babar et al. 2019). A key argument of this book is thus that while the category expatriate is central to the racialised politics of migration and belonging, its functioning in these politics is not best understood by presuming that the category maps easily onto the racial category whiteness. Indeed, the fact that expatriate now has a privileged association with white Western migration itself merits historical excavation and explanation. The precise working of the category expatriate in racialised politics thus deserves further analytical attention. This work also requires expansion of the range of voices considered. As Hindman (2009ab) and Grover (2014) note, those commonly labelled expatriates interact professionally and socially with nationals of the country they reside in, as well as with less privileged migrants – two groups of people that play an important yet underexplored role in fashioning the category expatriate.

Today, migration scholarship on privileged migration, including those labelled expatriates, is thus a burgeoning and diverse field and includes a debate on the term expatriate. In her research on US Americans in Europe, Klekowski von Koppenfels (2014:139) notes that the very act of calling someone an expatriate is already part of the 'widespread social hierarchization of migrants' (see also O'Reilly 2000; Croucher 2012; Kunz 2020a). This is echoed in heated media and public debates on the racialised and classed politics of the term, as exemplified by Koutonin's (2015) *Guardian* commentary cited in the Introduction. Such growing critiques might be partly responsible for the decreased use of 'expatriate' and its replacement with alternative labels such as 'internationals' (Chapter 5). Given its association with migratory privilege, some scholars too have rejected the term expatriate altogether, and instead favour conceptual framings such as 'privileged migration' or 'lifestyle migration.'[1] 'If "expatriate," as commonly used today, essentially implies immigrants of privilege', Croucher (2012:23) argues, 'it seems preferable to simply call them that'. Rather than delimiting a homogeneous group of migrants, the framing of privileged migration invites attention to the ways in which some movements are shaped by intersecting and relational dimensions of privilege in the context of broader social inequalities (Croucher 2012; Kunz 2016). This framing explicitly repositions migrants not usually labelled migrants *as migrants*, and disrupts the common racialised and classed disassociation between 'migrants' and 'expatriates' (Kunz 2020a).

However, as argued, expatriate does not always denote privileged social positions. And even when expatriate connotes a position of privilege, 'ignoring' the term does not allow us to analyse the work the category does in its own right. While the noted biases and tensions render expatriate a problematic category of analysis, they make it an interesting object of study. Studying the expatriate as a 'category of practice' (Brubaker and Cooper 2000) is thus the aim of this book. This analytical move decentres the individual migrant to focus on the multifaceted making of mobility categories and the mobility of these categories. Crucially, even in its academic usage expatriate is, to borrow Brubaker and Cooper's (2000:34) words, 'riddled with ambiguity, riven with contradictory meanings, and encumbered by reifying connotations'. Thus, even the analytical category expatriate of IHRM and migration studies demands to be studied *as a category of practice*. This book thus displaces the expatriate as *analytical* category to further examine what work it does as a category of *practice*. It does so precisely because the term is contested, charged and difficult.

The making of postcolonial migration

Migration is a discursive and material site where social difference is produced and social ordering achieved, and as such a terrain on which imperial and colonial power relations are reproduced, reworked and translated. As outlined above, research on privileged migration has productively employed the diverse and sometimes contending perspectives of postcolonial and decolonial scholarship as analytical and methodological tools to examine these dynamics. This is not equally the case in migration studies more generally, as Mains et al. (2013:132–133) note: 'Despite the material links between colonialism, postcolonialism and migration, social scientists in general have been slow to address this intersection' and the 'potential for postcolonial theory to fundamentally change how we understand migration is underexplored'. Relatedly, migration scholarship has been critiqued for largely ignoring the ways in which 'race'/racism structures migration and belonging (Essed and Nimako 2006; Lentin 2014; De Genova 2016; Schinkel 2018). In response, and especially in the wake of resurgent anti-racist activism and the increasingly recognised need to decolonise academia, a body of scholarship has emerged to examine the ongoing, reworked and recuperated ways in which imperial and colonial formations, and their accordant racisms, shape the governance, experience and representation of migration (e.g. Walter 2015; Achiume 2019; El-Enany 2020; Samaddar 2020; Mayblin and Turner 2021; Favell 2022).

In this book, I use postcolonial in its plural sense. The hyphenated 'post-colonial' refers specifically to the period after a colony has gained independence, or more generally to the period following the mid-twentieth-century wave of political decolonisation that brought an end to European colonial empires. 'Postcolonial', in turn, refers to a social reality that continues to be shaped by the social structures and institutions, epistemologies and discourses of the colonial era – i.e. the term notes the manifold 'continued and troubling presence and influence of colonialism' today (Jazeel 2019b:4). Jazeel (2019b:4ff), wa Thiong'o (2012:49ff), Bhambra (2014), Shohat (1992) and Colpani et al. (2022) offer further discussion of the multiple interlocking meanings, conceptual challenges and critiques of the concept 'postcolonial' that render it an inherently 'plural enterprise' (Jazeel 2019b:4). Postcolonial scholarship has been critiqued for ignoring or downplaying the fact that geopolitical, economic and often militarised imperial formations remain a forceful material reality, as do the various racisms that already served European colonial empires; and, as indigenous critiques of settler colonialism remind us, in many contexts there is nothing 'post' about the colonial. Scholars working in the decolonial mould, like Ndlovu-Gatsheni (2013) and Grosfoguel et al (2014), similarly highlight the ongoing 'coloniality of power/knowledge/being'. There is thus a good deal of 'neo-in-the-post of postcolonialism' (wa Thiong'o 2012:50), or in what Ndlovu-Gatsheni (2013), following Spivak, calls the 'postcolonial neocolonized world'. The postcolonial present still requires multilayered decolonisation for an anti-colonial future. Recognising the productive differences and debates between these approaches, in this book I thus employ both postcolonial and decolonial approaches, alongside anti-colonial scholarship and critiques of (neo) imperialism, as ultimately aligned analytical and methodological tools that can help us 'decolonise' migration and thinking on migration.

Another crucial intellectual resource in thinking about the expatriate and the making of migration (categories) today is critical work on 'race' and racism. 'Race' is a social construct that asserts the existence of essentially different human groups that have come packaged in reified geographic, religious, national or colour categories (Fields and Fields 2014). As Goldberg (1993:107) puts it, 'race' is conceptually 'chameleonic and parasitic in character'. That is, racial ideology has variously drawn on visible and invisible criteria, on physiological markers, cultural habits and religion, environmental and climatic conditions, biologised and economic pseudoscience, history and 'common sense', to position as *natural* and *right* the outcomes of individual and systemic acts of social categorisation and ranking, and their accordant discrimination, domination, exclusion, exploitation, expulsion and even genocide (Fields and Fields 2014; Stoler 2016). Many of today's most virulent forms of racism can be traced to European and North American imperial and colonial projects. As denoted by the notion of 'white supremacy' (Winant 2001), the racial category whiteness – commonly called 'European' in colonial contexts – was the imagined pinnacle in Euro-American racial formations which were materially predicated on the domination and exploitation of various racial Others. In the mid-twentieth century, internationalised anti-colonial and civil rights movements, often overlapping with organised labour struggles, achieved a 'worldwide break with the customary practices and entrenched institutions of white supremacy' and 'forced at least the partial dismantling of most official forms of discrimination and empire' (Winant 2001:134). What Winant (2001) calls the mid-century 'racial break' occasioned a 'sea change in racial epistemology and politics' in many contexts worldwide, a shift from state-enacted white supremacy to a liberal race paradigm that 'secures a liberal symbolic framework for race reform centred in abstract equality, market individualism and inclusive civic nationalism' (Melamed 2006:2). Notwithstanding this momentous historical challenge to racism, Stoler (1997) cautions against the view that past colonial racism was necessarily more secure and ferocious than post-colonial racism. Not only does racism remain virulent and violent today, but its seemingly more protean 'cultural' enunciation does not necessarily signal fundamental change or waning potency: already colonial racism's essences 'rested not on immovable parts but on the strategic inclusion of different attributes, a changing constellation of features, and a changing weighting of them' (Stoler 1997:200; see also Stoler 2009:174).

Migration has been a key site where racism is enacted, as 'race' is evoked discursively and socially produced as material and institutionalised inequality. Migration scholars have largely addressed the racialisation of migration through histories of immigration control that document the transposition of imperial and colonial forms of governance into present-day migration regimes. Immigration legislation that the US, European countries and self-governing white settler colonies began to develop in the later nineteenth century was bound up with colonial and imperial politics, and often a direct response to the arrival of sometimes relatively small numbers of non-white imperial subjects or Jewish refugees (Solomos 2003; Rosenberg 2006; Lake and Reynolds 2008; Anderson 2013; FitzGerald et al. 2014, 2017; Achiume 2022). McKeown (2004:2–3) shows that basic principles of border control and individual identification that have since become 'universalized as the foundation of [state] sovereignty and migration control' were first developed in white settler contexts, frequently to exclude free, i.e. non-indentured, Asian immigrants. Mongia (2007:403) similarly traces the responses to free Indian migration within the British Empire, concluding that 'state control of migration and attendant definitions of state sovereignty have a crucial colonial genealogy'. From the late nineteenth century, as Lake and Reynolds (2008:3) show, whiteness spread as a 'transnational form of racial identification' and as 'the basis of geo-political alliances' as white men across continents 'exchanged knowledge and know-how' in 'building and defending white men's countries' (Lake 2005:2012). Immigration legislation was mobilised to enact 'racial segregation on an international scale' (Lake and Reynolds 2008:5), for instance by repurposing the 'literacy test', first used to disenfranchise Black voters in the US South, as a tool of racist immigration control. The specific appeal of such discriminatory technologies – especially to imperial Britain, which officially proclaimed the equality of British subjects – was that they were formulated without direct reference to 'race' while being designed to be racially applied (see also Ghezelbash 2017). As Walters (2015:15) argues, 'like development policy (Mitchell 2002), migration policy takes shape in the space opened up by the breakdown of colonial systems and the formal shift away from the kind of state racism Foucault identified (Foucault 2003), while also carrying over and reorganizing key practices invented by colonial power'. It is thus important to trace 'possible connections between the rationalities, technologies and programmes of migration governance and the histories of colonialism' (Walters 2015:11).

The ongoing relevance of such histories is documented by a growing body of work that shows how, as Weiss (2005) argues, social positions in a global system are now powerfully structured by differential 'spatial autonomy' and determined by the 'quality of the spaces' people have access to. (Im)mobility across national borders has become a key factor structuring global socio-economic inequality, with Bauman (1998:9) going as far as to argue that 'mobility has become the most powerful and most coveted stratifying factor'. While explicit racial discrimination is nowadays mostly considered illegitimate, many countries still rely on 'hidden mechanisms of ethnic selection' (FitzGerald et al. 2018:17) and Mau et al. (2015) document a 'global mobility divide' that particularly benefits Euro-American citizens and disadvantages citizens of African countries. One's access to international mobility relies to a large extent on one's citizenship. Shachar (2009) has conceptualised citizenship as a form of unearned property, and Boatcă (2016:4) diagnoses that citizenship is 'a core mechanism not only for the maintenance of global inequalities, but also for ensuring their reproduction in the postcolonial present'. As Mohanty (2003:201–202) argues, 'unlike the colonial state, the gender and racial regimes of contemporary liberal capitalist states operate through the ostensibly "unmarked" discourses of citizenship and individual rights' enacted also via immigration and naturalisation legislation. In this context, Carens (2013:226) calls Western citizenship 'the modern equivalent of feudal class privilege – an inherited status that greatly enhances one's life chances'. As a result, Achiume (2022:46–47) argues, international borders are still 'racial borders' that rely on 'facially neutral institutions, policies, and practice' to 'sustain international migration and mobility as racial privileges, especially privileges of Whiteness'.

Such critical analyses of the governance of migration and citizenship are complemented by analyses that situate migration in the context of post/neocolonial racialised capitalism. As already argued by Sassen (1988:27), migration is embedded in larger transnational geopolitical and economic processes and the 'international circulation of capital and labor' demands a single analytical frame. In what was by no means an automatic process, 'states have successfully usurped from rival claimants such as churches and private enterprises the "monopoly of the legitimate means of movement"' (Torpey 2000:1). Yet this monopoly has never been complete or uncontested. Capital is not only a key factor in initiating and shaping migration flows, but states' immigration regulations are often oriented towards its needs. Samaddar (2020:59ff) notes that the history of migration is to a large extent the history of the movement of labour, and the techniques that governments – but also employers and labour intermediaries – have deployed to mould, manage and mobilise labour in their interest can similarly trace a genealogy to the earlier era of imperial globalisation. Imperial and colonial elites centrally relied on articulations of 'race' and class to justify the forced (im)mobilities – including transatlantic slavery and indentured labour, the facilitation and at times enforcement of settler emigration, and the (im)mobilisation of colonised subjects in the service of settler economies – that enabled their profits and helped establish today's transnational capitalist economy (Robinson 1983; Melamed 2006; Achiume 2019).

Accordingly, twentieth-century anti-colonial movements targeted *political* as well as *economic* domination and inequality, and racism in capitalist societies became a chief 'propaganda weapon' for the Soviet Union in the Cold War (Melamed 2006:4). Getachew (2019), for example, highlights that anti-colonial nationalism was not solely a project of nation-state building but one of 'worldmaking', with its 'most ambitious project' being the New International Economic Order (NIEO) that politicised the global political economy and contended that sovereign statehood and equality required changed economic structures. The NIEO was quickly rejected and displaced in the neoliberal counterrevolution after the 1970s (Getachew 2019). Formal political independence was thus achieved within a largely unchanged international economic system which, together with most institutions of international governance, remained organised in favour of the former imperial metropoles turned Western nation-states (Achiume 2019; Getachew 2019). Such analyses also throw into question migration studies' prevalent assumption that there exist sovereign, autonomous and equal nation-states (Achiume 2019; Getachew 2019).

The economic basis of ongoing global inequality was theorised and critiqued by radical work ranging from Nkrumah's (1965) account of neocolonialism to Robinson's (1983) formulation of an oppositional radical 'Black Marxism'. This critique now often continues under the heading of 'racial capitalism' (Melamed 2015; Bhattacharyya 2018; Virdee 2019), and points to lasting uneven political-economic relations to argue that formal decolonisation was incomplete at best, and that capitalism continues to rely on racism and sexism today, also enacted via migration. Lowe (1996) notes how immigration legislation became a key tool in the racialised organisation of the US economy and El-Enany (2020) argues that twentieth-century UK immigration and nationality law-making extends British colonialism to enact racialised material inequality. Britain's borders, El-Enany (2020) shows, legislate for enclosure and dispossession that rob formerly colonised peoples and their descendants of their fair share in the spoils of empire amassed in British institutions and on its territory.

Also 'uprooted' and 'free-floating' professionals are labour migrants caught up in the same highly differentiated and racialised migration regimes as their disadvantaged counterparts, and their 'hypermobility' ultimately depends on facilitation by states and employers. Indicatively, many states 'have provided new visas and renovated old types of visas for global firms and professionals' that amount to 'a new legal "infrastructure"' (Sassen 2006:n.p.). As work on expatriates and an emerging literature on migration industries and intermediaries (Gammeltoft-Hansen and Nyberg-Sørensen 2013) shows, corporations and non-state actors continue to shape and direct mobilities in significant yet underexplored ways to produce and profit from unequal racialised, classed and gendered migration – and from positioning some movements as not migration at all.

Mainstream migration studies has until recently remained largely silent on the racialised imperial and colonial genealogies of current migration dynamics. Accordingly, Walters (2015) diagnosed an 'amnesia that inflects migration studies when it comes to the colonial' and Raghuram (2009:30) noted the 'foreshortening of the time' that often marks thinking about 'brain drain' and renders us unable to see it as a 'postcolonial legacy'. Given the pronounced coloniality of migration, this 'amnesia' of scholarship might be better understood as a form of 'colonial aphasia' (Stoler 2011, 2016). In this reading, the colonial aphasia of migration studies is not mere oversight or neglect, but a sustained act of Eurocentric research production. Stoler (2016) argues that silence on colonialism is often less a matter of forgetting than the result of processes of evasion and occlusion, the epistemic techniques of which demand analysis. She points to limiting frameworks and conceptual vocabularies, to 'categorical errors that produced distinctions that did not matter as they missed those that did' and to how 'pathways' can be blocked by the dissociating categories in which we operate (Stoler 2016:161–163). Colonial aphasia thus centrally hinges on 'acts of obstruction – of categories, concepts, and ways of knowing that disable linkages to imperial practice and that often go by other names' (Stoler 2016:9–10). Fields and Fields (2014:18) share a similar concern in their analysis of 'racecraft' – that is, of the ways we think, speak and act that reproduce 'race' insidiously and often unwittingly by turning '*racism*, something an aggressor does, into *race*, something the target is' (Fields and Fields 2014:17). These mental operations and habits of speaking are easily missed, but they are crucial to the reproduction of racialised injustice by allowing an ideology to appear as 'uncontroversial everyday reality' and turning a collective societal past into a group or individualised trait (Fields and Fields 2014:11, 76). Such critiques are essential for a reflexive migration studies, which aims to examine the material and historical conditions of knowledge production on migration (see Chapter 7).

Migration categories and the ordering of movement

Categories of migration are significant sites where the ordering of movement and belonging as a key technology of power takes place. Jones (2008:762) argues that 'typologies of migration' are 'subject to dominant political forces and hegemonic discourses' and it is 'always necessary to examine whose interests such definitions serve and to understand that the conceptual landscape these terms construct is embedded within specific historical, political, and geographical terrains'. McKeown (2004) even finds that when it comes to comparing the historical magnitude and character of international migration, 'shifts in categories used to measure migration may be of more significance than the actual numbers themselves. We cannot understand migration without simultaneously understanding the social processes by which they have been produced, recorded, and processed as "refugees," "guest laborers," or "illegal aliens"'

(McKeown 2004:185). The categorisation of migration is thus a contested exercise with significant material effects.

Besides attending to the political, organisational and social production of the category expatriate, this book examines knowledge production *on* expatriates as part of the making *of* the category expatriate. From the outset, postcolonial scholarship has operated at 'a dual level of investigation' (Jazeel 2012), examining how colonial relations of power are sustained or recuperated 'out there' as well as in the knowledge we produce, with Edward Said 'urging us to examine the taxonomic conventions of colonial knowledge, how these conventions have shaped contemporary scholarship and why students of colonial knowledge did not ask about them' (Hall 2004:240). Melamed (2015:77) similarly recognises 'the complex recursivity between material and epistemic forms of racialized violence'. Scholarship takes part in the social construction of, and governance via, migration; it is 'an essential part of this institutionalized migration apparatus' (Dahinden 2016:2011).

From the late 1990s, critical mobilities research has demonstrated the ways in which (im)mobilisation is central to the making of power relations and the fashioning of social subjects (Cresswell 2010; Sheller 2011). A critical mobilities lens helps shift the focus from those who move to an analysis of the material and discursive production of (im)mobilities, to understand migration as an inherently political framing of only *some* movements and people (Anderson 2019). Mobility as an 'inclusive category' (Glick Schiller and Salazar 2013:184) allows all movement to be studied 'through the same analytical lens' and 'the division between categories such as international migrants and temporary travellers' to be questioned. As Kotef (2015:138) notes, the differentiation of movement 'cannot be understood separately from schemas of race, gender, ethnicity, or class, in which bodies are produced and organized'. As a tool to govern and circumscribe people's access to rights and resources, migration is central to social organisation: 'migration today is a matter of worldmaking' (Walters 2013:10).

Raghuram (2021) notes that understanding the imperial-colonial genealogies of the categorisation of migration is key to addressing racism and racialised inequality today. Helping us understand the role of categorisation in colonial rule, Mamdani (2012:42) has identified twentieth-century British colonialism in Africa as not simply based on 'divide and rule' but on 'define and rule', involving the (re)making of subjectivities in the interest of colonial rule. Indirect rule, Mamdani (2012:43) argues, was a form of Foucauldian governmentality based on the 'understanding and management of difference': the invention and legal production of 'natives' and 'strangers', 'races' and 'tribes'. Bringing these insights to today's context of migration helps us see that not only the differentiation among migrants but the very stipulation of who constitutes a migrant in the first place is deeply political. Anderson (2013:29) accordingly discusses the colonial and imperial genealogy of the categories 'citizen' and 'migrant' and shows that 'how "the Migrant" came to exist as a category of person whose mobility was to be controlled … cannot be analysed in isolation from the history of colonialism and the development of modern nation states'. In Europe today, Anderson (2017:1532) notes, '"migration" already signals the need for control and in public discourse is often raced and classed'. Crucially, the social ordering and governing achieved through migration policy and discourse is a means to govern not only those legally positioned as 'migrants' but society more broadly, including 'citizens' (Anderson 2013, 2017, 2019). In other words, categories are sites of wider social politics inasmuch as migration categories 'work through particularizations that serve to discipline and normalize the population as a whole' (Fortier 2006:324).

Migration research has tended to focus on political institutions, primarily the state, as the producer of migration categories. Dividing up international movers is a central way in which states assert control. Castles (2000:270) argues that 'there is nothing objective about definitions of migration: they are the result of state policies, introduced in response to political and economic goals and public attitudes'. Yet although states have substantial symbolic and material power to name and differentiate people, state practices alone can neither account for powerful migration figures nor explain the processes that bring legal or statistical categories into being. Accordingly, Dzenovska (2013:2010) shows for the Latvian case that the figure of the migrant is not only 'a state-based category' but also an ethically and morally saturated figure in the 'social imaginary'. And Elrick and Farah Schwartzman (2015:1539–1541) argue that German state actors use the category 'persons with a migration background' in ways that 'transform this nuanced statistical category into a homogenized social category', excluded from the imagined national community based not on principles contained in the statistical category itself but emerging from 'Germany's national cultural repertoire'. They thus conclude that 'in order to understand how the state uses statistics to draw boundaries within a society, it is necessary to go beyond the content of statistical categories themselves'. Power operates in the categorisation of movement below and beyond the state. This is especially the case given that, as Bigo (2002:71) aptly argues, 'Immigration is now problematized in Western countries in a way that is very different from the distinction between citizen and foreigner. It is not a legal status that is under discussion but a social image, concerning, to quote Erickson, the "social distribution of bad".'

Migration categories are never simply about legal or technical distinctions and the making of migration categories is not a straightforward outcome of state policymaking, but situated within broader economic, political and social processes. Corporations, academia, media and cultural institutions, individual migrants and non-migrants alike participate in the production of migration categories, and thereby in struggles about the interpretation and differentiation of movement. This is the case in particular for the category expatriate. The USA is one of a few countries (if not the only one) that use 'expatriate' as a defined legal category. As a legal construct, 'expatriation' has here consistently denoted termination of citizenship. Yet, the legal specifics of who loses US citizenship, why, and the meanings attached to the act, have shifted significantly in line with sociocultural changes and political struggles about who belongs. Accordingly, Green (2009:310) argues that 'expatriation must be understood as both a legal and a social construct' and that the 'imagined expatriate' has played an important role in shaping citizenship legislation. A common reason for US citizens to denaturalise today is to avoid paying tax, and the expatriate of US tax law is thus a *non-citizen* residing abroad (IRS 2022). This is unlike the expatriate of the cultural imagination, who is more likely to be a US citizen who carefully maintains their legal and cultural allegiance with the US while living abroad. In the US, the legal meaning of the expatriate has thus become increasingly incongruent with the term's sociocultural uses, and it is arguably as a social category rather than as a legal or statistical category that the expatriate functions most powerfully today.

This book thus primarily traces the career of the expatriate as a *social category* – that is, as a category taken to delineate a group of people that are seen to share some defining characteristic(s). Social categories are cognitive tools that help us think, communicate and learn (Croft and Cruse 2004). They create temporary generalities to stabilise an unstable world and fix imprecise and changing phenomena (Stoler 2016). Social categories are also always rooted in sociomaterial processes and power relations. Historically attuned and grounded in a relational ontology, Foucault (2004:30) recognised power as not only prohibitive, but also productive and generative, and the individual emerges as 'one of power's first effects'. In this reading, the classification of humans does not so much denote 'social substances' but constitutes a 'normative regulation' of society (Butler 1990). Conceptualising power as relational and socially distributed does not deny the disproportionate sway that the state, or other powerful institutions and social groups hold over the categorisation of people; nor does it deny the power effects emanating from coercion, force and violence that often accompany and, indeed, realise states' legal and administrative categorisation. However, power operates below and beyond these facts, and no one is outside or above it. If we understand power as relational, circulating and multidirectional, we need to pay attention to the microdynamics of its exercise.

Studying the expatriate as a social category means not presupposing a certain meaning but examining the expatriate in its different uses and moments of (in)stability; examining the subjectivities, social relations and social hierarchies it organises; and studying the emotional states it narrates, and aspirations and anxieties it conveys. It means, following Brubaker (2004:11), to not assume the category expatriate as a pre-given entity, but explore it as the result of 'situated actions, cultural idioms, cognitive schemas, discursive frames, organizational routines, institutional forms, political projects, and contingent events'. This means studying the expatriate as a performative and embodied category (Butler 1990) that places individuals within symbolic, social and spatial arrangements: examining how the expatriate creates borders and 'groupness' (Brubaker 2004) in diaspora space, with what allied categories and against which 'constitutive outsides' (Hall 2001). And it includes interrogating the knowledges and narratives, imaginative geographies and broader sociocultural discourses that the expatriate organises, the connections it makes visible and the dissociations it achieves. In general, it means inquiring to what uses the category is put and what the consequences of its mobilisation are; that is, how the category participates in the socio-political ordering of movement.

Studying the expatriate as a social category also means paying attention to its changing membership, its shifting boundaries and hierarchical inner life. As cognitive linguists tell us, categories are far from stable, discrete and clearly bounded entities whose members share properties definable in terms of necessary and sufficient features (Croft and Cruse 2004:76ff). Instead of thinking of categories as containers with fixed boundaries, thinking of them in relational terms suggests that boundaries are formed contextually, in relation to varying Others. Prototype theory, as first articulated by Rosch (1973) posits that category boundaries are 'vague' and 'variable', shaped by social and discursive context (Croft and Cruse 2004:91). In other words, while boundaries might be a constant feature of categories, their target, shape and location are not stable. Stoler (2016:69) thus highlights the need to interrogate concepts' 'capacity to expand and contract, to be capacious and constricting'. If mutable boundaries are fundamental to the functioning of categories (just like, as Balibar (2002:78) writes, mutable or 'polysemic borders' are fundamental for nation-states), the contextual boundaries of the category 'expatriate' are instructive of the situated social and political work the category is asked to do. Additionally, categories are also uneven within their boundaries. Prototype theory suggests that categories are assembled like 'radial networks surrounding one prototype' (Nerlich et al. 2011:10). This accounts for the phenomenon of 'graded centrality': the fact that 'Not all members of a category have the same status within the category' and some category members are always seen as more representative than others (Croft and Cruse 2004:77). Social categories are thus not evenly and technically assembled. They are contextually moulded and have a dynamic 'life within', are internally differentiated and hierarchical, and can be conditional on unacknowledged domains of operation (see also Gullestad 2002).

Following Stoler (2011), we also need to take seriously and explore the polysemy of categories. Polysemy refers to multiplicity of meaning, and is a 'graded phenomenon' that ranges from *unrelated* homonyms to a polysemic word holding multiple *interrelated* meanings (Nerlich et al. 2011). Polysemy is a social product and encodes a word's social history. It is 'one of the driving forces of language change', as, for instance, ad hoc meanings can become 'conventionalised' or previous meanings dropped (Falkum 2015; Koskela 2014). Moreover, polysemy not only reflects sociohistorical processes, but can also be mobilised for rhetorical purposes. For instance, the ambiguity enabled by 'conventionalised' polysemy is a discursive resource as we can 'exploit' polysemy for our purposes and leave two or even multiple meanings 'hanging in the air' (Nerlich and Clarke 2001:12). Such 'purposive ambiguity' (Kittay 1987), or 'calculated ambiguity' (Gilroy 1987), can be mobilised for many different purposes, including for example the communication of racialised content or the creation of 'intimacy and social bonds' through a shared ability to decode unspecified double meanings (Nerlich and Clarke 2001:14). Mobilising ambiguity results in the 'strengthening of conceptual and semantic connections between senses' and keeps meanings alive and connected (Nerlich and Clarke 2001:11, 18). In fact, when we cognitively process polysemic words, 'inappropriate senses' can remain activated for quite some time (Nerlich and Clarke 2001:13) and polysemic words can thus be 'unruly' as listeners 'access the most salient (frequent, conventionalized) meaning first, which is sometimes neither the literal meaning nor the intended meaning' (Nerlich and Clarke 2001:13).

This discussion of linguistic category-making and polysemy provides several entry points for thinking about the expatriate in relation to power. Power relations inhabit the category's polysemic constellations and shape the coordinates and intensities of their daily realisation, as well as underwriting the ambiguities allowed or prevented in uses of the expatriate. Such 'polysemic games' (Kunz 2020a) can do vital political work. Further, if polysemy emerges from us creatively using words in unusual ways to make sense of our world, what does our choice of words in our 'polysemic operations' reveal? For example, when do we use expatriate rather than migrant if both can mean the same thing? Moreover, while there might be no 'true' meaning of an inherently polysemic expatriate, claims about true meanings are themselves worth examining. The book thus attends to the malleability and mobility of meaning, to ambiguities, internal fault lines, rearrangements and remakings, abandoned usages and those that failed to become conventionalised, to moments of uncertainty and disagreement and instants where the category becomes ungraspable or even 'useless'.

Following the expatriate as methodological strategy

Towards a bricolage of meaning

This book *follows the category* expatriate. Following the expatriate as an analytical strategy here means studying this social category ethnographically and historically, in its material, discursive and sociospatial production, experience and effects. In the wake of the globalisation and mobility turns, ethnography has been mobilised and stretched to examine social dynamics beyond the boundaries of specific locales. Multisited ethnography, as conceptualised by Marcus (1995:105), is 'designed around chains, paths, threads, conjunctions, or juxtapositions of locations in which the ethnographer establishes some form of literal, physical presence'. To do so, Marcus (1995) suggests 'tracking' as methodology, following connections or associations, people, things or metaphors. Following as methodological strategy has since been productively deployed by researchers following money, commodities, supply chains, people and even data (Akbari 2020). Geographers have researched transnational production and consumption chains by following fruit (Cook et al. 2004) and flip-flops (Knowles 2014) to defetishise commodities and reveal the everyday and situated production and relational nature of transnational capitalism.

Taking its cue from these approaches, following a *category* as an analytical strategy includes following the term geographically, textually and historically, as well as following up on its uses and effects. It also includes thinking about what might follow: how to move beyond problematic categories and articulate a more just politics of migration. Rather than assuming expatriate to have a particular meaning, following means investigating what expatriate has been taken to mean by those embracing or rejecting it, and what the consequences of its usage are. Gluck and Tsing (2009:3) suggest that following 'moving words provide[s] methodological entry into social and political experience'. That is, we can study 'the relation between words and worlds by tracing the social and political life of words – specific words in specific places at specific times'. Similarly, in her research into the social categories populating colonial archives, Stoler (2016:79) suggests to 'follow the trajectories of the term itself': study its shifting enunciation, membership, moments of use but also moments of insecurity, confusion and rejection. This research strategy avoids reifying the expatriate and allows its charged relationship with various Others to be examined. It goes beyond studying migrants labelled expatriate and includes investigating academic, cultural and organisational uses of the term. Learning from Valentine's (2007) ethnography of the social category transgender, it means exploring how and with what effects social positions, relations, movements and spaces are assembled and organised through the category expatriate.

Ladwig et al. (2012:12–13) further develop the 'following' approach for historical studies by conceptualising a multisited ethnography that not only includes research in 'actual contemporary locations' but also in 'archival field sites', by following mentions of their study object into colonial archives. Following historically here means tracing situated genealogies of the expatriate to provide what Foucault called 'an ontology of the present' (cited in Garland 2014:372). Instead of using the category as an analytical frame to investigate past migrations, I thus make it the object of my analysis. This means inquiring into the career of the category expatriate *itself*, investigating its past uses and politics. Rather than searching for true origins or straightforward continuities, this genealogy of the category aims to 'trace the struggles, displacements and processes of repurposing out of which contemporary practices emerged, and to show the historical conditions of existence upon which present-day practices depend' (Garland 2014:373). In this vein, postcolonial genealogies produce histories of the colonial present. They trace postcolonial connections, ruptures and recuperations in relational 'transborder' spaces to provide non-linear histories, without universalising or teleological claims. This genealogical work relies on historical traces and flashbacks, on moments where the expatriate 'pops up' in archives in ways that help make sense of contemporary predicaments (Ladwig et al. 2012). Using Benjamin's (1968:255) metaphor, working historically 'means to seize hold of a memory as it flashes up at a moment of danger'. Where a present and a past form a 'dialectics at a standstill', they do not simply shed light on each other, but come together to form a new object of history (Benjamin 1999:462, 865). This constellation that far apart events can form together, effectively 'explodes' the linear historicist 'continuum of history' (Benjamin 1968:261). In Benjamin's dialectical constructivist approach, history is thus essentially open and unfinished. There are unrealised alternatives at every historical conjuncture that may yet be realised. This book accordingly places past and present snapshots of the expatriate from a variety of social contexts into a constellation, to make sense of each other, allow new understandings to emerge and to possibly help us imagine a future that fulfils past struggles.

This book does *not* provide an exhaustive ethnographic or historical account of the category expatriate. Instead, it is better described as a bricolage, or constellation of meaning across three disparate sites. The category expatriate spans and organises an array of sites that, although 'not coterminous or homologous', form part of its 'wider polysemic cultural formation' (Fortier 2013:71). This book follows the expatriate to and within three sites where expatriate is a central category, a vital organising force, and which in turn give it actuality and authority: anglophone IHRM literature, the *Expatriate Archive Centre* (EAC) and social spaces of privileged migration in Nairobi, Kenya. No directionality or teleology has guided my movements across these sites besides the fact that all three share a central reliance on the category expatriate. Nor am I arguing that the three sites need to be considered a unified whole. They tell their own situated stories of how the expatriate is produced, lived and negotiated. Ultimately, there is no true or original meaning of this slippery and unstable category. There is no universal notion that stands above its local enunciations. While each site needs to be recognised in its 'incomparable singularity' (Jazeel 2019a), they also offer crucial insights *together*. Ladwig et al. (2012) attend to how unalike sites that moreover differ in space and time can be analytically linked, and suggest this resembles Benjamin's method of montage, rather than a reconstruction of wholes. Far from a random piecing together, this is a conscious and 'constructive' process grounded in a relational understanding of knowledge production. Putting different and seemingly disparate sites in 'fresh juxtapositions' allows different conversations to happen and opens up the past for 're-examination'

(Ladwig et al. 2012:21). Approaching the sites as a constellation thus allows the entanglements of the category expatriate to be examined, not assumed; it reveals connections and coherences as well as fractures and friction; it generates insights that no single site could provide.

The three sites and their methodologies

Given my concern with attaining a situated, in-depth and nuanced understanding of meaning-making processes, social relations and power dynamics, the research for this book was of a qualitative nature. Different sites demand different research strategies, and key methods included participant observation, interviewing, archival research and document analysis of material gathered both offline and online. The first site to which this book follows the expatriate is Nairobi, Kenya. Nairobi is the *perfect place* to study expats, I was told repeatedly and with emphasis during my five months there. Nairobi is a young city. From its inception in 1896, 'Nairobi has always been a transnational city', a city of migrants, its creation as a regional imperial centre bound up with rural-to-urban, regional and trans-continental migration flows, ranging from the highly privileged to those experiencing various forms of oppression and exploitation (Campbell 2005:5; Rahbaran and Herz 2014). These migrations conditioned each other within highly unequal immigration regimes, and arrivals in urban space were sociospatially segregated along the racial categories 'Asian', 'African' and 'European' that British rule relied on (Lonsdale 2002). Nairobi today remains East Africa's economic hub, and many companies and international organisations have regional headquarters there (Charton-Bigot and Rodrigues-Torres 2010). Nairobi hosts a UN headquarters, and more recently became a regional 'tech hub', attracting local start-ups and multinational players like IBM (Henry 2015). In this context, Nairobi has continued to receive significant numbers of privileged migrants: a *perfect place* to study expats (Doro 1979; Uusihakala 1999; Dickinson 2016; Kunz 2018, 2021). Chapter 5 discusses how locating the 'expat' in Nairobi proved trickier than this statement suggests.

In Nairobi, following the category took the form of urban ethnography, including archival research on the expatriate. In 2016, I spent five months trying to be guided through the city by the category expatriate, focusing on places and institutions that explicitly addressed expatriates or were recounted to me as nodal points of Nairobi's expat scene. I became a member of the social and professional network *InterNations*, a regular visitor at the *East Africa Women's League* (EAWL) and took up yoga. I spoke to people who called themselves or were introduced to me as expatriates, as well as those that socialised or worked with them. I collected a range of data in this loosely networked expatriate social space, including daily field notes based on participant observation and 58 semi-structured, life history and expert interviews with 60 people (including two paired interviews with elderly couples), besides many more informal conversations. Interviewees included 28 men and 32 women from diverse demographic backgrounds. Migrant interlocutors (42) had lived in Nairobi between three weeks and over six decades. They were all socio-economically well off in the Kenyan context and held citizenship of Australia (1), India (1), Malawi (1), Pakistan (1), unknown (1), the USA (8), Zimbabwe (1), with a majority (28) being European citizens, mostly British (18). Those I met at InterNations or through yoga were in their twenties to late forties, single and in relationships, and worked in a range of professions at various levels of seniority. Through the East Africa Women's League, I met mostly older interlocutors, in their sixties to their eighties, who had lived in Kenya for decades and with whom I primarily conducted life history interviews, some across several meetings. I also interviewed 18 Kenyan citizens, some with dual citizenship, about their perceptions of and interactions with people they considered expatriates, and in some cases about their own experiences living abroad. They had various socio-economic backgrounds, with some being well-paid professionals frequenting Nairobi's upmarket bars while others made a more modest living as yoga teachers. Five interviews were with immigration experts and practitioners, both Kenyan and foreign citizens, including immigration lawyers, NGO staff and former policymakers. Informally, I also spoke to many taxi drivers, and staff like security guards, who took me to or worked at venues I frequented.

Additionally, I reviewed the InterNations Nairobi website, read blogs and articles aimed at expats in Nairobi, and joined a number of Facebook groups such as 'Nairobi Expat Social', 'Nairobi Expat Housing' and 'Nairobi Expat Marketplace'. I visited the Kenya National Archives and Documentation Service (KNADS) and the East Africa Women's League organisational archives and searched for appearances of the term expatriate to guide me through the vast amount of material. In the Kenya National Archives, I found a file on 'Asian expatriates' protesting their exclusion from the 1961 Overseas Service Aid Scheme (Chapter 2), a topic I then researched further at the British National Archives at Kew (where the bulk of relevant archival material for this chapter was held), and by reviewing British parliamentary debates and Kenya Legislative Council debates (available via Hansard online and Google Books). As critical literature on archives has argued, which historical records are retained, where these records are held and how they can be accessed is a highly political matter (Featherstone 2006). Kenya's colonial history is a prime example, as shown by revelations around the 'Hanslope files', which detail systematic torture and abuse of Kenyan freedom fighters during the 1950s, and which were repatriated and kept hidden by successive British governments until their court-ordered release in 2011 (Este 2013). The existence, location and accessibility of sources thus speaks to the ongoing geopolitics of historical knowledge production on the category expatriate.

The *Expatriate Archive Centre* in The Hague is the second site to which I followed the expatriate. The Expatriate Archive Centre is a small archive dedicated to documenting worldwide expatriate social history. The archive grew out of a project by 'Shell wives' – the Shell Ladies' Project (SLP) – to document their lives on the move with Shell. The SLP resulted in two anthologies (SLP 1993, 1996) and the establishment of a *Shell Outpost Family Archive Centre*, which in 2008 transformed into the independent and expanded Expatriate Archive Centre. My research strategy at the EAC was two-fold. Besides conducting archival research at the archive, I also explored the history and work of the archive itself. From late 2015, I spent three months at the EAC, conducting an internship and doing archival research. At that time and during subsequent visits, I also took field notes and conducted 19 interviews, mostly with EAC staff, founders, volunteers and collaborators, but also with a few people running other expat organisations based in The Hague. The research also led me to other archives, including the Amsterdam-based *Institute on Gender Equality and Women's History* (ATRIA). My research strategy at the EAC responds to critical engagements with archives that recognise archives as sites where social power is negotiated and knowledge is produced: as 'full-fledged historical actors' (Burton 2005:7). Here, archival processes as much as documents become objects of research. As Schwartz and Cook (2002:1) argue,

> through archives, the past is controlled. Certain stories are privileged and others marginalized. In the design of record-keeping systems, in the appraisal and selection of a tiny fragment of all possible records to enter the archive ... archivists continually reshape, reinterpret, and reinvent the archive. This represents enormous power over memory and identity.

Recognising this power, Stoler (2002:87) calls for ethnographic approaches that 'move from archive-as-source to archive-as-subject', for research that treats archives not only as sites of knowledge retrieval, but also as sites of knowledge production. Moreover, such approaches recognise archives themselves as 'historical artifacts' resulting from 'specific political, cultural, and socioeconomic pressures' (Burton 2005:6).

The third site of this study is international human resource management literature, which I similarly conceptualise as an archive documenting the production and uses of the category expatriate in corporate practice and its associated academic field. That is, IHRM literature is an archive of the making of the expatriate through the ways it has become known. Recognising academic knowledge production as a social practice situated within specific socio-political contexts allows us to 'adopt a particular kind of disposition to ... knowledge and theory conceived as "archive"' (Jazeel 2014:92), and to study this archive with the aim of understanding the societies and power constellations it was produced by and for. This methodological tactic is especially indebted to Said's (1993:xii) examination of the 'cultural archive' of Orientalism which centrally included 'specialized knowledge available in such learned disciplines as ethnography, historiography, philology, sociology, and literary history'. Approached as such, IHRM literature tells us not only about the expatriate as a contested socio-political formation always-in-the-making, but about the social contexts that have required and moulded, but also challenged it. By bringing IHRM literature *as an archive* into the fold of migration studies, I also hope to advance debates about what we imagine as migration and which histories of migration we write by help of what sorts of archives.

Conceptualising IHRM literature as an archive implies rereading what poses as technical matters of business organisation as matters of the hierarchical ordering of human movement and labour. Supposedly technical IHRM accounts can be seen as 'rhetorical sleights of hand' (Stoler 2002:99) that erase conflict and struggle from their accounts. Inquiring what is seen as the problem, who gets to speak on the problem and what the offered solutions are reveals the political nature of ostensibly technical and value-neutral writings on labour rotation in multinational corporations. Such conceptualisation as an archive thus means analytically approaching IHRM literature by reading it against but also along its grain. 'Reading against the grain' is a postcolonial tactic grounded in the Subaltern Studies Collective's project of wrestling a subaltern South Asian history from colonial archives by retrieving subversive acts and interpretations that are sidelined, hidden in omissions or inhabit undrawn conclusions, by uncovering suppressed experiences and recovering discontent and resistance (Guha and Spivak 1988). More recently, Stoler (2002, 2010) has called for a renewed reading of colonial sources 'along their grain', implying a methodological refocusing on the language of power to reveal narrative strategies but also instabilities and fragilities. As Stoler (2010:50) argues, such a careful yet critical engagement with colonial scripts is necessary, because often,

> Assuming that we know those scripts rests too comfortably on predictable stories with familiar plots. ... Not least, it leaves unaddressed how often colonial categories reappear in the analytic vocabulary of historians rather than as transient, provisional objects of historical inquiry that themselves need to be analysed, if not explained.

Questioning the narratives that colonial and corporate scripts seek to tell us thus includes interrogating their vocabularies and assumedly innocent categories, and locating tensions and disorder within the archive's ostensibly smooth genres (Stoler 2010). Here, this means engaging in the field of IHRM literature to probe the social categories this literature thinks with, centrally the expatriate, and to trace their imperial genealogies and colonial presents.

In practical terms, I assembled my archive of IHRM literature in 2016 through a search for academic articles on expatriat* in the academic citation databases SCOPUS and Web of Science, in the fields of 'Business, Management and Accounting', 'Psychology' and 'Economics, Econometrics and Finance'. In order to understand the key themes, approaches and concerns of the field over time, I selected from this archive the most cited articles for coding and thematic analysis in NVivo.[2] I limited this initial investigation to journal articles, given that the publishing requirements in organisational science favour journal articles over books (Prasad and Prasad 2002). While this search brought up several thousand articles, few were published before the 1980s. I thus additionally searched the JStor Management & Organizational Behaviour journals for articles on expatriat* published prior to 1980, and systematically reviewed the *International Executive* (launched 1959, now *Thunderbird International Business Review*), *Human Resource Management* (launched 1961) and *Columbia Journal of World Business* (launched 1965, now *Journal of World Business*) along the same criteria. I then worked through the reference lists of review articles to source further pre-1980 articles. Finally, I read articles and chapters offering reviews of the field, and articles on key categories and themes that emerged from my thematic analysis. In total, my archive of IHRM literature contained over 3,000 articles, of which I read over 350 articles and systematically coded 125.

How we study migration is closely entangled with the politics of migration. Although the possibility of reflexivity is contested (Lynch 2000) and its achievement remains necessarily imperfect (Kobayashi 2003), to attempt reflexivity seems indispensable given the intersubjective and political nature of knowledge production. As Rose (1997:318) puts it, 'I worry that my work may exclude or erase, I worry about its effects. … feminist geographers should keep these worries, and work with them.' Reflexivity thus remains a necessary ambition that can never be fully realised. Reflections on 'studying up' have been key for research on privileged migration (Fechter 2007). Coined by Laura Nader (1972:289), the idea of 'studying up' encourages scholars to 'study the colonizer rather than the colonized, the culture of power rather than the culture of the powerless' in order to understand the social processes that produce both. 'Studying up' proves especially useful for situating research on the category expatriate in a field that habitually assumes a privileged researcher and disadvantaged migrant interlocutors. In research contexts marked by multiple and intersecting power relationships there is of course no 'easy positioning' (Anderson-Levy 2010; Stich and Colyar 2015). My own white Europeanness and status as a PhD researcher meant that I was more realistically 'studying sideways', rather than 'up', vis-à-vis many interlocutors. Even if I did not call myself an expatriate, I was certainly positioned as an expatriate by others, and for good reason. Especially while researching the expatriate in Nairobi, I shared what were understood to be expatriate routines and habits. The symbolic capital of my whiteness and nationality and the cultural capital of speaking English proved salient. It affected what was said to me and around me, as when someone casually complained about immigration to Europe or joked about 'locals', assuming I shared or at least tolerated their sentiments. Especially as a researcher in Nairobi, I was able to use strategically my own privilege to access spaces of power. At the same time, my privilege arguably made it harder to get at the knowledges and opinions of those less privileged in those same spaces, including staff working at venues or for interlocutors. How my positionality thus ultimately shaped, helped or complicated my research remains indeterminate (Chapter 5). Throughout the research I was thus never outside the social phenomenon I studied, and if the expatriate emerges as a shifting category, so does my own relationship to it.

Notes

1 The term lifestyle migration has attracted similar critiques to that of expatriate. As Jaji (2019), Hayes (2018) and Huete et al. (2013) note, economic *and* lifestyle considerations are intertwined and crucial for most migrants. Whether these people are framed as lifestyle or economic migrants often depends as much on the migrants' motivations as on the researcher's assumptions about them: 'The fuzzy distinction between economic and lifestyle migrants shows that categories are not produced by essential attributes of mobilities' but largely premised on 'country profiles and the reasons they articulate and inscribe on mobile bodies' (Jaji 2019:37), so that 'Movement by the [African] continent's peoples is cloaked in a migration lexicon that depicts it as induced by

economic and political problems. This is contrasted to migration from the global North, which is connected to adventure and lofty aspirations' (Jaji 2019:19).

2 I read and coded all articles I found that were published pre-1980; for articles published between 1980 and 2010, I selected the 5 per cent most cited articles *per decade* for coding in NVivo; from 2010 to 2015, I coded the top 5 per cent cited articles *per year.*

Part I

The historical expatriate

2

From colonial civil servant to expatriate at the eve of Kenyan independence

It is sought, I fear, to inflict upon a future Government of Kenya this baby of racial discrimination that has unfortunately been one of the features of colonial administration throughout the century ... whether we like it or not what is in fact going to happen in a future independent country of Kenya is that we are going to get one class of persons – persons of one race – getting a particular salary, a very high salary, and another group of persons, whether they are Indians or Africans, who are going to get a lower salary for exactly the same job. Now, Sir, if this is not racial discrimination in fact – whatever the theory behind it may be – what is it going to be?

Fitzval de Souza, Kenya Legislative Council, 23 May 1961[1]

In 1967, 26-year-old Paul Theroux published a polemical article titled 'Tarzan is an expatriate', caricaturing expatriates in East and Central Africa. His expatriate is self-important, obnoxious and, by definition, white in a black country as 'the old order does not alter, the revolutions change nothing and still to be white is to be right' (Theroux 1967:19). Theroux's article documents the persistence of white privilege in post-colonial East Africa and shows the category expatriate to be key to this articulation of whiteness. His scathing commentary is still echoed today. As Fechter (2007:2) writes, 'the words "colonial" and "expatriate" are regularly employed in conjunction with each other in accounts of late colonial life', especially in reference to 'British gentlemen who, after prolonged exposure to the tropical climates of South or South East Asia, suffer from world-weariness, alienation and alcoholism'. Scholarship, too, deploys expatriate to denote colonial and postcolonial white migrants, as evidenced by Smiley's (2013:2015) work on the segregation of Dar es Salaam 'into European/Expatriate, Asian, and African areas'.

Others use expatriate specifically for (semi-)temporary white migrants. As Darwin (2010:332) notes, 'conventional usage' today is to contrast permanent 'settlers' with 'the expat' who 'lives overseas for a term. The reason is usually employment.' In such usages, the expatriate is often assumed *by default* to be white, so that the label expatriate makes the adjectival 'white' unnecessary.

This chapter explains but also problematises such uses of expatriate. It shows that in mid-twentieth-century East Africa, expatriate was not used exclusively for those racialised as white. Neither was the category primarily associated with temporary mobility. Indeed, assuming as much erases historical struggles. This chapter discusses the transformation of the Kenyan colonial administration into a national civil service. In the process, the British passed a number of measures to induce 'expatriate' civil servants to stay on until 'local' replacements had been trained, centrally including the 1961 Overseas Service Aid Scheme. The category expatriate proved a lynchpin in this process of decolonisation, and heated debate developed about who qualified as expatriate. The British government lobbied aggressively, and successfully, to define the category in a way that restricted it almost exclusively to white male officers, excluding most 'Asian' and 'African' expatriate officers and women. By recovering this debate, the chapter shows that it was far from decided who was an expatriate. OSAS *created* rather than *identified* expatriates and adapted rather than abolished colonial racism, although without mobilising explicitly racist terms, to structure postcolonial hierarchies of work and mobility and secure British influence through 'technical assistance'.

(Not) preparing the colonial civil service for independence

The colonial civil service at the eve of independence

The territory that is now the Republic of Kenya first came under British control in 1888 through the Imperial British East Africa Company. It became the East Africa Protectorate in 1895 and the Colony and Protectorate of Kenya in 1920. Kenya attained internal self-government in June 1963, full independence on 12 December 1963, and became a republic on 12 December 1964. It thus followed

Britain's other major East African territories, Tanganyika, which gained independence in December 1961, and Uganda, which won independence in October 1962. The British made Kenya a settler economy to try and recover the costs of the Uganda railway and preferred settlers 'of independent means', leading to Kenya's reputation as the aristocratic colony (Lonsdale 2010). Consequently, the number of white settlers remained small, and by 1962 the white population (56,000) was only a third of the Asian population (177,000) and a fraction of the over 8 million Africans (Vinnai 1974). While South Asians had come to East Africa long before British colonialism, many were brought as indentured labour to build the railway, while others came to fill mid-level clerical, technical and commercial positions, including in the civil service. They were positioned as the 'middleman minority' within the tripartite racialised hierarchy that British colonialism was built on; though privileged over Africans, they were discriminated against vis-à-vis Europeans (Lonsdale 2010). Africans, and to some extent Asians, opposed colonial rule in Kenya from the outset. Resistance erupted in the 1890s, 1920s, and again more forcefully in the 1950s, with the Kenya Land and Freedom Army uprising, labelled 'Mau Mau' by the British. Britain responded with a policy of 'multiracialism' stipulating a sharing of political power among racially defined groups, with a predominant role for Europeans and least power for the African majority (Maxon 2011). Within this framework, Kenyan Africans were first granted (very limited) electoral representation in 1957. Kenya's independence and constitutional framework were negotiated at the three Lancaster House conferences in 1960, 1962 and 1963.

The Colonial Service, to which all colonial civil servants belonged, was a key imperial institution and administered most of Britain's colonies under the authority of the Colonial Office and the Secretary of State for the Colonies in London. In Kenya's colonial civil service, as elsewhere, Europeans held virtually all the senior posts, while Asians and Europeans staffed the middle ranks and African personnel – by 1960 about 80 per cent of the service – filled most clerical, semi-skilled and unskilled grades (Vinnai 1974:177). While many civil servants in the higher and intermediate grades were recruited directly from the UK and South Asia, others were drawn from East Africa's European and Asian settler communities. The role of the colonial civil service was to maintain 'law and order', implement policy decided on in London, and collect revenue to make the colony self-supporting; until quite late, the civil service was not concerned with socio-economic development except to create favourable conditions for the European-dominated agricultural sector (Vinnai 1974). Tom Mboya (1970:163) accordingly recounted that pro-independence politicians viewed civil servants as 'antagonistic perpetrators of colonialism and domination' who were 'extravagantly paid' and 'not really interested in the welfare of his country'.

    British authorities at the time considered the transformation of colonial into national civil services one of the most important practical problems of decolonisation (Kirk-Greene 2000; Seidler 2018). The British faced the dual task of handing over functioning civil services to national governments and taking care of civil servants who lost their careers in the process. While colonial civil servants were servants of the Crown and their employment conditions were set down in colonial regulations, they were technically employed by their individual colonial governments, mostly on permanent and pensionable (P&P) terms (Kirk-Greene 2000). Independence was 'not foreseen' in their employment contracts, and with decolonisation accelerating by the early 1950s, officers began to worry what would happen 'once the legal entity with which they had contracted ceased to exist' (Seidler 2018:292). As a result, recruitment into the service was becoming difficult, officers were beginning to resign, and in many colonies fears arose of the breakdown of the civil service. As Seidler (2018:292) writes, this 'was a fairly well-known issue in the 1960s that has been overlooked by the more recent literature on colonial history'.

    Britain's first response to this challenge was the transformation of the Colonial Service into Her Majesty's Overseas Civil Service (HMOCS), announced in the 1954 White Paper Colonial No. 306. The White Paper's interconnected aims were to provide assurances to increasingly anxious colonial civil servants and prevent the breakdown of colonial civil services (Kirk-Greene 2000). It is often argued that the introduction of HMOCS 'involved little more than a change of name' (Williams 1964:24) to 'get rid of the "trigger" word, "Colonial"' as MP Bernard Braine specified.[2] Indeed, more significant to officers at the time was not the establishment of HMOCS but the assurance contained in the same White Paper that, prior to independence, Britain would negotiate agreements with independent governments to protect civil servants' employment conditions and ensure their compensation when they eventually left the service (Ireton 2013). Yet the creation of HMOCS proved consequential in East Africa in two important ways. First, unlike the Colonial Service, membership in HMOCS was not automatic, and civil servants had to reapply to join HMOCS. Second, a distinction between 'local' and 'overseas' civil servants was introduced and HMOCS was no longer open, as the Colonial Service had been, to 'locally recruited officials' – which included almost all African civil servants but also Asian and European staff recruited directly from Kenya's settler communities (Kirk-Greene 2000:149). The 1954 White Paper did not succeed in stemming the tide of officers leaving the service, with especially mid-career officers, most vital to the service, taking advantage of lump-sum compensation payments to leave sooner rather than later (Kirk-Greene 2000; Ireton 2013). In the mid-1950s, a breakdown of the service was looming in West Africa, especially Nigeria. And by 1960 the matter had become particularly urgent in East Africa, where over half of the remaining 21,000 HMOCS officers were based[3] and where localisation efforts had been so slow that Europeans continued to hold nearly all senior posts.

This resulted in Britain's next major measure, the 1960 White Paper 'Service with Overseas Governments',[4] which came into law in 1961 as the Overseas Service Act, generally known as the Overseas Service Aid Scheme (OSAS). OSAS financially supported independent governments to keep overseas officers for up to ten years. The scheme covered all remaining British colonies but each had to negotiate a separate agreement with the British. Officers 'designated' under OSAS would be employed by independent governments on local rates of pay, however they would also receive, at British expense, an additional 'overseas inducement allowance', and an allowance for children's education. The British also shared with independent governments the cost of officers' passages home and, eventually, their compensation and pensions.[5] OSAS was recognised as a generous provision for designated civil servants and the Minister of State for Colonial Affairs, Lord Perth, declared that the 'expensive and costly White Paper scheme at a time when the UK was subject to many other major financial pressures' was proof that 'HMG were more concerned about the future of the Overseas Civil Servants than about almost any other matter affecting Colonial policy'.[6]

Throughout the 1950s, the British thus put considerable effort into inducing European civil servants to stay on. They expended significantly less effort on training, recruiting and promoting Africans for senior roles. Although – or because – the British recognised that a 'competent and experienced Civil Service composed of local people' was a condition for 'responsible self-Government',[7] Africans were systematically excluded from positions of responsibility in the middle and upper ranks until the end of colonial rule (Kooperman and Rosenberg 1977). During the 1950s, the number of European civil servants in Kenya actually increased, to support the fight against 'Mau Mau' and in the context of the 'second colonial occupation', as coined by Low and Lonsdale (1976, cited in Kirk-Greene 2000) to refer to Britain's post-World War II colonial policy of 'development' and 'trusteeship' and the 'concomitant increase in European civil servants at a time when their reduction and a policy of localization might have been expected to be the order of the day' (Kirk-Greene 2000:317). Settler resistance further obstructed African advance-ment in the civil service, and until 1960 European civil servants were still recruited on permanent and pensionable terms (Vinnai 1974). Consequently, in 1960, HMOCS membership was at its peak while only five Africans had held senior posts in the colonial civil service (Kirk-Greene 2000). Only in 1961 did Britain announce its localisation policy for the civil service[8] and begin systematically training Africans to replace 'the key administrative cadre composed of Europeans' (Vinnai 1974:177). Between July 1960 and April 1962, the number of Africans above the lower clerical scales nearly doubled, but even then Africans only constituted around 12 per cent of staff in the higher scales.[9] At independence, Kenya still had a comparatively high percentage of European civil servants, especially in the upper and middle-ranking pay scales, but even in the lower clerical grades there were 'a large number of Europeans … drawing salaries that were not commensurate with their minor responsibilities' (Kirk-Greene 2000:256). As the Kenya Legislative Council (LegCo) member Mohamed Jahazi scathingly noted in 1963, 'you find that in some municipal councils the simple job of refuse collecting is headed by a European expatriate. I do not see how it will take years of training to instruct a man on how to collect refuse in the town.'[10]

It was precisely this failure, or disinclination, to 'Africanise' the civil service which resulted in Kenya having to rely on many OSAS officers after independence. OSAS too did not incentivise, let alone fund, the training of African staff, but was dedicated solely to enabling the ongoing employment of expatriate officers.[11] Indeed, OSAS incentivised independent governments to employ OSAS officers instead of local officers for as long as possible, especially in more expensive senior positions, to avoid costly compensation and pension payments. Kenya's Temporary Minister for Finance and Development, Joseph Nyagah, pointed out in 1961 that 'the country does not save any appreciable sum of money by replacing a designated expatriate officer by a local officer. In fact, the immediate effect is a quite considerable increase in the costs to the Kenyan government.'[12] As Sylvester (1999:704) puts it, 'decolonising processes culminating in political independence were usually sloppy, rushed, insensitive, violent or just haphazard'.

The Flemming salary revision: inducement and uneven salary increases

Besides offering guarantees of privileged employment through OSAS, Her Majesty's Government also increased the salaries of East African civil servants to induce them to stay. In 1960, the British government appointed a commission headed by Sir Gilbert Flemming – the Flemming Salaries Commission for the Civil Service in East Africa – to recommend revisions of civil service salaries. Significant salary increases were demanded by East African staff associations and supported by British parliamentarians,[13] who argued that East African salaries had not kept up with the increased cost of living and, in any case, salary increases were required to keep qualified officers in the territories. The Flemming Report was published in January 1961. Its recommendations exceeded staff demands and were enthusiastically welcomed in London. In the House of Commons, member of parliament (MP) Hilary A. Marquand noted that the Flemming Commission recommended 'very substantial salary increases, ranging from 25 to 30 per cent', which MP Henry Clark celebrated for going 'a lot further' than the 10 to 15 per cent most officers had expected.[14] When MP Sir Hendrie Oakshott mentioned 'some local criticism' among non-European officers, he went on to suggest that this criticism was 'founded more on political emotion than on logic', highlighting the to-be-expected 'discrimination with the arrival of independence in favour of the African civil servants' so that 'if the Flemming Report taken with the [OSAS] Bill is in the other sense discriminatory also, there is good reason for it'.[15]

Indeed, the Flemming salary revisions were harshly criticised – both for their discriminatory effect and for the way they had been implemented – by African and Asian members of the Kenya Legislative Council (LegCo) and the majority-Asian *Clerical and Allied Civil Servants' Association* (CACSA). A fact largely unremarked upon in London was that the salary increases were regressive in nature, i.e. the largest increases went to the upper salary bands, which included, by colonial design, primarily European officers. Accordingly, LegCo member Chanan Singh was critical that the Flemming revisions implied a 30 per cent salary increase for the highest-paid civil servants, 10 and 7.5 per cent increases for the next groups and a 15 per cent increase for the bottom group of 'subordinate staff'.[16] Fellow LegCo member Zafrud Deen agreed and noted that the Flemming report was 'largely condemned for its discriminatory nature' because it reproduced 'the racial discrimination which was the perpetuation of the old scale where Europeans and non-Europeans were divided into different compartments'.[17] This was echoed by Fitzval de Souza (see chapter opening quote) and Tom Mboya, who asked rhetorically, 'What benefits has the non-European element of the Civil Service derived from the implementation of the Flemming Report?'[18] The answer was, of course, significantly less than the European.

The way that the Flemming Report was implemented suggests that its sponsors were well aware of its discriminatory nature. The report was released in January 1961, when there was no sitting Legislative Council because Kenyan general elections were due to be held that February. The Kenyan government had therefore, in December 1960, obtained permission from the previous LegCo to implement the Flemming Report, the details of which were still unknown.[19] Upon the report's release in January 1961, the caretaker government immediately proceeded to implement Flemming's recommendations, with salary increases dated back to 1 April 1960.[20] This hurried implementation before the new Legislative Council was in place was necessary, the government argued, to put an immediate end to officers leaving the service. However, another consideration must have been that the new LegCo was for the first time elected in a general election with universal suffrage, and hence as expected dominated by the pro-independence Kenya African National Union (KANU) led by Jomo Kenyatta.[21] That the Flemming Report was published and implemented at a time when there was no Legislative Council to debate it, and certainly before the new LegCo was in place, was thus hardly accidental. The British and the colonial Kenyan government must have been well aware that the new LegCo would be highly unlikely to approve salary increases that principally benefitted the already highly privileged European civil servants. Indeed, furious protest erupted on 23 May 1961, when the new LegCo was asked to retroactively approve the additional costs that had arisen from the Flemming salary increases. The protest proved futile, however, not least because the payments had already been made.[22] The already generous renumeration of primarily European senior civil servants thus became even more lavish at the eve of independence. As discussed below, this not only produced a privileged postcolonial expatriate but also helped entrench inequality in the Kenyan civil service.

Colonial category-making for postcolonial times: the politics of defining the expatriate

Negotiating OSAS: who's an expatriate?

Like the Flemming salary increases, the Overseas Service Aid Scheme aimed to induce expatriate civil servants to stay on in the service of independent governments and proved similarly discriminatory. OSAS did not identify expatriates as much as *create* them as a privileged class of employees. It did so by translating the explicitly racialised inequalities that had structured the colonial civil service into ostensibly non-racial criteria for designation under OSAS. As a result, debate over the terms of designation turned into full-blown political struggle. After the announcement of the October 1960 White Paper 'Service with Overseas Governments', colonial governments were invited to negotiate individual OSAS agreements with Her Majesty's Government. Talks with Kenya commenced instantly and the 'Overseas Service (Kenya) Agreement, 1961' was passed as Ordinance Nr. 12 without division by Kenya's Legislative Council on 5 July 1961.[23] The application of the OSAS principle to Kenya – and East Africa more generally – was considered problematic from the outset. Theoretically, OSAS was to cover expatriate civil servants. However, who qualified as an expatriate was far from clear. Consequently, MP Sir Oakshott noted during the second reading of OSAS in the British Parliament that the 'most important question' was 'Who does the Bill cover? Who is an expatriate? Who is a designated officer or person?'[24] In response, the Secretary of State for the Colonies, Iain Macleod, stressed that expatriate status was *not* dependent on nationality although he expected 'the great majority' of designated officers to be citizens of the United Kingdom and Colonies. Instead, Macleod argued, expatriate status depended on being *not* 'locally domiciled', which was to be decided based on the original mode of recruitment: 'it is not the country of origin but the method of recruitment which is the test'.[25] But what seemed easy in theory proved difficult in practice and the eventual rules for designation under the OSAS Kenya Agreement covered the better part of a page.[26] While the rules thus became incredibly complex, their racial effects were strikingly simple: in March 1962, designated officers included 1 African, 32 Asians and 3,890 Europeans.[27] Yet the British and Kenyan colonial governments denied all charges of racism. So how was a racialised outcome achieved through ostensibly non-racial measures? A closer look at how the rules for designation were arrived at proves instructive.

The London meetings, December 1960

After Macleod had presented the OSAS White Paper to Parliament in October 1960, meetings with representatives from the Kenyan government and Kenya Staff Side were convened at the Colonial Office in London in December 1960 to discuss the proposed OSAS Kenya Agreement, including 'the most important issue, namely that of the definition of the term "entitled officer"'.[28] The Colonial Office argued that the scheme was

> for expatriate officers, the term expatriate having a geographical connotation. The scheme was intended to meet a situation in which officers whose permanent homes were outside a particular territory might leave that territory, to the detriment of public administration.[29]

However, the Kenyan delegation, led by Kenya's Attorney General and Acting Chief Secretary, Eric Griffith-Jones, called for broader rules for designation than those proposed by the British government. Griffith-Jones argued that OSAS would not achieve its objectives unless it covered 'officers who, whatever their origin, were recognised throughout Kenya to be "expatriate"' and who 'had never at any time had any cause to suspect that differentiation would be introduced between them and their colleagues'. As Griffith-Jones noted, even the differentiation between 'local' and 'overseas' introduced by HMOCS in 1954 had never been understood to imply any differential treatment such as was now proposed. He argued that if the proposed rules of designation based on a 'geographical connotation' of 'expatriate' were to be adopted,

> a large number of officers who had hitherto been regarded as expatriates,[30] and acknowledged as such by the Government of Kenya and indirectly by HMG by virtue of the application of the Holmes and Lidbury Salary Commission awards, would be excluded from the benefits and, more importantly, the security of their conditions of service which were inherent in the White Paper scheme. In these circumstances there would be a serious danger of a breakup in the Kenya government service and the exodus of significant numbers of key officials. The core of the problem was the definition of the word 'expatriate'.[31]

By thus conjuring the breakdown of the civil service, the Kenyan government delegation indeed achieved the inclusion of additional officers under OSAS (see below). That these additionally included officers were primarily European is revealed by Griffith-Jones's reference to their Holmes and Lidbury salary awards. It is confirmed by the Assistant Under-Secretary of State, Philip Rogers, who specified that three groups of officers were up for additional inclusion, including 'local' members of HMOCS, who all currently received 'inducement pay', which was by colonial design paid almost exclusively to European officers. Rogers then closed the meeting by noting 'that the question of guarantees to Asian and other officers excluded from the White Paper Scheme would be discussed at a subsequent meeting'.[32]

While the Kenyan delegation in London only lobbied to expand OSAS to more European officers, they did communicate to the Colonial Office that around 1,850 Asian officers recruited from 'overseas' before 1954 would expect the same guarantees as their HMOCS counterparts, noting that 75 per cent of them were expected to retire overseas. They were therefore also recognised as expatriates in Kenya.[33] Yet, while the Kenyan delegation asked for assurances for these Asian officers, they did not attempt to bring them under the umbrella of OSAS, which would have guaranteed their treatment on the same terms as their European counterparts. The participants at the London meetings thus agreed on rules for designation under OSAS, and agreed that the forthcoming public announcement of OSAS would also attend to the question of guarantees for those not designated. Staff representatives later stated that they left London under the impression that the Colonial Office had in principle agreed to essentially the same treatment for non-designated and designated overseas officers.

The vote, Nairobi, January 1961

No public announcement had been made by mid-January 1961. On 17 January, A. Z. A. Quraishy, the president of CACSA, which represented the mostly Asian non-designated officers, and the sole Asian representative at the London talks, wrote to Philip Rogers in London to highlight the 'grave doubts and anxieties' mounting among officers in the absence of any definite government statement.[34] When a draft text of the public statement on OSAS finally reached Kenya a few days later, it included the rules for designation but did 'not specifically mention the right to leave the service with compensation on transfer of power' for the mostly Asian 'non-designated officers on overseas terms'.[35] The Kenyan government thus anticipated staff opposition, but it still submitted the statement to the Central Whitley Council – the official forum of consultation between the Kenyan government and its civil service employees – to obtain the necessary Staff Side agreement. As anticipated, controversy ensued.

The Whitley Council consisted of 17 members: one chairman and eight members each of the Senior Civil Servants Association (SCSA) and the Clerical and Allied Civil Servants' Association. While staff associations in Kenya were now officially 'multiracial', the continuing racial hierarchies in the civil service meant that the senior SCSA was still dominated by Europeans, while CACSA represented the mostly middle-ranking Asian staff.[36] Accordingly, two SCSA members and seven CACSA members voted against the statement on OSAS. The Staff Side thus stood opposed to the statement with a narrow nine to eight majority. Another meeting was scheduled for 26 January.

In the meantime, the majority-European SCSA called a meeting for 23 January where its leadership revoked the nomination of the two members who had voted in opposition, and replaced them with acquiescent members. The two disqualified members protested to the Chairman of the Central Whitley Council, who refused to intervene, arguing that these were matters internal to the association. In response, on 25 January CACSA announced its withdrawal from the Central Whitley Council in two protest letters addressed to the Whitley Council Chairman and the Secretary of State for the Colonies in London.[37] In these letters, CACSA highlighted that if it acted in the same way as SCSA – namely, forcing members to vote in (racialised) line with association leadership – there 'would be no room for any compromise at Staff Side meetings and it would … be impossible for the Staff Side to function in the normal way'. SCSA had broken the implicit multiracial social contract under which the Whitley Council operated. The protest letters also noted that the proposed public statement did not fulfil what *both* staff associations, together with the Kenyan government, had agreed on as 'minimum requirements' prior to the London meetings, namely that non-induced overseas officers should receive guarantees equivalent to those of their European colleagues on inducement pay.[38] CACSA moreover declared its disagreement with the just published Flemming Report – which was nonetheless implemented during CACSA's boycott of the Whitley Council.

Despite CACSA's resignation, the Kenyan government went ahead with the meeting scheduled for 26 January where, with only SCSA members present (now all acquiescent), a Staff Side 'agreement' to the proposed statement was obtained.[39] Thus, on 8 February 1961

a joint communique by the Colonial Office and the Kenyan government announced the OSAS Kenya Agreement, including a summary
of its rules of designation and the much-debated Paragraph 6 which
promised further news for non-designated overseas officers to be
released by early March 1961 at the latest.[40] The racialised separation
of 'designated' from 'non-designated' officers was thus achieved.

Interlude: reproducing a racialised workforce from Holmes
(1948), via Lidbury and HMOCS (1954), to OSAS (1961)

OSAS included the reclassification of a racially hierarchised workforce
to recreate racist discrimination in non-racial terms. As CACSA's
protest letters noted, the differentiation made by OSAS between
'designated' and 'non-designated' officers did not in fact hinge on
whether staff had been recruited overseas or held overseas terms of
service. Instead, OSAS effectively sorted between those who received
inducement pay and those who did not, which was a racialised and
gendered distinction that rested on earlier colonial policymaking:
the 1948 Holmes and 1954 Lidbury salary revisions.

The fact that the 'Asian non-designated officers' (as they were
now regularly called in correspondence between the Treasury and
Colonial Office)[41] served on expatriate terms of service was recognised
by the Kenyan government. Accordingly, a 1962 memorandum by
the Staff Side of the Whitley Council noted:

> The pre-Lidbury overseas non-designated officers were originally
> recruited on the same terms as some of the officers who have now
> been designated ... The only difference between the designated officers
> referred to above and the overseas non-designated officers is that the
> former converted with inducement pay under the Lidbury Revision
> because prior to the revision they were serving on the then existing
> European salary scales, but the fact remains that the claims of both
> these officers for compensation rights, pensions guarantees, option
> to retire at independence, etc., are equal; this fact has been accepted
> by the Kenya Government in the past and was brought to the attention
> of the Secretary of State at the Civil Service Conference which took
> place at the Colonial Office in December, 1960.[42]

The 1961 CACSA protest letters had similarly laid out that many
of the Asian officers recruited pre-Lidbury were serving 'on terms
which clearly included an expatriate element in the form of overseas

leave and passages to their country of domicile'.[43] Moreover, CACSA president Quraishy noted the 'grave injustice' that

> some of the officers who later converted with inducement pay [under the Lidbury revision] were not only recruited locally but were born, bred and educated locally, whereas some of the officers who fortuitously did not convert with inducement pay were neither born nor bred locally and cannot be regarded as locally domiciled in accordance with your proposed definition of a 'designated officer'.[44]

Indeed, across East Africa, many civil servants were recruited on 'overseas terms' from the British Raj, later independent India and Pakistan. They served on permanent and pensionable (P&P) terms, received regular home leave, and their recruitment had to be approved by the Secretary of State for the Colonies (Lidbury 1954:24). They were thus recognised as expatriates by the East African colonial governments. The main differences between them and their European colleagues were rank and remuneration. Crucially, Asian expatriates were not granted inducement pay under Holmes (1948) and Lidbury (1954).

In 1947, the British government appointed a commission chaired by Sir Maurice Holmes to 'inquire into the structure, remuneration and superannuation arrangements of the Civil Services in East Africa'. The Holmes Commission recommended 'racial scales and terms of service thereby entrenching, not only in the civil service but in the private sector as well, the traditional structure of European administrator, Asian clerk, and African labourer' (Clayton and Savage 1974:293–294). Holmes introduced, for equal positions, a 3/5 wage differential based on race and a 4/5 wage differential based on gender, meaning Asians and Africans were pegged at three-fifths the salary of Europeans, while women received four-fifths the salary of men (Vinnai 1974:176).[45] Yet, Holmes claimed, this discrimination rested 'not on racial but on other and more fundamental grounds', namely that,

> subject to individual exceptions, the African is at the present time markedly inferior to the Asian of the same educational qualifications in such matters as sense of responsibility, judgement, application to duty and output of work [and] … the European civil servant surpasses the Asian in such matters as sense of public service, judgement and readiness to take responsibility.[46]

The Holmes Commission further argued that to arrive at 'fair wages', colonial governments must have 'regard to the law of supply and demand in determining what those salaries and wages should be', and:

> For many years to come, the employment of Europeans and Asians in the Civil Services will be necessary and, even if it were admitted that the quality of the work of the African was in all respects equal to that of the European or the Asian ... it would still be necessary to offer higher salaries to the European to induce him to leave his native land and to the Asian to deflect him from comparable posts in commerce and industry, which in East Africa are open to him in large numbers. In other words, the economic law of inducement must operate.[47]

There was, according to Holmes, not only an essential difference between the quality of the work of Europeans, Asians and Africans, but also between their 'native lands', so that the European (notably not the Asian) must be induced to come to the assumedly less appealing East Africa.

By 1954, in the face of growing anti-colonial resistance and in line with its multiracial policy, Britain was keen to abolish the explicitly racist 3/5 rule. It thus appointed another commission, chaired by Sir David Lidbury, to develop a unified non-racial salary scale. However, racist differentiations were reproduced also by Lidbury. The Commission again concluded that skilled Africans were not yet available in sufficient numbers and hence 'the need for recruitment in the external recruitment fields for some time to come, and in considerable numbers is inescapable' and for this, again, 'further inducement must be offered'.[48] Although recruitment overseas was now seen merely as 'a necessary phase in the evolution of an indigenous service', pay differentials were here to stay: 'We are dealing here with two separate sets of market values. The prospective candidate ... looks first at the salary which he would expect to earn for comparable employment in his own country.'[49] This time, induce-ment pay was considered necessary only to lure Europeans to East Africa. In contrast, Lidbury suggested that

> we do not think it necessary to schedule India or Pakistan as recruitment fields in which inducement pay should be offered ... we think that the administrations should have no difficulty in obtaining such recruits as they may need from these two countries without recourse to the inducement factor.[50]

On the other hand, Lidbury recommended that also 'local candidates', regardless of their place of birth and upbringing, should receive inducement pay if appointed by the Secretary of State in London to the administrative or professional services. As Clayton and Savage (1974:376) note, this proviso ensured that 'the best of the Kenya Europeans, who normally received their advanced education in Britain, could be recruited in this manner and would, therefore, still have a superior wage scale as compared with local Asians and Africans'. Even after 1954 (post-Lidbury), wealthier European settlers could thus bypass 'local' (i.e. lower) rates of pay, while Asians and Africans received 'local' pay even when recruited overseas because of their countries' lower 'market values'.

Regarding the conversion of officers on the existing pay scale for European officers, Lidbury concluded that given that 'No officer's net emoluments on conversion should be less than his present ones … There is no other practical course but to convert every officer at present on an "expatriate" scale to the appropriate point on the new scale inclusive of the "inducement" element'.[51] This meant all previous European staff, whether recruited overseas or locally, were converted with inducement pay under Lidbury. In contrast, Asian and African officers, previously pegged at 3/5 of European salaries, converted without inducement.[52] It is noteworthy that Lidbury did not acknowledge Holmes's (1948) explicitly racist justification of the 3/5 rule, but reproduced only his rationale of 'local and external market values'; in fact, he even argued that,

> although the [Holmes] Report attributed the difference to the 'additional expenditure to which the expatriate officer is put', the local officer *came to read into this fixed ratio an implied comparison of worth,* liable to be permanent and therefore an object of resentment.[53]

Lidbury pretended that Asian and African officers *read into* the 3/5 rule a 'comparison of worth'. He pretended that the 3/5 rule had differentiated between 'local' and 'expatriate' officers, rather than between 'races', and thus actively misrepresented the racist origins of pay inequalities. This allowed him to largely reproduce past discrimination within a nominally non-racial system. He abolished racialised pay hierarchies in name but largely reproduced them in effect via 'inducement pay' based on countries' different 'market values'.

In the same year as the Lidbury revisions, in 1954, Britain replaced the Colonial Service with Her Majesty's Overseas Civil Service (HMOCS), which was only open to 'overseas' officers. It was later argued that overseas officers 'are *normally* appointed to the service on inducement rates of pay', and hence 'admission to HMOCS ... has been restricted to those officers who are in receipt of inducement pay'.[54] Already in 1960, before publication of the OSAS White Paper, CACSA had written to the Secretary of State for the Colonies to demand that the discriminatory rules governing admission to HMOCS be changed so 'that all officers who are at present serving on expatriate terms, i.e. those who are eligible for overseas leave and passages to their country of domicile, are admitted as members'.[55] These calls went unheard – as of 12 November 1960, all HMOCS members in the Kenyan Civil Service were European (2,041).[56]

The economic rhetoric of differential geographical 'market value' reappeared during the OSAS debate. In 1961, Kenya's Minister for Finance and Development, K. W. S. MacKenzie, argued that OSAS did not distinguish by race but between 'the local civil service and the expatriate civil service' and that the OSAS 'overseas addition' was calculated 'with regard to the levels of salary reigning in the country from which the bulk of the expatriate officers are drawn', and hence 'based of course on United Kingdom standards'. As regards 'expatriate officers recruited in Asia',

> The basic rate of pay here is considerably higher than that in most countries in Asia already, and therefore there would be no justification in paying overseas addition to attract overseas officers to come here. That, Sir, is the basic reason for these scales of pay, and that explains what the hon. Members opposite describe as dis-crimination, but what I would call is *merely accepting the facts of economic life.*[57]

While past inequalities remained largely intact, the development from Holmes (1948), via Lidbury and HMOCS (1954) to OSAS (1961) reveals a rhetorical shift in racism. Racial ideology has frequently deployed essentialised and reified – i.e. ahistorical and unrelational – geographies, ranging from continents to nations (Mamdani 2012). Moreover, racism also increasingly drew on economic language and the supposedly non-political 'market logic'. Key to the production of inequality from Holmes to OSAS was the sorting of populations according to where they supposedly originated and thus *really* belonged. Yet, while talk of intrinsic differences between 'races' was gradually abandoned, the imaginary geographical units – Europe, Africa, Asia – which had been made into categories of human 'races' now had to stand in for them, in what represented a sort of rhetorical back and forth. As people came to embody geography, geography was used to fix them in their social situation. It was ascribed and hereditary geography, not simply the colour of one's skin, that established whether one became African, Asian or European. The geographical racial categories that British imperialism concocted denied the historical events and social relations that ultimately produce 'national' and 'economic' space. 'Europe' signified modernity, wealth and skill, while 'Africa' signified backwardness, poverty and immaturity, and 'Asia' was placed somewhere in between. These ascribed differences underwrote the ongoing argument that Europeans required higher pay because Europe was wealthier, while Asians did not need such emoluments because Asia was poor and salaries there low. Never mind that this wealth distribution was a relatively recent development and that the knowledges, labour and resources systematically extracted from the African and Asian continents by European states and corporations were critical to producing the wealth and skill amassed in Europe. Never mind, too, that Asians receiving low wages in Asia, and Africans in Africa, was neither natural nor automatic but the result of discriminatory European colonial policy often violently enforced. Never mind the actual poverty and miserable wages widespread in post-World War II Europe, including Britain. Such arguments that locked people into geography also ignored the fact that, theoretically, all 'British subjects' turned 'Citizens of the United Kingdom and Colonies' were free to move to the UK until at least 1962 – many East African Asians until 1968 – so that, theoretically, the British labour market with its supposedly higher wages should have been available to many 'Asians' and 'Africans'. Finally, such reasoning ignored the fact that many of the Asians and Africans who did reach higher ranks in the civil service had been educated in Europe too (Adu 1965). Hence there is no reason to assume that they could not also have found employment in Europe, were it not for racial discrimination. Fields and Fields (2014:24) call racism 'the practice of applying a social, civic, or legal double standard based on ancestry' – from

Holmes to OSAS, the practice remained even if its ideological garb changed.

The reproduction of white privilege now also demanded different temporalities of migration. If British colonial administration previously relied on the offer of a permanent career, the continued dispatch of British civil servants depended on them being seen as temporary staff. Those civil servants who became designated under OSAS were normally 'permanent and pensionable' staff, who operated on behalf of the metropolitan government but typically served out their career in the colonies. It was precisely the *permanent* nature of their employment that was highlighted when advocates called for salary increases, generous compensation or other benefits for expatriate civil servants who faced the eventual loss of their careers. Officers on fixed-term contracts were the exception, and their exclusion from OSAS was a much less political issue. Hence, when European LegCo member Reginald Alexander[58] discussed in 1960 'the very large problem, of the substantial number of civil servants who are outside Her Majesty's Government's White Paper', he specifically noted that the problem of excluded 'temporary and contract officers ... is not so acute because of the very nature of their appointments, either temporary or on short term contracts'. Independence itself necessitated an increased reliance on temporary staff – and the framing of expatriates as temporary staff. Independent governments did not want to depend permanently on their former colonists, and temporary 'contract terms' indicated that any such reliance was fleeting, a transitional stage in the process towards full independence.[59] In this context, the British government was increasingly unwilling to promise permanent careers, and in 1962 the Department of Technical Co-operation (DTC) officially stated that henceforth all recruitment would be on a contract basis (Kirk-Greene 1999). It was thus with decolonisation that expatriate 'overseas' employment became associated with temporariness – and that white migratory privilege increasingly reproduced itself via its nominally temporary status (see also Chapter 3).

The treatment and resistance of Asian and African expatriates, East Africa, 1961–62

The joint communique that announced the OSAS Kenya Agreement in February 1961 promised further news for non-designated overseas officers to be released shortly. Yet negotiations dragged on with particularly the Treasury increasingly unwilling to agree to even the most limited provisions. The promised guarantees did not materialise until October 1962 and were considerably less favourable than those for designated officers. Throughout this time across East Africa, Asian civil servants lobbied for their inclusion under OSAS on the grounds that they too were expatriates. While various East Asian staff associations, such as the Kenyan CACSA, threatened 'positive action',[60] civil servants also fought individually, as evidenced by the memorandum from civil servants Pinto and D'Cunha cited in the introduction of this book. Their petition, like others, was rejected by the Permanent Secretary because the officers 'did not convert with an inducement addition following the Lidbury Revision'.[61]

Asian and African members in the Kenyan Legislative Council also condemned OSAS. In May 1961, LegCo member Chanan Singh – who had come to Kenya to work on the railways, retrained as a lawyer and was to become Assistant Minister in Kenyatta's first Independence Cabinet and Judge of the Kenyan High Court – highlighted that 'the very idea of an inducement pay', or 'overseas addition', was introduced by Lidbury 'to keep the old racial differentials in being' and that 'only a negligible number of non-Europeans benefit from this new arrangement [OSAS] so that to all intents and purposes the arrangement is racial'.[62] He then picked apart the government's notion of 'overseas recruitment': 'If you exclude people recruited in India and Pakistan, but apply the addition only to officers recruited in the United Kingdom, then obviously you're making a racial discrimination.' In any case, Singh goes on, until 'quite recently', Europeans born and recruited in Kenya were accepted as members of HMOCS and thus included as 'expatriate' officers under OSAS. So, Singh exclaims, 'will the Government make up its mind and say what they really mean by expatriate officer? It is no use referring us to a definition which is arbitrarily contrived to give financial assistance to certain classes of officers.' The 'basic question', Singh concludes, is, 'does the Government accept the principle of equal pay for equal work or not?'

Faced with growing opposition, Kenya's Attorney General Griffith-Jones wrote to London in summer 1961, complaining that the British proposals submitted in the meantime for non-designated officers 'fall lamentably short of the minimum defensible on grounds of equity', especially given that 'at one time it was intended that the non-designated officer should be covered by the limited compensation scheme now introduced for the designated officer'.[63] From Uganda, Governor Sir Frederick Crawford declared his agreement with Griffith-Jones, noting that he expected 'serious discrimination' of this group of 'virtually all Asian' officers in Uganda, too.[64] As predicted, the latest British proposal was rejected by the Staff Side in the Whitley Council in summer 1961.

In London, fears grew that the impasse over Asian officers might jeopardise the OSAS agreement. In September 1961, Sir Arthur Hilton Poynton, Permanent Under-Secretary of State for the Colonies, at the Colonial Office, wrote to Sir Ronald Harris at the Treasury about the great 'political and financial risk' that 'unless we can achieve a settlement of the case for the Asian officers the East African leaders will decline to foot, even initially by way of loan, their proportion of the bill for British overseas officers'.[65] He reported that the Kenya Staff Side were planning a 'press and political campaign' coupled with 'non-cooperation in the localisation [programme]' and notes, 'we have already been under fire in the United Nations over this in connection with Tanganyika and the subject is coming up again at the forthcoming session'. His concerns proved right. In November 1961, the UN General Assembly passed a resolution requesting that the British government 'extend … similar considerations in the matter of compensation for loss of career to all civil servants without regard to race, colour, creed or origin'.[66] Meanwhile, the Indian government approached the British government to voice their 'concern' at 'the acute uncertainty and anxiety that prevails among Indian nationals employed by the Governments of Kenya, Uganda and Tanganyika, in regard to their future careers and prospects of employment', and note that 'so far the compensation scheme has been made applicable only to a certain category of officers, the bulk of whom are of European origin; while the great majority of officers of non-European origin have been excluded from it'.[67] All this proved to little avail. In January 1962, Tanganyika became independent without granting a general right to retire to non-designated officers, while Kenya and Uganda seemed on a similar course.

In February 1962, the Treasury and Colonial Office still disagreed. The Treasury rejected all responsibility and argued that non-designated officers should simply become local citizens and 'absorbed in the community'; and declined to even provide Kenya grant-in-aid for a compensation scheme.[68] The Colonial Office responded that this idea 'bears no relation whatever to the facts of life in Kenya as they are to-day. There is not the slightest doubt that the non-designated officers serving on overseas leave terms will be replaced by Africans as quickly as possible.' The Treasury replied that it very well recognised that Asian officers may become Africanised but that if the Kenyan government 'chooses to indulge in this luxury, they must pay for it themselves'. In what might now be called 'methodologically nationalist' fashion, the Treasury thus constructed the matter as a conflict between a Kenyan nation-state and its Asian civil servants – obscuring the fact that the imperial British government had created the situation in the first place. It was not until October 1962 that a 'Limited scheme of retirement benefits for non-designated officers serving on overseas leave terms' was agreed.[69] While OSAS officers were 'induced' to stay with generous terms of service, non-designated Asian officers were in effect coerced to stay, as leaving before an agreement was in place would have meant forfeiting even their pensions earned to date.[70]

Finally, some, like Tom Mboya, were critical that African officers were a priori excluded from expatriate status:

> there are Africans who are entitled to inducement pay, they have not been told how they convert. Their counterparts who were equally entitled to inducement pay will convert to the expatriate terms which means a much higher salary than the African or Asian and then the criterion is most interesting. The criterion here is that when you are an African automatically you are not an expatriate civil servant.[71]

Overseas African officers were by British default classed as local. Already Lidbury had noted that in the category African 'are included Africans of the mainland, whether born in any of the three mainland territories or immigrants, and a relatively small number of Seychellois, Mauritians and Comorians'.[72] In 1961, LegCo member Nzioka Mulli critiqued the fact that while Europeans were induced to stay, non-Kenyan Africans were barred from even entering the civil service:

> The hon. member who spoke, I forgot who it was, said that there were no Africans who have qualified as expatriate officers in this country. I know of one who is a very highly qualified man; he does not come from either East Africa or West Africa, but he comes from

somewhere else in Africa; he is highly qualified and he was very interested in joining the Kenya Civil Service, but he was denied the opportunity. There are many hundreds of them, especially from a country like South Africa.[73]

The post-colonial tethering of expatriate status and whiteness, institutionalised by HMOCS and OSAS, hinged on the active exclusion of Asians and Africans from this privileged category. Yet the British continued to deny all charges of racism and maintained that their 'special obligation' to designated OSAS officers simply did not extend to others who had been hired directly by colonial governments. Kenya's Acting Chief Secretary, Griffith-Jones,[74] similarly argued that 'no question of race as such enters into it', and while 'quite clearly, the bulk of expatriate officers are European', he also pointed to the 'considerable number of Europeans in the Civil Service who will not qualify for these expatriates' supplements'.

'Trying to find a way round this difficulty', London, 1961–62

The 'Kenya problem' was repeatedly debated in the British Parliament. However, the problem as conceived in London was the ongoing exclusion of some European officers from OSAS. In the bill's second reading, in January 1961, the Secretary of State for the Colonies, Iain Macleod, announced:

> There is one matter which is of great interest to the House. It arose out of the problems of definition and of officers designated under the scheme [sic]. It has particular application to Kenya where a considerable number of people who are not, according to the definition, genuine expatriates and, therefore, would not qualify under H.M.O.C.S. because, in a sense, they are Kenyans instead of people who have come from this country, would be excluded from the benefits of this scheme. We have been trying to find a way round this difficulty, and I think that we have succeeded.[75]

Macleod went on to inform MPs that the British agreement with the Kenyan delegation provided for the inclusion of approximately 700 additional civil servants.[76] MP Sir Hendrie Oakshott was 'delighted' about 'this very generous and broad definition' which included the 'comparatively large number of European officers who were not recruited through the usual machinery of the Colonial

Service in the United Kingdom but who joined locally'.[77] The 'problem' as understood by many in the imperial metropole was the protection of white privilege abroad – rather than equal pay for equal work. Only rarely was the fate of Asian civil servants debated in Parliament. In a rare mention, Labour MP and future Minister of Overseas Development, Barbara Castle, confronted then Secretary of State for the Colonies, Reginald Maudling, in May 1962 about the 'quite unjustified distinction' that OSAS included 'about 1,000 European officers in Kenya who were locally recruited, in many cases were locally born' while there were 'Asian officers in exactly the same position, but who have not been designated simply because they had not reached the salary stage arbitrarily fixed for the right to convert under the Lidbury provision'.[78]

Although Macleod had declared the 'Kenya problem' solved in January 1961, British parliamentarians continued to raise the issue when it transpired that some Europeans were not included even under the extended rules of designation. In January 1962, MP Patrick Wall argued that 'non-designated expatriate officers' and 'local officers' 'believe that Her Majesty's Government have broken their pledges to them'.[79] The Under-Secretary of State for the Colonies, Hugh Fraser, responded that the government's obligation to these officers was not the same given their direct recruitment by colonial governments, and explained that while some of them were Europeans, the majority were Asian and 'the danger could emerge of attempting discrimination'.[80] Yet, some British MPs continued to call for the designation of *all* European officers, like MP Patrick Wall, who saw a 'considerable difference' between locally recruited European and non-European officers, with the latter being 'generally speaking … an indigenous inhabitant of the country and he intends to stay on there'.[81] Moreover, while in 1961 the Minister of State for Colonial Affairs, the Earl of Perth, had still supposed that the problem of designation was probably unique to Kenya,[82] in 1965 MP Henry Clark pointed to the 'non-designated officers, particularly in Northern Rhodesia and Malawi, and those that are still left in Tanganyika, Zanzibar and Kenya, and a large number of other territories'. He explained,

> We probably hear most about the non-designated officers in Northern Rhodesia. This is because Northern Rhodesia had probably more

people who were, in a technical sense, locally recruited. However, it is quite wrong to pretend that they were not expatriate officers in every sense of the word. In the early 1950s we were encouraging people to go to Rhodesia to build up an inter-racial State and we were trying hard to persuade Europeans to become Rhodesian citizens. In that atmosphere a large number of people travelled to Rhodesia, looked around for a job and decided on Government service, but they were expatriate employees of the Rhodesian Government as surely as anybody else.[83]

The OSAS Kenya debate is thus a case study with broader relevance in the politics of turning colonial populations, and the hierarchies that divided them, into post-colonial ones. Yet the debates about who was an expatriate were quickly and conveniently forgotten in political debate and academic literature that increasingly conflated expatriate with European. There is no mention of Asian expatriates' struggles to be counted *as expatriates*, either in Adu (1965) or in Kirk-Greene (1999, 2000), for whom the expatriate is, without question, European. Yet it was British colonial policy that *created* the postcolonial expatriate officer as by default socio-economically privileged and white vis-à-vis Asian and African 'local' staff.

Expatriates' uses from administration to development

The expatriate in British development practice

This chapter's history of the OSAS expatriate speaks to a growing body of work on the imperial origin and effects of international development. The British government framed OSAS as technical development aid and funded OSAS officers as technical assistance personnel. As such, OSAS was welcomed in the British Parliament across political divides. The Department of Technical Co-operation was established in July 1961 (and replaced by the Ministry of Overseas Development in 1964) and OSAS was recognised as a 'major vehicle of technical assistance overseas'[84] and 'the rock on which the Department of Technical Aid [*sic*] was founded'.[85] OSAS accounted for more than half of Britain's expenditure on technical assistance between 1962 and 1965,[86] and was extended and broadened in 1965 to include staff in public sector bodies like universities and statutory corporations.[87] Kothari (2005:47) discusses the narratives of former colonial administrators turned development practitioners to show how their colonially acquired experiences and skills 'shaped the culture and direction of post-independence development'. Hodge (2010:43) similarly argues that the 'remobilization of former colonial personnel' by European governments and institutions of international governance constitutes an 'important and hitherto neglected legacy' of late European imperialism and needs to be examined for a 'fuller and more critical understanding of the origins and history of the so-called "Age of Development"' (see also Hindman and Fechter 2010; Mosse 2011; Redfield 2012; Wilson 2012).

After World War II, British colonialism in Africa was increasingly justified as 'a welfare-developmental system' (Wasserman 1974:427). White (2002:411) draws on Mudimbe's theorisation of colonialism to show how postcolonial development – via new subject positions, institutions and discourses – replicated essential features of colonialism, including 'the integration of colonised economy and history into Western economy and master narrative' (see also O'Brien 1974). Parliamentary debates about OSAS evidence this use of development as a strategic tool to secure symbolic, geopolitical and economic objectives. As Lord Hastings declared in 1960, 'expatriate officers' needed a higher salary than 'the local men' and 'If we are able to give indirect aid by paying the differential, I think that is going to be one of the best investments that this country has ever made'.[88] The payrolling of expensive British civil servants in the service of independent governments was thus a calculated cost to serve British interests (see also O'Brien 1974; Cohen 1977; Bennell 1982). Nairobi was East Africa's economic and political centre, Kenya a strategic military location and British capital investments, as well as British settlers' property and prosperity, remained entrenched in Kenya's most crucial industries (Rothchild 1970; Ogot and Ochieng' 1995). Without returning to the structuralist terms of dependency theory, a materialist perspective seems crucial also because, as Wilson (2012:211) writes, the 'discourse of developmentalism' has been 'extensively analysed' in post-development and postcolonial work but significantly less attention is paid in this literature to the fact that 'Development was conceived both as a Cold War antidote to communist revolution and as a means by which ex-colonies could be maintained as subordinate suppliers of resources and raw materials for Northern capital.'

Britain's investment into the continued functioning of Kenya's civil service was thus to no small degree motivated by intertwined economic, geopolitical and military interests in the Cold War context. From the outset, OSAS was justified by raising the spectre of communism. Before the announcement of the OSAS White Paper, MP Bernard Braine declared in July 1960:

> I find it well-nigh incredible that anyone in high authority in this country should be willing to risk the break-up of this unique Service, which is unrivalled in its African experience, at a time when the Soviet bloc countries are straining every effort to lay hands on anyone they can find to instruct in African languages and in knowledge of African culture in order to take over where we leave off. As the *Economist* put it neatly last week, The Communist powers are donning the khaki shorts as the Britons reach for their pinstripes.[89]

White (2002:410) notes that development 'was forged in the era of the Cold War', and in the Cold War context could be understood as 'a continuation of war by other means'. Yet the defence of British influence was required not only to counter Soviet advances, but also vis-à-vis an increasingly powerful US ally and institutions like the United Nations that professed anti-colonial views (Clayton and Savage 1974). A changed ideological context required a symbolic reframing of colonial administration that began with the rechristening of Her Majesty's *Colonial* Civil Service into Her Majesty's *Overseas* Civil Service in 1954, and continued with OSAS. Lord Milverton accordingly argued that

> The habit, from Soviet Russia to the United States of America, of depreciating the honourable record of British colonial rule should be fought on every occasion it arises. You have only to look round the world to note the achievements rendered possible by thousands of colonial civil servants.[90]

Similarly, the Secretary of State for the Colonies, Macleod, stressed that 'the function of the modern Colonial Service is not one of Imperial domination' but one of development: 'we have the finest organisation in the world for providing professional and technical assistance to under-developed territories. In fact, we already have the kind of service for which the United Nations is now groping.'[91]

Rhetorically, justifications for the financing of expatriate civil servants thus relied on the spectre of the 'communist threat', and reproduced well-worn notions of colonial tutelage and the civilisational mission. In parliamentary debates, the colonial civil service was constructed as a quintessentially British institution that epitomised civilisational achievement, with the British civil servant its missionary. MP Bernard Braine was moved to exclaim that

> upon this relatively small but select body of men depends in very large measure the success of everything that we are trying to do in the emergent countries. These men are much more than civil servants; they are teachers of the most important skill which our country has to impart to others – that of fair and just administration ... they are ambassadors for our way of life ... upon these men will depend whether the new States elect voluntarily to maintain close and cordial relationships with our country, particularly in matters of trade, in the years to come – long after the power to compel them to do so has been relinquished.[92]

British emigration remained tethered to economic and political influence. The Marquess of Lansdowne imagined expatriate civil servants, yet again, as pioneers, the vanguard of a much bigger undertaking:

> I am convinced that the British people will continue to want to go overseas and to serve abroad. In the future, they will not be going as Governors, as High Commissioners or as District Commissioners; they will go (as they used to go in the old days before the creation of our Empire) as missionaries, teachers, nurses and doctors. We must give them encouragement and help.[93]

Similarly, MP Dr Barnett Stross hoped that 'this tiny Bill' might inspire a 'crusade' of

> talented young men and women to go out into other parts of the world, particularly into the newly emergent territories and the Colonial Territories, in order to offer a term of service under contract ... because we believe that there are aspects of our culture, which have been gained at very great expense over the centuries, which are well worth handing on to people who need them.[94]

Colonial-era notions of civilisational superiority grounded in historical and cultural achievement were repurposed to support a burgeoning development industry still dependent on the continued emigration of people moving in the service of British interests, now called expatriates. Ultimately, British political elites did not just introduce OSAS to take care of those they recognised in intersecting classed, gendered and racialised terms as 'one of theirs'; OSAS was also an investment in longer-term British geopolitical and economic interests. The *aim* of racism, Fields and Fields (2014) remind us, is not always solely or even primarily the implementation of racist beliefs but also the justification of self-serving double standards, uneven political relationships, socio-economic inequality and unearned material gain.

The expatriate in the Kenyan civil service

From internal self-government in June 1963, Africanisation of the Kenyan civil service greatly accelerated, and in an 'almost complete personnel turnover' more than 75 per cent of higher-level posts were 'Africanised' by 1967 (Werlin 1973:253). While Africanisation implied a change in personnel, it did not, at least initially, imply a rectification of the vastly unequal pay scales, or the restructuring of an 'authoritarian' state administration (Adu 1965; Vinnai 1974; Kooperman and Rosenberg 1977; Bennell 1982; Ogot and Ochieng' 1995). OSAS and the Flemming reforms played a direct role in cementing colonial structures inasmuch as they further inflated top salaries, ensured the continued presence of a disproportionately remunerated foreign staff, set the baseline for future international recruitment and helped keep the colonial administrative system largely intact. Africans entering the senior ranks expected their pay and privileges to compare to those of their 'expatriate colleagues' (Adu 1965:20–21), and some 'exerted pressure on the Government to retain the colonial salary structure' (Vinnai 1974:180). The transformation of privileged senior civil servants into even more socio-economically privileged expatriates thus exacerbated the already stark inequality in the civil service. The problem was further compounded by the fact that all Europeans, whatever their responsibilities, had been in the senior service and hence their African replacements also entered the senior service, even in roles such as stenographers (Vinnai 1974; Bennell 1982). Adu (1965: 112, 30) accordingly notes that 'a large element of expatriate staff in the senior ranks' had 'a distorting effect' on the local salary levels and diagnosed that 'the structure of the civil services in former British Africa bears ... the stamp of its original racial sources of recruitment'.

The ongoing presence of privileged white expatriate civil servants thus helped entrench socio-economic inequality in the civil service and, as independence politician Oginga Odinga warned, contributed to 'the replacement of a non-African by an African privileged elite' (cited in Rothchild 1970:746). The Holmes Commission (1948) had already recognised that racialised difference in civil service remuneration was so large that paying senior Africans the same as Europeans would introduce an undesirable degree of inequality among Africans, with consequences far beyond the civil service: 'The disadvantages of so remunerating any class of Africans as to create a Mandarin caste, divorced in income and interests from their fellows, would not be confined to the economic field' (Holmes 1948:27). The same inequality considered appropriate between 'races' – which was crucial to producing 'race' – was recognised as a concern *within* a social group. Yet the subsequent Lidbury reforms did precisely that and thus 'marked a major step in the creation of an expensive African social elite' so that, as a contemporary observer noted, 'at a time when all over the world the tendency is to draw rich and poor together, in Kenya the Civil Service Salaries drag them apart' (Clayton and Savage 1974:375).

As predicted, this had broader social repercussions. Public sector salary structures had a strong influence on the distribution of incomes in the private sector (Bennell 1982) and reinforced the position of civil servants as a separate and privileged social class (Vinnai 1974). The role of civil services in the formation of national elites in newly independent African countries has been much discussed, with public sector employees so overrepresented among the rich that 1960s/70s dependency theorists spoke of a 'rentier class' of politicians and public servants who aligned themselves with foreign interests (Simson 2020). Also Fanon (1967:123) saw a 'bourgeoisie of civil servants', trained by the former metropolis and 'geared toward intermediate activities' ultimately serving metropolitan interests. At the time, Western-oriented capitalist Kenya was considered a prime example of this development (Bennell 1982; Simson 2020). Finally, while OSAS was hailed as development aid in the UK, the terms of the agreement meant that Kenya inherited a financial burden of expatriate compensations and pensions that amounted to a significant proportion of its total budget in the early independence years (Vinnai 1974). As LegCo member Reginald Alexander critiqued, 'surely the employer … must pay the compensation. In this case the employer of HMOCS is clearly Her Majesty's Government, and why, why on earth by any stretch of imagination we in Kenya should be expected to pay this compensation is something beyond my comprehension.'[95] To pay these sums, Kenya took out loans from Britain and thus remained tied to the UK by bonds of debt. Only in 1971 did the British government take on the pre-independence pensions of former expatriate officers after ongoing protest by East African governments due to the financial burden on their economies.[96]

With independence, the Africanisation of the Kenyan civil service thus began in earnest. Officially African status was now non-racial, dependent on holding Kenyan citizenship, so that formerly Asian or European staff who had opted for Kenyan citizenship should be counted as African staff, not expatriate. Yet the usage of expatriate in the Africanisation process reveals the complex ways that race, belonging and power continued to be intertwined in the new nation. In August 1966, the Provincial Commissioner of Kenya's Coast Province requested that all provincial government offices and departments 'compile a tabulated list of all expatriate officers in your department serving in this Province indicating thereon the name of the officer, time and date of appointment, designation, nationality and the terms of service'.[97] The lists submitted in response include 'Americans', 'Germans', 'Irish', 'Indians', 'Pakistanis' and 'Seychellois', but most were 'British' and 'British subjects'. The latter comprised many Asian officers, like 'British subject' C. E. Lobo, on permanent and pensionable 'Non-designated Overseas Terms', who had worked in *G. K. Prison* in Shimo-la-Tewa since 1949.[98] The Education Department list even created a new category: 'N.D.O: Non-Designated Officer (Asians with Passage Privileges)'.[99] These lists not only suggest the fate of many Asian expatriates but also the racialisation of belonging in independent Kenya, and the ongoing usefulness (and limits) of the category expatriate as a racial sorting tool. While the communication submitted by G. K. Prison explicitly stated that it did *not* include Kenyan citizens on its list, the lists of expatriate staff submitted by the *Provincial Veterinary Office* and the *Nyali VOK Transmitting Station* include Asian Kenyan citizens.[100] In one instance, 'Asian', a racial category, is listed under 'nationality'. Kenyan citizens were thus counted as expatriates, positioned as Other to the nation, on racial grounds. So, did the staff compiling these lists misunderstand the task or was the task ambiguous on purpose? In other words, what were these lists supposed to capture and what work was the term expatriate expected to do: designate citizenship, colonial-era racial categories or possibly both? The latter might be suggested by the Kenyan government's parallel exclusion of Asians from key positions in the economy (Hansen 1999).

In these lists and the accompanying correspondence, the category expatriate thus captures both colonial notions of race, and also loyalty to the new state as evidenced by the decision to take up citizenship. This ongoing tension between the 'expatriate as non-citizen' and 'expatriate as non-racially-African' reflects broader struggles about belonging in the new Kenyan nation that arguably remain unresolved today (McIntosh 2016; Dickinson 2016; Kunz 2018). Ultimately, the Kenyan government's ambiguous use of the category expatriate in the service of Africanisation shows that Kenyan citizenship and national identity remained racialised in ways inherited from the colonial period, or 'structured by colonial exclusionary logics' (Mamdani 1996, 2012; Achiume 2019). The Kenyan government, like the British, used the term expatriate in tacitly racialised ways to serve their political ends. The ordering of who belongs where, so central to colonial racism, continued to be an important technique of governance. The fluctuating-yet-always-insecure positioning of 'Asian' civil servants – whether they were legally British, Kenyan, Indian or Pakistani citizens – further evidences the messy politics of categorisation in the context of the disintegrating British Empire. Asian officers continued to be positioned as expatriates by African Kenyan elites, and accordingly excluded from access to state and economic power; meanwhile, even those that remained British citizens became positioned as immigrants in the UK, excluded from what El-Enany (2020) calls the 'spoils of empire'. The British betrayal of its Asian civil servants foreshadows the 1968 Commonwealth Immigrants Act, designed to stop Kenyan Asians coming to the UK and leaving up to 200,000 essentially stateless (Hansen 1999). In this way, HMOCS and OSAS, just like immigration and naturalisation legislation, were tools used by the British government to fashion and govern (im)mobilised populations.

Conclusion

The expatriate emerges as a lynchpin category from the archive of Kenyan independence: actively reinterpreted, usefully ambiguous and deeply contested. It is entangled in the adaptation of racialised colonial inequalities and the renegotiation of geopolitical and economic influence for the postcolonial Cold War context. Despite ongoing resistance, the end of the British Empire here reveals itself as a re-racialising process, involving the reformulation rather than abandonment of racial politics. The sorting of who belonged where and thus deserved what, that had been so central to colonialism, continued to be a useful political tool. This sorting was now enacted along ostensibly non-racial lines and expatriate status became a tool that could justify the ongoing practice of unequal pay for equal work along racialised lines without naming 'race'.

(Re)shaped at this particular historical conjuncture – moulded in colonial for postcolonial contexts – expatriate continued to mean different things to different people. Where it served its economic and geopolitical interests, the British government actively attempted to import colonial hierarchies and discourses into postcolonial arrangements like national civil services and British development aid. This included translating colonial articulations of mobility, belonging and work in ways that reproduced many of the accordant inequalities. While individual OSAS expatriates did not necessarily act as the defenders of British interests that British politicians evidently wished them to be, the OSAS agreement, Flemming salary revisions and other late colonial policies, and the discourses they came couched in, transported and translated colonial inequalities for the postcolonial period. However, while the category expatriate was used to reproduce white privilege and British influence, it was never only white people who were recognised as expatriate, nor did all white people become expatriates. Some such incongruency was arguably necessary to allow the British to continue denying the racialised nature of their policies. OSAS and its expatriate officer thus stand in the British imperial tradition of enacting racist discrimination in non-racist terms, so as not to expose Britain's unequal treatment of its (former) imperial subjects (Lake and Reynolds 2008; Anderson 2013; Mongia 2018; El-Enany 2020). In the post-colonial period, enabling privileged white migration, as *expatriation* became useful also given Britain's increasing exclusion of Asian and African (former) British subjects and citizens as 'immigrants'. Although with less sway and arguably less interest to impose its usage beyond its borders, the new Kenyan political elite deployed a different reading of expatriate in a similar way: as a tacitly racialised tool of governance useful to redistribute profit, power and privileges.

The essentialisation of ascribed origin, which underwrote geographical articulations of 'race', continued. However, it was not filled only with rhetoric of culture and civilization but framed in 'economistic talk', where the market value of places stood in for the value of people while nation-states and 'the economy' were taken out of the imperial political economy that had produced them. Borrowing, redeployment and translation mark the history of racism, and the end of the empire thus involved neither a fundamental break with colonial racism nor direct continuity, but the 'discursive *bricolage* whereby an older discourse of race is "recovered", "modified", "encased", and "encrusted" in new forms' (Stoler 1995:61). In its postcolonial iteration, this racism was increasingly dependent on the imagination of *separate nation-states* and the language of *economic common sense*. Tracing this rhetorical shift from 'race' to 'national labour pools', 'market value' and 'facts of economic life' remains of acute relevance to understanding how racism is reproduced today not only through 'cultural racism' but also through 'economic racism'.

Today, the controversy about who would be designated under OSAS seems wholly forgotten and even scholars of the colonial civil service, like Kirk-Greene (2000) or Vinnai (1974), speak of expatriate civil servants as if this was a straightforward and uncontested grouping of (white) people. The erasure of the treatment and resistance of 'Asian' and 'African' expatriates is a political act, which endures in today's imagination of the past expatriate as by default a white and temporary subject. Such erasure also contributes to the reification of 'race', concealing the specific racist acts that ensured its (re)production, the ongoing resistance they were met with and the actual difficulty of fixing 'race', which as Stoler (2016) argues, has always been an ideological construct on unstable epistemic footings, securing its claims to essentialism by vague and varying measures.

This chapter has analytically linked the staffing of colonial administration and national civil services, British international development aid and the making of migration. Chapter 3 brings into the fold the study of international human resource management. Neither development nor multinational business in their current form would be possible without mobilities of people, practices, policies, categories and discourses that share colonial genealogies across the public/private sector divide. Yet few studies have examined the genealogies of the shared staffing conventions and categories that development and business depend on. The next chapter therefore examines the expatriate in early IHRM literature and shows that HR policies might seem technical (and dull), but they are certainly not unpolitical.

Notes

1 LegCo, 23 May 1961, p. 280.
2 Bernard Braine, HC, 11 July 1960, s5-vol626-cc1133–44.
3 Secretary of State for the Colonies, Mr Iain Macleod, HC, 24 January 1961, s5-vol633-cc36–107.
4 White Paper 1960 (Cmnd 1193): Service with Overseas Governments.
5 HC, 24 February 1965, s5-vol707-cc409–525; see also Ireton (2013).
6 'Overseas Service Aid Scheme: Kenya. Note of a Meeting held at the Colonial Office at 12 noon on the 23rd December, 1960.' TNA CO 822/1947.
7 The Earl of Perth, HL, 28 March 1960, s5-vol222-cc306–420.
8 Establishment Circular No. 15, 16 March 1961; TNA CO 822/1953.
9 The Lord Chancellor, HL, 15 May 1962, s5-vol240-cc531–618.
10 LegCo, 23 July 1963, p. 1812.
11 As Labour MP John Stonehouse lamented in a lone critical side note; HC, 24 January 1961, s5-vol633-cc36–107.
12 LegCo, 1 November 1961, p. 646.
13 E.g. MP Henry Clark, HC, 19 December 1960, s5-vol632-cc963–1024.
14 HC, 24 January 1961, s5-vol633-cc36–107.
15 Ibid.
16 LegCo, 23 May 1961, p. 253ff.
17 Ibid.
18 Ibid.
19 Chanan Singh later noted the 'very vague and general nature' of the previous LegCo's resolution and thus argued that 'The government has no business to proceed on the assumption that it has a right to accept the report without consulting this Council' (ibid.).

20 Mr MacKenzie, Minister for Finance and Development, LegCo, 23 May 1961, p. 247.

21 Although the still biased composition of the LegCo – which included seats reserved for Europeans (10), Asians (8) and Arabs (2) – meant that while KANU won 72 per cent of the popular vote, it only held 19 of 65 seats (Sanger and Nottingham 1964); also see the African Elections Database, available at https://africanelections.tripod.com/ke.html#1961_Legislative_Council_Election [Accessed 9 February 2022].

22 LegCo, 23 May 1961.

23 LegCo, 10 May 1962, p. 104.

24 HC, 24 January 1961, s5-vol633-cc36–107.

25 Ibid.

26 For a copy of the Overseas Service (Kenya) Agreement 1961, see TNA CO 822/3022.

27 Notes of a meeting held in the Colonial Office, 23 March 1962; TNA CO 822/1949.

28 The term 'entitled officer' was later changed to 'designated officer'; Philip Rogers, Assistant Under-Secretary of State, in 'OSAS: Kenya. Note of a Meeting held at the Colonial Office at 2:30 pm on 15th December, 1960.' TNA CO 822/1947.

29 Notes of a series of meetings held between 15 and 23 December 1960 at the London Colonial Office, with representatives from the Colonial Office and a delegation from Kenya, including representatives of the Kenyan government and the Staff Side of the Kenya Whitley Council. The objective was to discuss the model OSAS Kenya Agreement with a particular focus on defining who would be designated under the scheme; TNA CO 822/1947.

30 This begs the question on what grounds these officers had previously been recognised as expatriate. Griffith-Jones is accusing the Colonial Office of trying to switch from a racialised use of expatriate, which it so far supported, to a more limited 'geographical' one. This, he argued, would imply a breach of 'public faith', as Rogers himself soon admitted.

31 London meeting notes (see note 29); TNA CO 822/1947.

32 Ibid.

33 London meeting notes, December 1960; TNA CO 822/1947.

34 Letter from Quraishy to Rogers, 17 January; TNA CO 822/1947.

35 Telegram from Kenya (Sir P. Renison) to Secretary of State for the Colonies, 24 January 1961; TNA CO 822/1947.

36 Civil service staff associations had been racially segregated until the 1954 Lidbury reforms (Clayton and Savage 1974; see also Smith 1999).

37 TNA CO 822/1947.
38 Joint letter from CACSA members to the Chairman of the Central Whitley Council, 25 January 1961; TNA CO 822/1947.
39 Secret telegram by Kenya Governor to the Secretary of State for the Colonies, 13 April 1961; TNA CO 822/1947.
40 TNA CO 822/1947.
41 Ibid.
42 Memorandum on 'the future of overseas officers', 26 March 1962; TNA CO 822/1949.
43 TNA CO 822/1947.
44 Letter from Quraishy, in his role as president of CACSA, to the Secretary of State for the Colonies, 25 January 1961; TNA CO 822/1947.
45 Women were mostly invisible in the debate about designation under OSAS. However, SCSA submitted a petition on 21 June 1962 demanding that 14 women, mainly personal secretaries, be designated under OSAS, and MP Barbara Castle followed up on this matter with a question to the Secretary of State for the Colonies on 19 February 1963. This was denied on the grounds that these women did not convert with an inducement allowance under the Lidbury revisions. Indeed, Kenya was the only East African territory to decide in 1954 that women were categorically *not* to receive inducement allowances. See TNA CO 822/3022.
46 Holmes Report 1948:24–25.
47 Holmes 1948:24.
48 Lidbury Report 1954:20–21.
49 Lidbury 1954:21, 19.
50 Lidbury 1954:25.
51 Lidbury 1954:317, see also 291.
52 Except some Asian officers who had recently been moved to European pay scales – Lidbury mentions two such cases.
53 Lidbury 1954:19; emphasis added.
54 Letter by the Director of Establishments Office regarding the application of Mr. de Sa to HMOCS, 19th January 1961; KNADS Folder C5/5362.
55 TNA CO 822/1947; a similar request was voiced by LegCo member Zafrud-Deen to the Secretary of State on 21st October 1960.
56 TNA CO 822/1947.
57 LegCo, 23 May 1961, p. 258, emphasis added.
58 LegCo, 16 December 1960, pp. 1144–1145.
59 LegCo, 24 March 1960, p. 85.
60 TNA CO 822/1949.
61 Letter to the Provincial Commissioner, Rift Valley Province, 30 August 1961; KNADS Folder C5/5362.

62 LegCo, 23 May 1961, p. 266.
63 Letter from Griffith-Jones to Rogers (DTC), 3 August 1961; TNA CO 822/1947.
64 Letter from Sir Frederick Crawford, Government House (Uganda) to Rogers, 22 August 1961; TNA CO 822/1947.
65 Letter from Poynton (Colonial Office) to Harris (Treasury), 18 September 1961; TNA CO 822/1947.
66 UN General Assembly Resolution No. A/RES/1646(XVI).
67 Copy of the conversation, dated 9 October 1961, and aide memoire dated October 1961; TNA CO 822/1948.
68 Letters from 20 February 1962, 23 February 1962, 5 March 1962; TNA CO 822/1949.
69 Service Circular (No 27), 27 October 1962; TNA CO 822/1959.
70 Memorandum by the Staff Side of the Central Whitley Council; TNA CO 822/1949.
71 LegCo, 23 May 1961, p. 256.
72 Lidbury 1954:29.
73 LegCo, 23 May 1961, p. 263.
74 Ibid., p. 262.
75 HC, 24 January 1961, s5-vol633-cc36–107.
76 Ibid.
77 Ibid.
78 HC, 8 May 1962, s5-vol659-cc187–8.
79 HC, 26 January 1962, s5-vol652-cc662–72.
80 Ibid.
81 Ibid.
82 HL, 14 February 1961, s5-vol228-cc723–61.
83 HC, 24 February 1965, s5-vol707-cc409–525.
84 Barbara Castle, HC, 24 February 1965, s5-vol707-cc409–525.
85 Henry Clark, HC, 24 February 1965, s5-vol707-cc409–525.
86 HC, 24 February 1965, s5-vol707-cc409–525.
87 As Clause 2 of the 'Overseas Development and Service Bill'; HC, 24 February 1965, s5-vol707-cc409–525.
88 HL, 6 July 1960, s5-vol224-cc1161–1234.
89 HC, 11 July 1960, s5-vol626-cc1133–44.
90 HL, 14 February 1961, s5-vol228-cc723–61.
91 HC, 19 December 1960, s5-vol632-cc963–1024.
92 HC, 11 July 1960, s5-vol626-cc1133–44.
93 HL, 1 July 1965, s5-vol267-cc1019–1031.
94 HC, 24 January 1961, s5-vol633-cc36–107.
95 LegCo, 10 May 1962, pp. 94–107.

96 Pensions (Increase) Act 1971; TNA OD 16/807.
97 Letter to all provincial heads by the Office of the Provincial Commissioner, Coast Province, 2 August 1966; KNADS 'Expatriate Officers' Folder C5/7921.
98 Letter to the Provincial Commissioner, Coast Province, 9 August 1966; KNADS Folder C5/7921.
99 Letter to the Provincial Commissioner, Coast Province, 10 August 1966; KNADS Folder C5/7921.
100 KNADS Folder C5/7921.

3

Towards a new breed of expatriate manager in international business

Not much can be done to save international executivism from disappearing gradually under the impact of growing nationalism ... International 'executivism' will phase out from the global management scene by the year 2001. ... No free nation in the world ... wants its industry and commerce or any other sector of its economy for that matter to be under the domination and exclusive control of exogenous managers. The presence of aliens in strategic management positions in business organisations, particularly in underdeveloped countries, is not only considered detrimental to the national interest and 'managerpower', but also resented by the populace. No global movement started and supported by aliens, whether political, military, or religious, is likely to survive today in the face of rising nationalism. Two important worldwide movements, colonialism and evangelism (respectively dominated by foreign colonial powers and foreign missionaries) are virtually disappearing. International executivism (dominated by foreign managers) will certainly share the same fate.

Cecil Howard, 1970, *Management of Personnel Quarterly*

In international business, the expatriate is often taken to denote an 'intracompany assignee', transferred abroad by their multinational employer for a number of years. Researching these migrations is the aim of *international human resource management* (IHRM) studies. IHRM research is conventionally said to have emerged as an academic field in the 1980s, centrally in response to intensifying globalisation. This chapter instead shows that a vibrant debate on the type of labour migrant now thought of as the 'traditional expatriate' already existed in the 1960s and 1970s. However, what is now the 'traditional expatriate' was at the time called a 'new breed of expatriate'. Tracing the emergence of this 'new breed', the chapter shows that, then as now, IHRM's category expatriate was neither technical nor straightforward but enmeshed in social and political struggles and riven by internal fault lines. IHRM studies does not simply document matters of business administration but participates in the hierarchical ordering of human movement and labour.

Early IHRM literature reveals the imperial genealogy of corporate 'migratory management', but also shows modifications in response to political changes. In the 1960s and 1970s, the worldwide success of anti-colonial movements, and rising calls for economic decolonisation and a more just international order, posed serious challenges to European and North American multinational corporations (MNCs) and their imperial methods of control and coordination. Early IHRM literature not only recognises this political context but actively intervenes in it. While some scholarship critically records the imperial legacies of multinational management, most sanctifies the enduring asymmetrical power relations of multinational business, not least by translating imperial discourses of 'white trusteeship' and the 'immature native' into management theory to establish the necessity of expatriate management.

This history, the chapter finally argues, is rendered invisible by more recent IHRM scholarship that locates the field's origins in the 1980s and narrates an unsituated and ahistorical 'traditional expatriate'. Both epistemic moves achieve a 'colonial aphasia' (Stoler 2011) that obscures imperial origins, sanctions the reproduction of imperial business practice today and shields knowledge production from having to reckon with its own postcolonial genealogy. The chapter thus also documents how a body of literature has depoliticised a category by hiding its geography and history. It implies a historiographical effort of recovery, as well as an intellectual effort to understand the production of social categories like the expatriate as a technique of governance within racialised global capitalism. Digging into this archive of IHRM also implies excavating an archive of migration studies and achieves a change in focus from 'moving people' to knowledge production on moving people and the mobility of that knowledge (Madge et al. 2015).

IHRM literature and the rise of the expatriate

An ahistorical IHRM and its 'traditional expatriate'

IHRM studies and its expatriate are firmly fastened to the control of global capital. IHRM scholarship has established itself as a 'strategic business partner' (Wald and Lang 2012) and its concerns revolve largely around helping corporations manage the 'expatriate cycle': expatriate selection and training, adjustment, performance and failure, the role of families, compensation and repatriation (Dabic et al. 2015). Research focuses almost exclusively on managerial and senior professional staff of MNCs and habitually assumes the perspective of headquarters (Boussebaa and Morgan 2014). Scholarship has been largely inattentive to less senior mobile labour and to international staff transfers in non-corporate organisations such as churches or international organisations (Kaufman 2008; Berry and Bell 2012). Moreover, unlike in critical management and organisation studies, there is still 'very little written explicitly on issues of power, domination and ideology in IHRM' and the field has largely failed to reflect on its own role as an academic discipline (Peltonen 2012:536).

IHRM studies are also markedly ahistorical as neoliberal business practice is 'seen to be without history or geography' (Hindman 2009a:249). More specifically, IHRM literature is marked by a constitutive 'colonial aphasia'. As Cooke (2003a) argues, management studies have denied the historical roots of management theory and practice in antebellum slavery, while 'development management owes an unacknowledged debt to colonial administration' (Cooke 2003b:47). In short, the historiography of management has written out colonialism, empire and plantation slavery. Roediger and Esch (2012:31) similarly show that, whether on Southern plantations or in Northern factories, 'managers were never outside of the US racial system and in many ways made that system'. Their diagnosis remains acute: while US labour management, both domestically and abroad, was steeped in racial thought, this 'has until recently remained little investigated, scarcely theorized, and too often unnamed' (Roediger and Esch 2012:23). In organisational and management studies more broadly, emerging post/decolonial perspectives thus attend to how racism and imperial relationships 'remain deeply embedded in organizations not just in terms of structural features and patterns of material inequality but also as ways of conceiving of differences and capabilities' (Boussebaa and Morgan 2014:101; see also Prasad et al. 1997; Prasad and Prasad 2002; Prasad 2012). As Boussebaa et al. (2012:482) note, understanding these processes requires conceptualising the firm as an internally differentiated and uneven transnational social space, 'embedded in the wider, historic processes of colonialism and imperialism that have shaped, and continue to shape, corporate globalization'.

In a stark exemplification of its colonial aphasia, recent IHRM literature habitually references the 'traditional' (Froese 2012; Shaffer et al. 2012), 'typical' (Baruch et al. 2013), 'prototypical' (Bonache and Zárraga-Oberty 2017) or 'conventional' expatriate (Collings et al. 2007; Alshahrani and Morley 2015). This generally refers to a senior employee posted to a foreign subsidiary for several years with their family and a generous compensation package. Alternative labels are 'assigned' (Jokinen et al. 2008), 'organizational' (Froese 2012) or 'traditional corporate' expatriate (Cerdin and Pargneux 2010). The 'typical' or 'traditional' expatriate seems an uncontested category, the historical standard against which novel forms of 'international work' are defined, as when Cerdin and Brewster (2014:248) note 'the diversification of expatriate assignment types … beyond the traditional expatriates'. Rhetorical mobilisations of the 'typical' or 'traditional' expatriate, often in a seeming aside, regularly lack historical perspective and sociostructural context, rendering this a timeless and contextless figure. Occasionally, the traditional expatriate is historically situated in a brief sketch that does not actually discuss the relevant political context, as when Altman and Baruch (2012:246) outline that the 'traditional expatriation path … was followed since before and particularly after World War II until the 1980s as the common expatriation route'. Elsewhere, the historical horizon is painted so broadly as to effectively dehistoricise, rather than contextualise, the traditional expatriate as the eternal order of things:

> entrepreneurs have recognised the importance of physically relocating managers to foreign locations where business operations are based since approximately 1900 BC. Indeed, even at this stage, locals were viewed as inferior and restricted to lower level jobs while parent

country nationals (PCNs) were afforded superior conditions, similar to modern day expatriates. (Collings et al. 2007:199)

Yet IHRM's expatriate is not as ageless or uncontested as the adjectival 'traditional' or 'typical' might suggest. Instead, much like the historian Yusuf Bala Usman argued about European colonial historiography of Africa, 'the discourse on tradition was actually an admission of historical ignorance' and its political effects include the ossification of social relation (cited in Mamdani 2012:94).

Although the emergence of IHRM scholarship on expatriates is often located in the 1980s, and publications certainly multiplied from then on, research on international staffing existed much earlier (see also McNulty and Selmer 2017). In the 1960s lively discussions took place on themes such as expatriate selection and compensation, adjustment and culture shock, failure and return, and the role of families. While debates and approaches have certainly diversified since, IHRM's central concerns were already established research topics in the 1960s. Interestingly, throughout the 1960s and 1970s, the now 'traditional' expatriate was understood to be a 'new breed' of expatriate, a social role that emerged out of previous forms of imperial migration which were being transformed in response to decolonisation. Early IHRM literature thus proves insightful, offering historical perspectives sorely missing from today's scholarship.

Decolonisation, the Cold War and the new breed of expatriate

Early IHRM literature was (and to some extent remains) US-centric, primarily concerned with US multinationals, before beginning to turn to European and Israeli MNCs in the 1970s, and Japanese firms in the 1980s (Zeira 1976; Tsurumi 1978). After World War II, European countries lay in ruins and clambered to hold on to global dominance, while anti-colonial movements were winning political independence, and the USSR and the US emerged as the world's two military, economic and political superpowers. MNCs were central to US ascendancy. Between 1945 and the mid-1960s, the United States accounted for an estimated 85 per cent of all foreign direct investment (Jones 2005), and by 1960 about 64 per cent of the largest 250 industrial companies were headquartered in the US (Roach 2005). The oil and automobile industries had first driven US multinational expansion abroad and one 1955 study found that, reflecting the importance of the oil industry, 31 per cent of US expatriates were stationed in Saudi Arabia, 24 per cent in Venezuela and only 8 per cent in Western Europe (Reynolds 2004). Not only did US corporations increasingly enter foreign markets and move production processes abroad, but overseas profits also became increasingly significant compared to domestic business (Dickover 1965). As US corporations orientated themselves to the world, the MNC itself changed and grew in importance: 'the emergence of the multinational firm as an institution of global importance must rank as one of the major features of mid-twentieth-century history' (Fayerweather 1972:2). Today, MNCs distribute 'trillions of dollars' of foreign direct investment and their power to decide 'who gets what' makes them key actors in the international political economy (Bakir and Woods 2018:279).

It is thus hardly surprising that an academic field like IHRM studies emerged to support the intertwined US imperial and corporate expansion, also by depoliticising this project. In the Cold War context, 'scientific management' and 'human relations' became soft power tools in the US geopolitical strategy of containment: 'they were a mechanism to foster wealth and prosperity, but also, and more importantly, cultural, social, and political alignment' (Salles-Djelic 2019:402). As a form of labour discipline, human relations promised harmony and engagement as antidotes to workers' struggles, union power and potential Soviet influence; symbolically, it became part of the US 'modernization' agenda as a model of modern labour organisation grounded in US cultural and civilisational superiority (Salles-Djelic 2019). Against the Cold War backdrop, European and Japanese economies, too, became 'Americanised' through the import of US management practices (Salles-Djelic 2019), and despite competition over global influence, US and European elites collaborated, if on uneven terms, to preserve the 'Western'-dominated capitalist global system (Achiume 2019). Accordingly, the Seven Sisters oil cartel controlling the post-war international oil industry was underwritten by a broader Anglo-American coalition and, as Louis and Robinson (1994:487) argue, from the mid-1950s British and American officials agreed that their interest in Africa was best served by speedy independence organised 'in such a way that these [successor] governments are willing and able to preserve their economic and political ties with the West'. It is in this context of a US-dominated postcolonial capitalism integrating a system of unequal nation-states that David Young, writing in the *Harvard Business Review*, detected 'a steady growth in what is almost a new breed of expatriate':

> Whereas the expatriate once was either a merchant residing in an overseas territory for most of his life, or an overseer employed in an extraction industry in a remote territory, the new breed consists of managers and technical experts who, in many cases, have counterparts in the host countries. Their role has changed from that of pioneering to instruction of local counterpart staff or, in some cases, to watchdog activity over the home offices' financial interests in operations otherwise run entirely by local nationals. (Young 1973:117)

This new breed was thus understood to have a genealogy in imperial business and labour regimes while also reflecting adjustments made in response to geopolitical change. The transforming expatriate of the 1960s and 1970s thus encapsulates broader geopolitical continuities and ruptures.

Indeed, growing US corporate power is revealed in the very uptake of the category expatriate by business literature. When the 'new breed' was first announced in the 1960s, corporate migration was not the sole nor even a prominent association with expatriate in the United States. As Nancy Green (2009) shows in her social history of the term in the US context, primary associations with expatriate in the early twentieth century were banishment, exile and estrangement. Prominent expatriates included the writers and artists of the 'lost generation', who were considered suspect by the US public for their bohemian lifestyles as much as for their unpatriotic choice to leave the country. Hence, expatriate is a rare occurrence in 1950s business scholarship[1] and in 1958, the *International Executive*'s 17-page reference list of relevant research titles makes no mention of expatriates. Similarly, although Fayerweather's (1959) monograph *The Executive Overseas* is considered an early example of 'expatriate studies' (McNulty and Selmer 2017), Fayerweather himself did not refer to expatriates but instead relied on the clunky 'United States executives stationed overseas', or simply 'executives overseas'. A 1966 publication by business historian Mira Wilkins exemplifies just how much the meaning of the term expatriate was changing. In her article titled 'The Businessman abroad' – part of a special issue called *Americans Abroad* – Wilkins challenged popular imaginations of American emigrants as bohemians, noting that most Americans abroad worked for US-headquartered corporations. She then described various motivations of American businessmen abroad:

> Some Americans go abroad seeking adventure ... Some go overseas 'to make more money.' Some see 'career opportunity' in foreign assignments ... Some are business expatriates – born overseas of American parents or residing for years abroad, they are more at home outside the United States than in this country. Others go overseas because coincidence or the need for a job has led them to their position. (Wilkins 1966:88)

This sole reference to expatriates in an article about US businessmen abroad does not denote corporate managers but implies permanent emigration. Similarly, writing in *MSU Business Topics*, Gonzalez (1967:69) still felt the need to justify his use of expatriate, writing that 'the 25,000 executives representing US business abroad are frequently called *expatriates*. The word has a reserved meaning and does not convey the usual meaning of banishment or withdrawal from one's country.' US business literature of the 1960s and 1970s thus wrote *against* the term expatriate's more prominent associations with emigration, estrangement and exile. This shift in meaning was tied up with an increase in US personnel abroad. Hiring US citizens to manage business abroad was by no means a new practice; the novelty lay in the size and significance of the phenomenon (Wilkins 1966). Accordingly, Richard Hays (1974:26) wrote in the *Journal of International Business Studies* that prior to 1940 there were only a few sizeable American multinational firms and 'Most expatriates needed could be found by tapping the pool of internationally experienced sons of military, diplomatic, or business fathers.' When international investment increased rapidly after World War II, US firms found 'a pool of eager expatriates' among veterans. Soon enough, however, demand outgrew supply, and by the 1950s firms began recruiting individuals for expatriate service who had never worked abroad. This, according to Hays, was when expatriation became a practical and academic concern in the US. The growth of US multinational business thus implied the intensification, increased importance and shifting interpretation of business-related emigration. US corporate migrants, increasingly figured as expatriates, thus gained in visibility and status in a country that had historically conceived of itself as one of immigrants and had been suspicious of citizens living abroad (Green 2009).

'Third World nationalism': the end of the expatriate?

The take-up of the term expatriate by US business literature thus reflects geopolitical and economic changes. The break-up of European empires implied a major business opportunity for US corporations. To realise this opportunity, US corporations relied on organisational structures and management hierarchies that paralleled European imperial practice. Yet this contradicted the country's professed opposition to European imperialism and its support for Third World nationalism, key moral legitimations for US supremacy. IHRM scholarship helped resolve this contradiction by proclaiming the novelty and distinctiveness of US business expansion. In the *Journal of the Academy of Management*, Gonzalez and McMillan (1961:34) announced that 'The US today occupies the place of eminence in the world of international enterprise which Britain occupied in 1913', while also noting that the majority of firms involved had 'little if any overseas investment' previously. This position as 'relative newcomers' to international business led scholars like Dickover (1965) and Hall (1960:87) to position Americans as 'all too often "innocents abroad"'. In such narrations, individual expatriates as much as corporations and the US itself became 'innocent'. This framing erases earlier US imperial, colonial and military ventures as well as 'the greatest US export in the quarter century after 1890': American mining engineers who 'replaced European experts in Asian, Mexican, South American, Australian, and African mines in significant measure because they so successfully proclaimed a knowledge gained at the intersection of race and management' and whose success prompted the *Engineering Magazine* to trumpet the 'Anglo-American industrial ascendancy' already in 1913 (Roediger and Esch 2012:236, 293). Rather than historical fact, the rhetoric of 'innocents abroad' thus signalled efforts by the US to dissociate itself from flailing European colonial empires – while US firms arguably picked up where European powers left off.

Despite such efforts at dissociation, IHRM literature recognised imperial expatriates as the most important progenitor of the 'new breed' of expatriate. European corporations had been key actors in imperial projects and historically relied on the same racialised labour arrangements as colonial administrations, tethering race, rank and remuneration (Leonard 2010a; Kunz 2020b).[2] Such explicitly racialised labour hierarchies were challenged by anti-colonial movements that achieved political decolonisation and increasingly called for economic decolonisation by the 1960s.[3] In this context, early IHRM literature recognised corporate migration as inherently political and 'political considerations' were, according to Young (1973:117), the central reason for the 'new breed' of expatriate. Business historians confirm the significance of decolonisation as possibly the most fundamental challenge for multinational business in the twentieth century (Vitalis 2009). Decker (2008a:609) writes that worldwide hostility towards multinational companies grew in the 1960s and the expropriation of firms, mostly in Africa and Latin America, reached its height in the 1970s, generally interpreted as a decade of 'severe challenge to the ownership and control of multinationals in less developed countries'. She also notes that 'What has received next to no attention in the literature is the fact that Western companies felt consistently threatened by the pressure to promote Africans, often more so than by localization and indigenization legislation' (Decker 2008b:606).[4] This political momentum subsided in the 1980s, as neoliberal agendas became entrenched and the 'new breed of expatriate' was relabelled the 'traditional expatriate': seemingly historically constant and organisational common sense.

Reflecting the significance of political and economic decolonisation for corporations, these were central themes in early IHRM literature. Notably, the 'new breed' of expatriate did not imply changed geographies of migration and control. Both Young (1973) and Vivian (1968) position expatriates, old and new, as moving from the metropole to its peripheries by evoking past 'pioneering' roles and the current 'training of locals' in 'remote' and 'overseas' territories'. In 1963, Francis Hodgson wrote in *MSU Business Topics* that US firms doing business abroad now faced many 'hazards', especially the 'spectre of nationalization' that 'lurks in many foreign areas' so that there were few business opportunities abroad where 'local participation' or 'rapid development of nationals into management positions' was not required by law or contractual agreements (Hodgson 1963:53, 49). While 'nationalism' was also recognised as a consideration for doing business in Europe (Howard 1970) and Canada (Lindeman and Armstrong 1961), US firms generally employed the most Americans in 'underdeveloped' countries (Wilkins 1966:85) and it was here that they faced the most severe challenges. Accordingly, Murray (1975:22–23) argued that while 'the underdeveloped countries represent a prime area for growth and profits', doing business there was challenging and 'things are likely to get worse' as

> multinationals are accused of such offences as repatriating excessive profits overseas and using capital-intensive methods of production that do nothing to alleviate widespread unemployment. These and similar allegations are used as justification for the expropriation of foreign investments and the nagging restrictions placed on the operations of multinationals.

In response to such political sensitivities, Wilkins (1966) writes, few companies had entirely American top management teams overseas. Some firms restricted Americans to key managerial positions, such as general and finance manager, while others had regional offices staffed mainly by Americans, while national subsidiaries were headed by national executives (see also Zeira 1976).

This 'economic nationalism' led the more pessimistic commentators to declare the imminent end of the expatriate. Cecil Howard (1970:11–12), cited at the beginning of this chapter, concluded that 'not much can be done to save international executivism from disappearing gradually under the impact of growing nationalism'. Similarly, Harbison (1963) saw expatriate employment as but a temporary means for developing countries to employ skilled labour while training their own nationals, and Harbison and Myers (1960:9–10) predicted in the *International Executive* that 'expatriate management too will become an anachronism in modern society'. From the late 1960s, this resulted in growing calls for the multidirectional rotation of staff to establish 'geocentric' and 'polycentric' firms (Perlmutter 1969). Vivian (1968:40) hence predicted that 'the very concept of "an expatriate" is becoming increasingly academic' as US companies were following older European multinationals in adopting 'a multinational management outlook' where 'management, and managers, will become international – better still, nonnational'.

Yet other commentators, like Negandhi (1966:57), argued that although 'costly and sensitive', there appeared 'no alternative' to sending Americans abroad. They observed that while the number of expatriates might be decreasing and the nature of their deployment changing, MNCs continued to place Americans in top subsidiary positions. If Third World government pressure to replace foreign managers and technicians with nationals was mounting, the response was lacking. Some, like Howard (1974), suggested that firms failed to effectively recruit, retain and develop host country national (HCN) managers, with 'mediocre' expatriates unwilling or unable to train their potential successors. More commonly, however, the slow rate of replacement was explained with the lack of suitable local candidates, and in any case the topic was not systematically researched in IHRM studies. Expatriates thus continued to fulfil functions of oversight and control; they simply had to be used more sparingly and strategically. While decolonisation thus challenged and changed multinational businesses' reliance on migrant management, it did not end it. The ascendancy of a 'new breed' of expatriate was fast under way.

Theorising the new breed of expatriate

Adapting to changing circumstances: new expatriate temporality, roles and personalities

The 'new breed' of American expatriate was seen to differ from *his* European colonial predecessor in three related ways: he moved for shorter periods of time, in different roles, and exhibited a new attitude and management style. First, the 'new breed' was seen to go on shorter assignments. In the *Advanced Management Journal*, White and McGowan (1977:16) noted 'a new breed of expatriate, the international expatriate' who moves 'from foreign assignment to foreign assignment'. Also the *International Executive* (1971:10) found 'the "career foreign service executive" formerly commonplace in European firms … disappearing in favor of the more mobile US-style men'. While this changing temporality of movement was certainly enabled by easier and cheaper travel, it was also due to a new unviability of direct and permanent foreign control of corporate interests abroad. Accordingly, Vivian (1968:32) identified four types of 'expatriates', with the most important one the 'temporary expatriate', who was sent on a 'medium term assignment, often at the initial phase of an operation, and training local personnel to take his place'. This 'temporary expatriate' was replacing the 'professional expatriate', who had 'worked abroad most of his career without being assimilated by his host country'. The 'professional expatriate', Vivian concluded, was 'a holdover from earlier days' and 'a disappearing group'. Importantly, it was not temporality that made Vivian's expatriate – he included permanent and short-term expatriates – but origin and organisational power.

This new temporary expatriate was said to be working *with* rather than reigning *over* host country nationals. The evolving narrative was one of short-term training and mutually beneficial cooperation. As Hodgson (1963:49) noted in the journal *Business Topics*, while the export of American capital and personnel was not new, 'today there is a fundamental difference' as now 'foreign economic involvement is related to national security'. This new sensitivity also required a new 'type of American' to be sent overseas,

> who sees his role as that of a co-operator rather than a carpetbagger, and as that of a supervisor-trainer rather than an unapproachable manager. The reasons for this are not centred in do-goodism but in cold economic fact. There are few business opportunities in foreign countries today, either established or planned, in which local participation is not required by law, or where rapid development of nationals into management positions is not required by contractual agreement … a cooperative partnership-type approach is simply good business. (Hodgson 1963:53)

Mira Wilkins (1966:90) similarly recognised changed circumstances:

> American businessmen have become highly sensitive to their positions as foreigners abroad. Corporation executives emphasize that their operations are 'identified' with the 'economic growth of the host country.' They insist on their companies and their employees being 'good citizens.' They stress respect for the host country.

Erik Cohen (1977:8) described the same developments in decidedly more political terms in his sociological review of 'Expatriate communities'. In many formerly colonised countries, he wrote, the 'legal position' of expatriates had changed and 'once lords of the land, they are now merely wealthy (and envied) foreigners' needed for specific purposes and allowed to stay for limited periods to train up nationals. However, he argued, this often turned out to be a 'pious wish' or 'ideological proclamation', as individual expatriates might be transient but 'expatriate enclaves' were 'permanent fixtures' (Cohen 1977:72–73). Moreover, while expatriates' shorter stay may 'reduce host hostility' it also precluded their 'deeper involvement' in the country and 'organizations often shift their personnel between jobs in different countries, precisely in order to prevent the development of such involvement and to safeguard undivided allegiance' (Cohen 1977:18). Notably, Cohen wrote all this in the journal *Current Sociology*, not in a management or business journal where the focus was on helping to solve corporate problems rather than critiquing corporations.

The third major change associated with the 'new breed' of expatriate were new attitudes and behavioural skills. As Howard (1974:138) described,

> The unprecedented demands placed on today's multinational executives by the mounting tide of nationalism and the drastic changes in their status worldwide call for new breed of expatriots [*sic*]. In view of this demanding situation, the overall suitability of an executive for an overseas position should be of utmost concern and importance to US multinational corporations ... It is equally important that his personal and environmental traits as well should be considered and analyzed, particularly where there is great diversity between cultures.

The new breed of expatriate required a new set of social and cultural skills to successfully manage American business interests in a changed global business environment. What exactly these skills looked like – and how they could be identified – became a key research focus in IHRM studies. Scholars thus developed an intense preoccupation with the expatriate's personality: 'personal qualifications are at least as important as the technical competence of candidates', John Ivancevich (1969:193) suggested. This reflected the heightened importance of expatriate staff. Precisely because their numbers were reduced and their deployment became a politically sensitive affair, while the profitability of US overseas business rose and subsidiaries became a geopolitically important means of proliferating US managerial culture, expatriates gained in strategic importance. Indeed, the very development of an academic field studying expatriates suggests their increased significance. Accordingly, Lesher and Griffith (1968:55) wrote in *Business Horizons* that while in the past many companies had used foreign positions as 'dumping grounds' for managers who 'had reached their peak in the domestic organization', this practice had 'changed radically in recent years' as firms now 'recognized the importance of committing top domestic talent to overseas operations'. In both the corporate and public sectors (see Chapter 2), expatriate staff now became not simply business-critical but positioned as national emissaries. George Dickover (1966:1) stated that overseas positions involved 'a twofold public relations responsibility in representing the company and United States to the community', and hence 'companies increasingly are exercising extreme care, as well as using the most modern devices and procedures, in selecting the individual – and his family – to be sent abroad' (Dickover 1965:144). Hodgson (1963:49) went as far as arguing that in the Cold War context, 'our business manager abroad has become an agent of US foreign policy'. As the expatriate became a key figure of US global hegemony, the role was seen to require skills beyond those required in domestic management. Identifying the right *man* and training *him* properly became central, while expatriate failure emerged as a growing concern,[5] resulting in incessant streams of scholarly and practical interventions.

Besides the expatriate's personality, scholarship also increasingly worried about their families. Lawrence Steinmetz (1965:15) reported in the journal *Human Resource Management* that many companies did not send US managers abroad unless accompanied by their wives, who played 'a critical role in the man's ability to adjust and be effective in an international environment'. Wives were assigned key responsibility for expatriate failure (their role was, unsurprisingly, emphasised less in discussions of their husbands' successes). Deciding on what personal qualifications were the right ones proved more difficult, a difficulty that itself secured the need for ongoing study. Scholars identified 'social adaptability' (Ivancevich 1969:193), 'sixth sense' (Negandhi 1966:58), 'special skills', or 'factor X', involving 'cultural flexibility', 'friendliness', 'lack of racial or religious prejudice' and an ability for 'acceptance and cooperation' (Shetty 1971:19). In the absence of precise definition the problem became visualised in the stereotype of the 'ugly American':

> Overwhelmed by the milieu of unfamiliarity, the expatriate and his family completely shun associations in the host country. Any number

of manifestations can occur: overt prejudice, social isolation, and possibly even direct conflict with the local citizens. Although aware he is jeopardizing his job, the 'ugly American' engages in a war with the feared environment. (Heenan 1970:51)

The looming spectre of the 'ugly American' and his unchecked wife continued to provoke a stream of scholarly interventions on the conduct of empire's elite emissaries. Seemingly unaware of the colonial lineage of their preoccupation with corporate wives (Hindman 2013), scholars mobilised new principles of scientific management and lamented, like Steinmetz (1965:28), that many companies considered 'evaluation' of wives 'improper', a 'taboo' which he considered 'a luxury they can ill afford' if they want to operate on 'sound management principles'. Expatriates and their families thus needed to be analysed and evaluated, measured and moulded with the help of a fast-growing scientific apparatus and an increasingly lucrative training industry (Jack and Lorbiecki 2003).

The figure of the 'ugly American' revealed concerns about expatriates' cultural, national and racist prejudices, recognised as obstacles to overseas business that depended on the goodwill of foreign governments. In *MSU Business Topics*, Hodgson (1963:53) warned that

> Caution should be exercised in transferring an individual raised in the Deep South to an overseas position where his assistants are of negroid origin or have dark skin colour. Equal caution should be used in regard to naturalized citizens from European countries whose early environmental training included a belief in their ethnic superiority to the nationals of Asia, Africa, Latin America, and other overseas areas.

While Hodgson recognised racist attitudes as a problem in overseas operations, he did not situate this problem within US structural racism, nor did he address the American tradition of 'race-based management', which labour historian John Commons had already in 1907 called 'the nation's paramount managerial innovation' (cited in Roediger and Esch 2012:21). Instead, Hodgson framed racism as a problem of individual attitudes and, moreover, conveniently associated racism with the Deep South and European imperialism. This effectively reconfirmed the US industrial North as the source of modern, superior management. He also assumed that expatriates would naturally be white Americans. Hodgson thus responded to firms' concerns about how the behaviour of overseas managers impacted their business, while ideologically defending US dominance in international business and offering strategies to advance it. Ultimately, an individualised focus on the personality of managers and their families mystified sociostructural conditions of inequality. Also in this sense the moulding of expatriates was intimately entwined with the furthering of international business.

Managing (across) culture

At the same time as scholarship worried about the cultural insensitivities and racism of expatriate staff, it redeployed racialised notions of difference to produce its field of intervention. In a sense, the expatriate was not allowed (to display) the very sense of Anglo-American supremacy that IHRM literature helped articulate. Despite concerns about expatriates' individual(ised) attitudes, scholarship generally espoused US management culture as the enlightened future awaiting the world. Such accounts could take on strong missionary overtones and echo justifications of European tutelage of colonised people not yet ready for self-government. As Roediger and Esch (2012) show, US management had long traded in race as a tool of labour management, at home and abroad. Scholarship on expatriates, too, engaged well-worn paternalistic racism, including notions of the civilising mission and colonial tutelage. Mildred Adams's 1961 article 'When tribesmen shift from jungle to jobs', published in the *International Executive*, discusses the alleged difficulties of Africanising mining in Ghana and relies on colonial racism par excellence – what Mamdani (1996:4) calls the 'honorable Western tradition' of infantilising 'Africans' as a 'child race'. In her account, Ghanaians still live in a childlike, pre-modern way: 'Out of the hot, humid forests surrounding the Ashanti gold fields, greatly daring and greatly scared, come Ghanians [*sic*] who want jobs' (Adams 1961:20–21). She then contrasts the ever-patient American boss with those demanding yet infantile Ghanaians who, after completing a basic group exercise, 'dance around' because 'They have proved themselves at the white man's game'. Their leadership skills are limited to being 'boss boy',

> Eager, bubbling, quick-witted, the boss boys give out a sense of infinite future possibilities. Even the best of them, however, are hampered not only by the short span of their experience in the higher levels of

occupation but also by fear of witch doctors, of spells, and of fetishes, a fear that is not easily replaced with reasoned caution. (Adams 1961:21)

While Adams's account stands out for its unabashed racism, its narrative logic is not unique but underwrote common assertions in IHRM literature that while deploying expatriates might be expensive and politically tricky, it was unavoidable because host country nationals simply were not ready for positions of responsibility. Even the most urgent calls for localising management did not avoid such paternalism. In their seminal article, Perlmutter (1969:125) declared a need not for revolutionary change but for 'evolutionary movement from ethnocentrism to polycentrism to geocentrism', where 'the polycentric stage is likened to an adolescent protest period during which subsidiary managers gain their confidence as equals by fighting headquarters and proving "their manhood"'. Again, the local employee is a childlike figure proving 'himself' under the patient and guiding eye of the corporate headquarters and its local emissary, the expatriate.

Grounded in assumptions of US superiority, IHRM scholarship positioned US expatriates as harbingers of modernity and development. Characteristically, Gonzalez and McMillan (1961:39) asserted that

> The science of management has reached its highest state of development in the US ... Transferred abroad, this know-how is first viewed with scepticism. Foreign national employees and partners are slow to respond and understand the American scientific approach to management problems. However, once fully indoctrinated they accept and support this way of doing things. The superiority of this more objective, systematic, orderly and controlled approach to problems is seen and accepted.

Similarly, the *Monthly Labor Review* published an article titled 'Exporting US standards to underdeveloped countries' (Shearer 1965), and in the *Columbia Journal of World Business*, Hannum (1967) positioned MNCs as more effective than any programme of development assistance in teaching business skills as well as basic hygiene, simply as a by-product of their profit-orientated activities in 'less developed countries'. Wilkins (1966:92–94) thus concluded that American businessmen abroad 'have a mission as much as the missionaries' and among their most important contributions was 'the communication of their methods and their skills', ranging from 'hard work ... in societies where such a virtue is often absent' to 'American management techniques', which had 'a marked effect on the "business revolution" taking place in Europe'. Now, as then, 'the argument that the "English-speaking race" embodied wise management continued to add its part to empire building' (Roediger and Esch 2012:206).

However, in the changed geopolitical context, overtly racist ideology and management practices could not simply be reproduced, especially for operations in now independent countries. Here, culture proved useful. In her article, 'Exchange of people among international companies', published in the *Annals of the American Academy of Political and Social Science*, Susan Holland (1976:57) finds that

> the United States international manager is conditioned by a socioculture that generally values objectivity, totally depersonalized decision-making, accuracy, directness and openness of communication and relationships, pragmatism, practicality, egalitarianism, problem-solving, competition and competitive self-advancement, individual responsibility, initiative, and so forth.

This American manager, steeped in an American culture supposedly animated by the creed of equality, opportunity and liberty, is positioned in marked contrast to those 'in the developing countries',

> who may place value on subjectivity, for example, or on abstract ideas rather than scientific formulas; or who cannot accept methodology and systematization and whose society may maintain personalized and hierarchical or vertical, family-oriented systems of human relationships. (Holland 1976:57)

From such accounts, the white American man emerged as the quintessential rational modern subject. The question thence was not whether others would gain by emulating the US (manager) but how US managers could best mobilise cultural empathy to make others understand this fact and guide them in the process. To this end, the US manager had to

> be able to adjust and modify his values and expectations to the extent necessary to make his perspective and goals understandable and acceptable to the HCNs ... even if he feels that his method of doing business is best, he needs to be able to communicate this to the HCNs in terms and language that they can understand .... (Holland 1976:56)

Cultural understanding and sensitivity were increasingly seen as business-critical skills, resources essential for management in the global economy. It was thus necessary that HQ's strategic representative, the expatriate, was able to transcend the confines of his culture and manage (across) cultural differences, just like previous American managers had exported their skills of managing different 'races' (Roediger and Esch 2012). Culture thus became a central research topic – as a generalising, homogenising and essentialising construct. Culture replaced race rhetorically, but recycled racist ideology in content and effect. It worked to establish the superiority of American management and thus the obvious right of Americans to manage.

Such IHRM literature on managing across cultures arguably did for US business what earlier anthropology had done for European empires inasmuch as it classified and explained Others for metropolitan interests and produced an ideological justification for US dominance. Hall and Whyte recognised as much when writing in the *International Executive* that

> Anthropologists have long claimed that a knowledge of culture is valuable to the administrator. More and more people in business are willing to take this claim seriously, but they ask that we put culture to them in terms they can understand and act upon. (Hall and Whyte 1960:14)

Now as in the past, 'cultural understanding' was encouraged inasmuch as it was useful for administration. Moreover, literature consistently presupposed a Euro-American subject as the bearer of such 'cultural empathy', and as best placed to decide about its limits. While the expatriate was expected to do the understanding and empathy, it was the HCN who was ultimately supposed to undergo cultural change by assimilating to US cultural norms. As Zeira et al. (1975:81) critically observed: 'While the international manager is instructed in the need to be sensitive and to adjust to the local culture, the major onus to change is placed on the host employees' (see also Prasad and Prasad 2002).

While research has noted the rise of a 'cultural racism' that relies on redefining 'race' as culture (Melamed 2006), Stoler (1995, 2011) cautions that culturally articulated racism was nothing new, but already central to European imperial projects and deployed prior to and alongside the 'bio-racism' (Fields and Fields 2014) popularised in the nineteenth century. The discourse of culture that served IHRM recycled and translated well-worn colonial racism which perceived culture 'as a given dimension of a people's existence and not a product of historical existence and development' (Mamdani 2012:101). Critical voices at the time cautioned against an analytical over-reliance on a simplified and reified notion of culture. In the *Harvard Business Review*, Sirota and Greenwood (1971:53) wrote that

> Cultural differences are often posited as a major difficulty encountered in managing employees from other countries ... however ... the problem could just as often result from automatic, stereotyped assumptions of differences on the part of management in multinational organizations.

Despite such warnings, an essentialised 'culture' and individualised 'personality' became the dominant framework for thinking about difference, power and conflict in IHRM (see also Prasad et al. 1997). This depoliticising framework facilitated a shift away from a concern with the political nature of expatriate management. Matters of political and economic power, as well as sociostructural discrimination and inequality, became reframed as problems of culture – a trend set to intensify from the 1980s with a booming 'cross-cultural training industry' (Jack and Lorbiecki 2003; Hindman 2013; Cranston 2014). Accordingly, Peltonen (2012:539, 532) notes that 'many personnel techniques are legitimized with a reference to cultural differences and cross-cultural adjustment' and defines IHRM literature as investigating human resource practices 'in cross-*cultural* contexts'.

Compensating expatriates: colonial difference in postcolonial times

While cultural management became one focus of IHRM literature, Reynolds suggests that expatriate compensation was its original function: 'the international personnel function started with and was built around expatriate compensation as its core competency' (Reynolds 1997:119; 2004). Hindman (2013:10, 8) similarly stresses the centrality of compensation practices for making expatriates, arguing that 'Expatria' is first and foremost 'a product of the package expatriate labor system', and at least until the 1990s the expatriate package was the 'most salient distinction' for defining who was a part of 'their self-understood community'. To remunerate their expatriates, many US companies used the 'balance sheet approach', which adapted the US State Department's practice of basing US expatriate salaries on home country pay – then among the highest in the world – and included tax equalisation and several differentials, premiums and allowances. Although expatriate compensation is much more differentiated today and many move on 'local contracts' (see also Chapter 4), Bonache and Zárraga-Oberty (2017:153) find the 'balance sheet' remains the most commonly used approach among global mobility compensation systems, and international staff still cost on average 2.4 times more than their domestic counterparts. They explain that the 'traditional' reasons for 'assignment premiums' have remained unchanged, for example 'family and personal issues' and the 'continued uncertainty regarding international terrorism and the political and social unrest in certain destinations' (Bonache and Zárraga-Oberty 2017:152). They do not address the fact that the need for special expatriate compensation arose at least partly from a concern with institutionalising postcolonial inequality.

In the 1960s, commentators like Vivian (1968) were already arguing that expatriates were 'grossly overpaid', with firms 'tacitly stating that to live outside the US is a hardship deserving of extra compensation', an attitude which 'is an obsolete holdover from the early days' and 'tends to alienate our overseas neighbors and customers' (Vivian 1968:34). Tellingly, Vivian's concern had its limits. He continued that hardship compensation is 'fully justified' for some locations, like Saigon or the Persian Gulf, places that presumably corresponded to 'the more savage fringes of Empire', to which British subjects had to be lured with hardship compensation in the 'early days' (Vivian 1968:34). Vivian (1968:30) thus noted that expatriate compensation programmes 'now in use by many [US] companies are derived from nineteenth century British colonial compensation practices', while Allard (1996:39) specifically pointed to the British East India Company, which he argued 'developed the overseas paycheck, the hardship bonus, the school allowances for children left behind and, of course, the foreigner's compound – complete with club and hospital – which is still home to oil company engineers and the like almost 200 years later'.

The oil industry developed expatriate compensation practices that were then adopted by MNCs more broadly. Lesher and Griffith (1968:55) discuss that US oil companies were among the first major

US firms operating abroad, and first to offer 'hardship allowances'. Notably, George Dickover, who coined the 'balance sheet approach', was himself a former expatriate in the petroleum industry (Reynolds 1997). White and McGowan (1977:15–16) further suggest that in the 'pioneering oil company days' Americans had travelled abroad, primarily to Europe, without ever receiving a 'foreign service premium', even if living conditions were worse than at home. Special expatriate compensation was only introduced when US oil companies began operating in the Middle East, especially Saudi Arabia, 'both as an inducement to attract qualified personnel overseas and as a compensation, of sorts, for the "cultural shock"'. Oil companies soon 'outdid themselves' to create an expatriate 'Shangri-La' while 'other companies followed suit with the foreign service premium even for nonremote European locations' (White and McGowan 1977:15–16). What White and McGowan (1977) do not discuss is that the 'foreign service premium' paid to expatriates working on the Saudi Arabian oilfields was part of a system of racialised inequality institutionalised across labour, pay, housing, health and education. The US domestic oil industry (Dochuk 2019; Pierre-Louis 2021) and the Anglo-American-dominated international oil and extraction industries were structured by white supremacy, and the 'Jim Crow' racial organisation of US oil camps in Saudi Arabia (Vitalis 2009), Venezuela (Tinker Salas 2009, 2015) and Panama (Roediger and Esch 2012) mirrored the 'ethnic segregation' of European 'company towns' and oil camps (Reem 2013:45; Kunz 2020b).

While the precise mobilities of racialised, classed and gendered expatriate compensation practices remain to be investigated, today's expatriate compensation can trace a direct genealogy to Euro-American oil imperialism. Shared logics of white supremacy shaped expatriation practices across corporate, national and imperial borders to institutionalise 'whiteness as management' (Roediger and Esch 2012). In a postcolonial world, compensation may have become an even more important tool for headquarters to establish the status of their expatriates, because mechanisms of direct political control and legislated discrimination were unavailable. Writing in 2017, Bonache and Zárraga-Oberty critique that the pay differential between expatriates and HCNs results in expatriates living 'in cultural bubbles', which 'is not the best way of encouraging enculturation or an understanding of what it is like to live and work in another country'

(Bonache and Zárraga-Oberty 2017:158). The authors, however, criticise the very effect that the pay differential was designed to achieve. Indeed, the 'balance sheet' quite effectively encourages an understanding of living in another country – as a 'European' under conditions of coloniality. Instead of addressing this colonial-imperial genealogy, the authors offer an abstract discussion of 'the inequity *perceived* among HCNs' (Bonache and Zárraga-Oberty 2017:154; emphasis added). They acknowledge that the balance sheet 'discriminates against HCNs' who are 'very likely to consider that this situation is unfair', which is 'unfortunate' not because it *is* unfair but because HCNs might refuse to play their role as 'valuable socializing agents, sources of social support, assistance, and friendship for expatriates' (Bonache and Zárraga-Oberty 2017:155). Indeed, this problem is considered of such importance that 'many studies have sought to identify the factors that may offset or attenuate the negative influence of pay differential on the inequity perceived among HCNs' (Bonache and Zárraga-Oberty 2017:155) – in other words, academics have not studied histories of structural inequality, or considered how to overcome them, but have instead studied how to convince HCNs that this inequality is quite acceptable.

Internal fault lines, hierarchies and expatriate Others

I have argued that the 'new breed' of expatriate implied the adaptation, not the end of imperial practices and ideologies, and traced the socio-political emergence of this new breed of expatriate with the help of early IHRM literature largely ignored by current scholarship. This final section investigates the ongoing internal differentiation of the 'traditional expatriate'. The category's internal fault lines and constitutive Others further confirm the postcolonial power geometries of international business. Americans were never the only expatriates, but all intracompany assignments were not treated as equal. IHRM's 'intracompany assignee' has been inconsistently defined and ambiguously bordered, as apparent in the differentiation between 'parent country national' (PCN), 'third country national' (TCN) and 'host country national' (HCN).

Whereas PCNs share the headquarters' nationality, TCNs have a nationality other than that of the headquarters and of the subsidiary where they work. While the expatriate is usually defined in universalist guise as *an* intracompany assignee, the socio-political history outlined thus far lives on in the dominant tendency to equate the expatriate with the PCN (Collings and Doherty 2011). PCNs have been critiqued as expensive, ill-adjusted and prone to failure yet, as Edström and Galbraith (1977) have already noted, the organisational choice to transfer PCNs has remained largely unexamined. To this day, the 'necessity' of PCN deployment is suggested by the very plethora of research dedicated to facilitating it.

Despite the centrality of the PCN to the category expatriate, the equation of the two was at no point absolute. From early on, some studied TCNs as expatriates, prioritising the fact that an individual worked outside their native country over whether they shared the nationality of headquarters (Edström and Galbraith 1977; Cerdin and Selmer 2014). This reflects the reality that PCNs were never the only employees sent abroad as expatriates. Yet, even where TCNs become (framed as) expatriates, they frequently remain 'alternatives' whose benefits or shortcomings are defined against the PCN and who are deployed, for instance, because 'the country of assignment is not that different culturally from their own' (Parker and McEvoy 1993:373). TCNs' secondary corporate positioning is also suggested by their compensation. Perlmutter and Heenan (1974:128) found that TCNs with identical credentials and jobs often received half to one third the total compensation of US PCNs. Indeed, one of the most often cited reasons to hire TCNs remains their lower cost to the firm (Schollhammer 1969; Reynolds 2004; Shaffer et al. 2006; Collings et al. 2007; Collings and Doherty 2011). As J. G. Trimmer (1980:344, 346), Head of Management and Expatriate Remuneration at Shell International Petroleum, put it, employing 'unconventional' expatriates from South America and Asia can help avoid 'the very heavy indirect costs of Western European expatriates', and so 'using "cheap" expatriates' has 'played its part in commercial-policy of some companies'. As argued in Chapter 2, the practice of basing pay on origin – or gender for that matter – does not only have colonial roots but remains a racialising practice inasmuch as origins cannot be changed. One remains trapped.

TCNs are thus generally positioned as secondary expatriates – if they are framed as expatriates at all. Positioned as expatriates' Other, TCNs have also provided the very justification for deploying and privileging PCN expatriates. This becomes evident in Burritt's (1988:108–109) account of the oilfields in Saudi Arabia where, he writes, multinational staff 'are generally drawn from Third World countries' and 'Commonly called Third Country Nationals':

> Possibly the one area that causes the expatriate manager in Saudi Arabia the most frustration is the lack of consistent, high-quality work output. The standards of quality which are generally taken for granted in the United States are the rare exception ... the TCN employee is at first bewildered by constructive criticism aimed at improving the cleanliness and neatness of his work. Accustomed to the standards in his home country, he simply fails to perceive that his work is not acceptable.

The US expatriate is here contrasted with a homogenised Third World TCN. These categories are situated within a paternalistic narrative of divergent ability and skill, once again echoing the 'white man's burden' of the 'civilising mission'. Indicatively, only two years earlier, Seccombe (1986) also looked at the relationship between TCNs and PCNs on the Saudi oilfields: he examined the labour struggles of Italian workers who had been recruited by Aramco after World War II 'as an alternative to importing costly American personnel'. Notably, 'white' management here did not include all those today recognised as white, with southern Europeans treated as 'lesser European races' and relied on as 'middlemen workers' (Roediger and Esch 2012). Tellingly, Burritt's (1988) article published in the *Journal of Management in Engineering* does not cite Seccombe (1986), which was published in *Immigrants & Minorities*. TCN – or 'migrant' – labour struggles against 'expatriate' management remain invisible in IHRM, also by being relegated to a different category of movement and hence a different academic discipline (see Chapter 7).

Unlike the PCN and TCN, the host country national (HCN) is generally said to work in their country of citizenship and, as discussed, the supposed lack of suitably skilled HCNs has been a key justification for expatriate assignments. While HCNs have thus been worked as the category expatriate's most obvious Other, the border between these categories also proves fragile. Already in 1971, Eldin and Sadiq (1971:130) suggested that firms might hire, as 'highly qualified expatriates', non-nationals resident in the US and assign them to their country of origin 'because of their familiarity with the local as well as foreign scene'. Alpander (1973:1–2) made similar recommendations to help American corporations 'appear indigenous' to host countries.[6] These cases of 'HCN expatriates' evidence potent inequalities, but also highlight that the choice to tether organisational role and origin is socially and historically contingent, rather than self-evident. The boundary between PCN expatriates and HCNs also proved fragile in another way. The distinction between these two categories of staff was secured via pay checks and privileges, but also required the management of PCNs' social habits and emotional allegiances, as suggested by Dickover's (1965:144) observation that companies preferred to send 'employees already indoctrinated in company policies and objectives'. Developing strong identifications with HCN colleagues, subsidiaries or societies was decidedly not part of PCN expatriate job descriptions. The concerted effort to uphold the boundary between PCNs and HCNs is maybe best exemplified by resurfacing concerns, already prevalent in European colonial projects (Kennedy 1987; Stoler 1995, 2010), that PCNs might 'go native'. As Wilkins (1966:90) notes:

> American managers of foreign subsidiaries often have failed because they did not understand the foreign nation in which they worked, but others have also failed because they understood the foreign country so well that their home office decided they had 'gone native'.

Tellingly, Zeira (1976:41) reported PCN expatriates critiquing the way rotation policies made it 'almost impossible' for them 'to develop meaningful and rewarding relations with primary groups within and outside the subsidiary', so that they 'have no choice but to develop lasting relations with those officials at HQ who determine their personal status' and thus 'adapt their managerial behavior' to HQ expectations. PCNs too emerge as a category of labour moulded and disciplined within particular organisational arrangements, governed by tropes of the 'failed expatriate' who 'went native' or turned 'ugly American' as much as by practices of excessive remuneration and frequent rotation.

There is little research on TCN and HCN perspectives, despite the fact that the research which does exist has consistently highlighted asymmetrical status, inequitable treatment and uneven career prospects. Already Fayerweather (1959) devoted a whole chapter to the views of Mexican HCNs, noting discrimination and asymmetrical relations rooted in colonial histories. In 1972, Clausen spoke about 'two classes of corporate citizenship' (Clausen 1972:15) and Daniels (1973:695) noted that although MNCs 'frequently complain' about the difficulty of finding qualified local managers, practically no research existed on local managers' 'need satisfactions, biographical profile, beliefs about success–failure determinants, and compensation' (Daniels 1974:9). Zeira (1976:2–3) and colleagues described the political nature of staff transfers in several publications, where HCNs criticised the fact that 'very few of them will be rotated to other subsidiaries' and TCNs 'usually feel very uncomfortable and insecure' in their position. Both HCNs and TCNs highlighted difficulties in getting positions at headquarters, and found that if they were transferred it was mainly to improve the firm's relations with host governments and did not result in key positions. Here and there emerge glimpses of how organisational structures, social positions and relations were experienced in the 'corporate peripheries'. Yet the experiences and perspectives of HCNs and TCNs remained marginal concerns in IHRM studies until today (Toh and DeNisi 2005; Bonache and Zárraga-Oberty 2017).

While the emerging tenor in IHRM was about culture as the key source of conflict in corporations, the issues that emerge here are not primarily, or at all, about cultural difference but about systemic power asymmetries and structural discrimination based on origin. This was, ironically, corroborated by research on foreign MNCs operating in the US (Harari and Zeira 1974; Holland 1976; Stopford 1976). In this context, Sethi and Swanson (1979:37) reported on a US lawsuit where

> Three white, male, American executives have charged a Japanese trading company ... with job discrimination based on race and national origin. They alleged that the parent firm's expatriate employment policies give preferential treatment to Japanese executives in its hiring, compensation, and promotion practices.

The authors note that reserving top management positions for PCNs might conflict with US civil rights laws, which had, ironically, been introduced to overcome white, male managers' discrimination against African and Asian American and women workers. It is ironic, too, that the practice critiqued in this lawsuit was common in US MNCs and constituted the very object of IHRM research.

Conclusion

Reading IHRM literature from the 1960s and 1970s against and along its grain reveals a corporate category expatriate in the making. Scholars at the time described a 'new breed' of expatriate. This 'new breed' did not trace its ancestry to those strange and estranged American bohemians living abroad who US publics had thus far imagined under the label expatriate. Instead, the new breed was placed in the lineage of imperial managers, merchants and administrators of the earlier era of European-dominated globalisation. Yet the new breed was a changed man. He moved merely temporarily, did not command but train and cooperate, was selected with great care and trained in cultural sensitivity. These qualities were seen to distinguish the new US expatriate manager from the former European expatriate administrator – and by extension US global leadership from European imperial domination. Beyond such rhetoric, these changes were arguably a response to the changed requirements of conducting business in now independent nations and, as Chapter 4 shows, became the professed canon of US as well as European multinationals. A new way of administering multinational business – i.e. a new expatriate – was necessary, as one observer put it, not because of 'do-goodism' but due to 'cold economic fact'.

Scholars thus recognised the tense geopolitical context of international business. US corporate profits and a capitalist vision for the world were threatened not only by Soviet military might but by Third World independence leaders who embraced social justice, even socialist ideas, and instead of control of their populace looked to control of their resources, the development of national industries and skill, and equitable terms of trade within a 'new international economic order' (Shilliam 2014; Getachew 2019). These independence movements moreover connected with a growing fraction of the US civil rights movement, which called not only for an end to racist segregation and equal civic rights, but for economic redistribution (Gaines 2006). More was at stake than access to markets and resources released from European control.

While the 'new breed' of expatriate professed a new creed, it also reveals continuities in practice and thought. The intertwined political, economic and social developments that challenged the racialised and gendered labour hierarchies of which the 'old expatriate' had been an important part, led to modifications rather than the end of the expatriate. The direction of managerial mobilities was still largely from HQ to subsidiaries, decision-making power remained as unevenly distributed as profits, pay and privileges, and expatriates were still normatively white and male. Temporary PCN expatriates helped produce US multinational corporations as uneven spaces, just like permanent administrators and managers had done in previous European empires. IHRM literature participated in the adaptation of corporate practices to a new international system, an adaptation that often meant change in the service of conservation. That means, practices of imperial control and coordination were changed ultimately to secure inherited power imbalances and inequities. IHRM studies aided this by frequently naturalising and rationalising social inequalities and injustices by recycling colonial ideology in changed terminological garb: 'race' was moulded into 'culture', 'natives' turned into 'host country nationals' and scientific management sounded like civilisational achievement.

Today, the birth of the 'new breed' and 'his' historical transformation seem forgotten in IHRM studies. The temporary, well-compensated intracompany assignee moving from core to periphery with their nuclear family is now the 'traditional expatriate'; this figure reveals the tacitly racialised and gendered logics still structuring management in the global economy. IHRM has depoliticised the category expatriate also by universalising abstraction: by hiding its geography and history. This detachment of the category from its imperial genealogy facilitates the ongoing (re)production of imperial practice and thought by other names, as argued in Chapter 7. But the ambiguities and self-contradictions of the traditional expatriate reflect the politics of staffing that the vast majority of IHRM scholarship does not address. Political not cultural conflict and resistance, shine through the internal fault lines of the traditional expatriate. We cannot understand the extent of this conflict and resistance by staying within the IHRM archive – read along or against its grain. Instead, we need to rethink and expand what we consult as the archive of corporations and capitalism. The next chapter further explores this topic by discussing the renewed pressures the 'traditional expatriate' faced, almost as soon as it had been declared traditional.

Notes

1 See e.g. Mangone (1957), Mandell (1958), Thompson (1959) and Wallace (1959).

2 Accordingly, a commentator writing in the *Monthly Labor Review* equated colonial administrators and corporate managers when writing that 'expatriate (colonial) administrators and managers were abruptly removed' in many territories at the end of colonial rule (Fisher 1961:955).

3 Though, as Decker (2008a:480) cautions, the movement for 'economic decolonisation' prevalent especially in Latin America and Africa in the 1960s and 1970s denoted a form of economic nationalism that was more than a simple imperial after-effect.

4 Localisation here implies the local incorporation of 'extra-territorial companies' (Decker 2008b:606).

5 That high expatriate failure has been critiqued as a self-reproducing myth, rooted in mis-citation rather than careful scholarship, has done little to reduce its popularity (Harzing 1995; Hindman 2013).

6 See Bird and Mukuda (1989) for similar practices in Japanese MNCs.

4

Remaking the Shell expatriate: from company wife to global citizen

I wish I was back as a Shell wife again.
With the wonderful family of Shell to sustain.
Life after Shell is not nearly so good.
I'd go back again to that life if I could.
Extract from poem 'Those were the days', Shall Ladies' Project,
1996

The *Royal Dutch Shell Group of Companies*, often called simply 'the Group', or 'Shell', consistently ranked among the largest and most profitable corporations of the twentieth century. Throughout the century, the Group depended on a set of elite employees, known as 'international staff', who migrated throughout its global business empire to deploy specialist skills and knowledge, instil company culture, and coordinate and control this highly dispersed concern. This system of migratory management came under pressure by the 1990s, and this chapter examines how the Shell expatriate changed at the turn of the millennium. In doing so, it also traces the broader fashioning of neoliberal elite migration and its ideological ideal-type: the transnational professional, commanding a global consciousness and skill set, self-directed and flexible, at home in the world.

The Shell model: family migration and management

The Group emerged in 1907 from the merger of the *Royal Dutch Petroleum Company* and British *Shell Transport and Trading Company*. The Group's parent companies were formed in the nineteenth century during a period of intense globalisation driven by the imperial activities of European states and capital. Both firms found their original sources of oil and significant markets for their products abroad, in territories directly or indirectly under British and Dutch imperial influence (Jonker et al. 2007). After Royal Dutch and Shell merged in 1907, their further expansion remained embedded in European imperial practice and the Group relied on a racially differentiated workforce with white men staffing virtually all posts of responsibility and power. By 1958, Shell was active in more than 50 countries, and while European and North American operations were managed largely by nationals of the respective countries, this was not the case in the rest of the world. Moreover, to rise in central Group management, one had to be classified as 'international staff' and have gathered significant 'experience overseas'. The vast majority of international staff were always British and Dutch men, alongside some other Europeans and North Americans (van Overstraten Kruysse 1985; Sluyterman 2020; see Kunz 2020b for a more detailed discussion).

This system of racialised and gendered corporate management first came under pressure during the post-war wave of political decolonisation (Kunz 2020b). The mid-twentieth-century 'racial break' (Winant 2001) brought about by intertwined civil rights and anti-colonial movements resulted in a partial abolishment of the 'racial order', accompanied by new forms of racial privilege and discipline (Melamed 2006). Shell, early among multinationals, responded to decolonisation with 'regionalisation'. As enunciated by Shell's Head of Recruitment Division, A. P. Blair, in 1959,[1] regionalisation included the increased promotion of nationals into the management of now more autonomous operating companies, encouraged to see themselves as national companies within an overarching corporate matrix structure (Sluyterman 2007, 2020; Kunz 2020b). To enable this business model of 'decentralised cohesion', Shell continued to rotate an elite cadre of employees around its business to fill staffing needs, transfer knowledge and, crucially, instil company culture and coordinate and control this dispersed corporate concern from London and The Hague headquarters. The group of expatriates now however included both 'international staff' (IS) and 'regional staff' (RS). 'Regional staff' were employed by national operating companies and could be 'cross-posted' for specific assignments, but their careers took place within their operating company. In contrast, 'international staff' were hired by Group headquarters. They were expected to work abroad for most of their careers and had the opportunity to move up into central Group management. The expatriate thus became an internally diversified category, and in 1959 Blair envisaged that the eventual logical conclusion of 'staff integration' would be the inclusion of 'local/regional' staff into the central cadre of 'international staff', i.e. to include formerly colonised subjects in central corporate management (Kunz 2020b). Yet, Shell's labour hierarchies, like those of the oil industry more generally, remained tacitly racialised, and by the 1990s this central cadre of international staff continued to consist almost entirely of white men (van Overstraten Kruysse 1985; Kunz 2020b).

International staff, and their partners and children who accompanied them on longer assignments, formed a networked group of elite employees whose personal relationships, shared socialisation and mutual recognition were central to Shell's system of corporate management. Evans (1991:3, 23) accordingly called the 'network of personal relationships' and 'long-term trust' among senior management the organisational 'nervous system' that enabled Shell's philosophy of decentralised control of autonomous operating companies. International staff were usually hired directly from universities and expected to stay with Shell for their whole careers (Sluyterman 2007). Migration was a key tool to train and socialise these men and their wives for senior management positions. Given its paternalistic micromanagement of employees' lives, Shell was often characterised as a benevolent but commanding patriarch, nicknamed 'Uncle Joe' (SLP 1993:185).[2] In a continuation of colonial administrative and business practice, wives generally moved with their husbands and, though unpaid, stood in Shell's service almost as fully as their husbands. As the anthologies published by the Shell Ladies' Project (SLP 1993, 1996) document, the on-demand-mobility, sense of community and performative privileged lifestyles that Shell relied on for its model of corporate control required women's social, emotional and organisational labour. Shell's incorporated migration was thus a racialised, classed and gendered project, a heteronormative family enterprise that depended on the set-up of the nuclear family, the prioritisation of male careers and on wives' multifaceted informal labour (see also Tremayne 1984; Gordon 2008; Hindman 2013). This interlinking and conflation of the familial and corporate is reflected in the notion of the 'Shell family' which came to denote both the migrant worker's nuclear family, the body of Shell's elite migrants (SLP 1993, 1996) and at times even all Shell staff, as in

Blair's 1959 report. Shell corporate management was also a racialised project that forged association and solidarity among a mostly white migrant elite whose status as international staff, frequent rotation and socio-economic privilege fostered co-dependency while forestalling integration into postcolonial places and identification with operating companies (Kunz 2020b).

Shell's case is of broader relevance. Expatriation policies are compared and shared across organisations and sectors. As one former Shell spouse put it, 'you eyed the other companies and their arrangements ... if one [company] decided to improve conditions, I think, generally others followed' (interview, 2016). Also, when it restructured its system of expatriation in the 1990s, Shell surveyed the expatriation policies of other major multinationals, as well as the Dutch and British Foreign Offices. Among multinationals, Shell not only consistently employed the largest number of expatriates but was generally hailed as a pioneer with regard to the 'internationality' of its staff and its responsiveness to the 'broader expectations of society' (Grant 2008:133). From early on, Shell was seen as an exemplary case of a 'geocentric' firm where 'an individual's skills counts more than his or her passport' (Pucik et al. 2017:12). Indeed, Shell has been called 'one of the world's three most international organizations, the other two being the Roman Catholic Church and the United Nations' (Grant 2008:123). That Shell's internationality has been considered a role model allows inferences about multinational business more broadly. It also shows that the term 'international' can hide as much as it reveals: because historically racialised labour hierarchies did not align neatly with national borders, Shell's exemplary group of 'international staff' could still be made up of mostly white men.

The Shell expatriate in the 1990s: unwilling spouses and neoliberal diversity

Family troubles and neoliberal responses: restructuring the Shell expatriate

By the 1990s, Shell's system of corporate control and coordination via well-socialised mobile managers had come under renewed pressure, which resulted in the most substantial changes to Shell's category expatriate since the 1950s. Again, these changes took place within a broader corporate restructure. The 1980s saw the acceleration of global integration and the widespread deregulation of capital, labour and commodity markets (Sluyterman 2009). In the rich Global North, organisational power relations were in flux as large-scale attacks on trade unions, the dismantling of protective labour laws and increased outsourcing abroad weakened employees, while the liberalisation of financial markets increased shareholders' influence over company management. Especially after the disintegration of the Soviet Union had spelled the end of the moderating effect of the 'Soviet threat', neoliberal privatisation, deregulation and casualisation became the order of the day and Shell planners agreed that 'there was no alternative' (Sluyterman and Wubs 2010). Power relations in the global oil industry were further shifting as the Organization of the Petroleum Exporting Countries (OPEC) had significantly challenged Anglo-American control, and the so-called '1980s oil glut' led to the collapse of oil prices, so that by 1995 the Shell Group declared 'lagging financial and retail results' (Mirvis 2000:69). In this context, Cor Herkströter, who had become Group Chairman in 1993, decided that Shell's organisational structure needed to be overhauled. In 1994, Herkströter enlisted the management consultant McKinsey and between 1994 and 1997 Shell abandoned the regional-focused matrix structure to globally integrate its business and centralise investment and business decisions. Undoing a lot of the decentralisation that 'regionalisation' had introduced in the 1950s, operating companies became grouped according to their business, which left far less room for national variation and autonomy. As Sluyterman and Westerhuis (2008:22) put it, 'Shell ended the "local fiefdoms" and created one global company'. In other words, Shell abandoned the model of '"local rule" as a technique of colonialism' (Hindman 2013:142) which it had adopted in the context of the mid-century push for political and economic decolonisation, to return to more centralised control. In this context the importance and role of expatriates also changed.

Against this backdrop, Shell enacted far-reaching neoliberal changes to its employment relations. In the name of creating a more cost-effective organisation, Shell enacted mass redundancies and increased outsourcing and 'offshoring' of headquarters functions – including the administration of expatriates – to locations with markedly lower labour costs, like Bangalore, Cracow and Manila (Birkenkrahe 2002;

Matthews 2019). Worldwide, the number of Shell employees fell from 137,000 in 1990 to 90,000 in 2000 (Bamberg 2010). For its remaining staff, Shell 'flexibilised' labour relations by abandoning expectations of lifetime employment, ending employee programmes in housing, medical care and entertainment, and introducing performance-related pay that increased the Group's internal income disparities (Sluyterman and Wubs 2010). These changes were driven by financial considerations, but also the stated wish to 'unleash talent' and increase staff involvement in decision making and financial stakes in performance (Mirvis 2000).

These reforms also included changes to Shell's system of expatriation. By the early 1990s, and thus predating its corporate restructure, Shell realised that expatriates, especially international staff, were less willing to move at the behest of the company. To find out what impeded their mobility, Shell undertook a large-scale survey of expatriate international and regional staff and their spouses in 1993: the '*Shell Expatriate Outlook Survey*'. The Outlook survey revealed two prime reasons for staff's decreased willingness to take global assignments: partners' careers and children's education.[3] In 1988, the vast majority, 96 per cent, of expatriate staff were still men (Sluyterman 2007:290). Yet many of their female spouses now had their own careers and were less prepared to give them up. Similarly, parents were increasingly unprepared to separate from their children at an early age by sending them to boarding school, as had been the practice in Shell previously. And 'while the latter meant a temporary restriction on mobility, the former implied a more serious, longer-term immobility' (Shell HRP 1994:4). The survey also found that spouses were generally less satisfied than staff. They felt that their expertise was neither valued nor utilised for improving expatriate assignments, and were critical that Shell did not assist them in finding employment abroad.[4] While Shell was relatively early in recognising these challenges, it was not unique in facing them. In 2019, Matthews still found that the two main reasons that expatriate assignments were being turned down were 'family concerns' and 'partner career/income'.

Yet, neither Shell's global corporate centralisation, its various cost-cutting exercises, nor expatriates' own resistance to moving spelled the end of the expensive institution of the expatriate. Even while Shell enacted mass redundancies, the number of expatriates increased from roughly 5,000 in 1991 (Barham 1991) to around 7,400 in 2005 (Mays et al. 2005), to 6,100 in 2019 (Matthews 2019). Like many of its competitors, Shell continued to adhere to a development philosophy of 'growing our own timber' (Mahieu 2001:122) for its prized international staff, which it continued to largely recruit early on in their careers to develop their often highly specialised technical skills and groom them for senior management by moving them through different roles and locations (Sucher and Corsi 2012). Shell also continued to believe in 'culturally immersed' managers, as Hugh Mitchell, Shell's Chief Human Resources and Corporate Officer (cited in EIU 2009:22) noted in 2009:

> the most successful companies, they have very powerful identities and strong corporate cultures. … A very large company can exercise control through governance and processes more easily if there is a common belief system and common norms and behaviors. There is a huge cultural element to their success.

Shell expatriates thus continued to fulfil key roles as communicators, coordinators and controllers. Accordingly, Marcus Birkenkrahe (2002:3) recounts that when he joined Shell in 1997, he found that the Group's best-functioning 'Knowledge Management system' was 'the community of expatriates; mostly senior managers who were rotated through overseas jobs in Shell's operations in more than 130 countries. The most-valued knowledge in Shell was created, shared, consolidated and used by people, not computers, and pushed around the globe through these expatriates.' Shell thus continued to rely on a group of mobile, well-compensated bearers of its corporate culture to enact control and headquarters' interests. It still considered 'mixing' local and expatriate employees the 'lifeblood' of Shell and mobility thus 'critical to the business', so 'expatriates and their partners must be content if the business mission is to succeed' (Solomon 1996).

Instead of abandoning its system of expatriation, Shell adapted it. Following the Outlook survey, Shell established six 'task forces' in the areas of children's education, spouse careers, spouse recognition and involvement, staff planning and consultation, relocation information and assistance, and health.[5] In 1995, Shell created a 'Spouse Employment Centre' that advised spouses on employment issues and provided financial assistance to cover costs associated with spousal careers (Solomon 1996). Together with other multinationals, Shell also founded (and chaired) the 'Permits Foundation' to lobby governments to eliminate legal barriers to spouses' employment (*Personnel Today* 2005). Finally, to better recognise and actively involve spouses, Shell together with spouses created a network of Shell-wide 'Expatriate Information Network Centres' which became known as *Outpost*. Outpost centres were staffed by spouses and provided information on, for instance, host country culture and spouse employment.[6] Such efforts to explicitly recognise spouses as integral to its management model, and to improve their experiences of expatriation, reflect the serious concern that 'unwilling wives' not only contributed to expatriate failure – which had become a central theme in IHRM scholarship by the 1990s – but now kept their partners from being mobile in the first place.

In addition to measures aimed at inducing spouses, Shell responded to the gendered challenges to its management model with neoliberal flexibilisation. Rather than abandon its expatriate, Shell allowed more individual choice but also internally differentiated this staff category, just as it had done in the 1950s, by introducing new disciplinary techniques of 'partitioning' and 'ranking' (Marsden, in Prasad et al. 1997). These to some extent remodelled the expatriate from loyal 'organisation man' to flexible 'entrepreneurial self' (Bröckling 2015). Partly to accomodate spousal careers, the Outlook survey had revealed a desire for 'more choice' and 'greater consultation' and 'openness' in planning expatriation.[7] As one former senior Shell employee noted,

> people were less accepting of Shell doing everything for them, people wanted to design their own lives rather than have their life designed for them by Shell. There was a lot more individualism coming in, particularly amongst the younger staff. (interview, 2016)

In response, the Group abandoned its tightly monitored career planning, the 'one-size fits all mobility model' and expectations of lifetime employment, in favour of more flexible, self-directed 'open resourcing', more expatriation pathways to choose from and variable pay. Employees now applied to assignments advertised on Shell's internal job market and entered a 'release period' around six months before the end of their assignment to apply for another Shell-internal role (Matthews 2019). Crucially, expatriates, too, could now lose their jobs if they did not find re-employment. Greater employee choice thus became an opportunity for greater employer choice, with expatriate assignments now also opportunities to dismiss staff who did not live up to expectations or yield to corporate demands. Just like job security was reduced, loyalty to the company was 'no longer expected nor rewarded' (Sluyterman 2007:288). Former 'Shell men' now circulated as mobile individuals within an exclusive but also more precarious labour market.

Expatriates thus got increased 'choice' and 'flexibility' but also found themselves more precarious and unequal. Payment structures were increasingly tied to individualised performance, implying greater inequality among expatriates and an emphasis on competition instead of the harmony thus far nurtured and expected. Notably, a proportion of expatriates now relocated on 'local' terms – called 'Local National and Non-national' (LNN) terms – especially if they were deployed *to* Europe and North America (Margolis 2009:13). This evidences a broader trend away from generous expatriate packages (for some) as 'improved living standards globally and pressure to reduce business costs means that increasingly "local plus" packages may be offered instead, without traditional add-ons such as hardship allowances, mobility premia and perquisites' (Matthews 2019:19). Shell also increasingly accepted unaccompanied mobility including 'grass widower terms', international commuter assignments and short-term international assignments. Those on grass widower terms moved without their family, while short-term assignments of 6–12 months meant an unaccompanied move with regular flights home, and a guaranteed role upon return. While these options became more common during the 1990s, they remained secondary. In 2014, of Shell's over 7,000 expatriates, around 75 per cent were still on long-term international assignments of three to four years and 60 per cent of those were accompanied by family; roughly 17 per cent were on local LNN terms; only 7 per cent were on short-term international assignments and 0.6 per cent on international commuter assignments (Fenton and Spyra n.d.:4). The number of expatriates on longer-term assignments did not decrease – Shell simply added more expatriates on 'unconventional' terms.

Shell's neoliberal flexibilisation and 'familial reframing' of its expatriate staff was partly a response to, but did not fundamentally change, the expatriate's patriarchal constitution. The number of women in expatriate positions remained low (see below). As Marsden notes (in Prasad et al. 1997:108), 'flexibility for the employer tends to mean the creation of a relatively secure and well-compensated core group of workers and a much larger and much worse off peripheral group' which often disproportionately includes women. It is also questionable to what extent the measures improved spouses' experiences overall. One former Shell wife, at least, felt otherwise. She recounted how from the 1990s 'internationally mobile staff privileges were diminished in many companies', including Shell, where

> A perception amongst partners particularly would be that the 'family care attitude' that had been part of Shell for many years was changing to a far more shareholder entitlement mentality. As HR moved all its expat services to cheaper locations (call centres in Poland, The Philippines etc.), there was increasing frustration with the lack of understanding and communication between employee and HR. A lack of personal engagement removing the 'warmth and feel good' impression that had been part of the company in the past. Times do change and this was the direction that many western companies have adopted. Shame really ... [also] as more and more employees work 4 weeks on, 4 weeks off (and families are not encouraged to be part of that expat experience), I believe this creates far more challenges for families and less impact on the employer. (personal communication, 2016)

Also, Hindman (2013:15–16) observes that between 1990 and 2000, expatriates in Nepal 'were starting to experience negative effects of business efficiency, rhetorics of global flatness and neoliberalism' and 'the claim that this new paradigm of flexibility would generate a more diverse group of international workers who are more closely integrated into the local economy was having the opposite effect'. Within Shell, it appears that instead of uniformly improving the experiences of staff and spouses, Shell replaced old with new challenges in the social reproduction of the Shell expatriate – still primarily a white male employee from the Global North.

Diverse expatriates?

In the 1990s, Shell faced not only financial but also social and political pressures. From the mid-1980s, it received bad press for defying economic sanctions by supplying oil to apartheid South

Africa. In 1995, the Group was hit by more scandals, including its role in the execution of writer and environmental activist Ken Saro-Wiwa by the Nigerian military dictatorship, and the environmental controversy of Shell's planned sinking of the North Atlantic oil storage platform Brent Spar. These events marked a reputational 'real low point' and caused Shell to fundamentally rethink, and centralise, its public relations and corporate social responsibility functions (Mays et al. 2005:313–314). Its response involved a series of roundtables convened in 1996 in 14 countries to solicit opinions from senior employees, non-governmental organisations, academics, media and government representatives on 'what society expected of companies like Shell'. One 'problem area' identified was that Shell appeared 'Eurocentric' (Paine 1999a:6).

In line with efforts at reputational management, and likely emboldened by its 'flexibilisation' of employment relations, Shell adopted a diversity and inclusion (D&I) agenda. Again, it was praised for taking a 'pioneering position' when few multinational corporations outside the US undertook diversity initiatives (Egan and Bendick 2003). Diversity efforts started in Shell's US subsidiary, which established a 'Shell Diversity Center' in 1996 and appointed its director, Leslie Mays, as the first woman on the subsidiary's board of directors (Mays et al. 2005). While US Shell lost much of its separate identity in the Group-wide business restructure, its diversity agenda was elevated to Group policy. In 1997, a report to the central Group's Committee of Managing Directors identified 'international diversity management' – with diversity defined as 'all the ways we differ' – as 'strategically important for global organizations in the twenty-first century' (Egan and Bendick 2003:720). The Committee agreed, designating diversity as a key priority, and decided on nationality and gender as the two Group-wide diversity focuses. According to Mays et al. (2005:316), the Committee even identified concrete 'numeric targets': 'to achieve capability to provide at least 100 percent national cover of all country chair positions by 2003' and 'to increase to 20 percent the number of women in senior executive positions by 2008'. It also created a 'Global Diversity Council' that was to define measurable success indicators and a timetable for implementation (Mays et al. 2005:316).[8] Yet, as Egan and Bendick (2003) diagnose, progress remained slow, and indicatively, diversity targets have become more vaguely articulated since.

Sucher and Corsi (2012) write that in 2005 Shell set two 'aspirational targets' – in contrast to binding targets or quotas – namely to 'continuously improve representation of females in senior leadership positions to 20%' and to 'continuously improve representation of nationals in senior leadership positions in regions and countries to majority of incumbents'.[9]

Sucher and Corsi (2012:4) note that US Shell first implemented diversity policies to 'comply with local legal requirements', and Sucher and Beyersdorfer (2010) note that Shell's acceptance of a 'business case' for diversity was helped by the fact that many of its competitors were adopting similar policies. Indeed, from the 1980s 'diversity management' became popular especially in North American firms, at least partly because it provided an upbeat voluntary, easily marketable and corporation-led alternative to the perceived dangers of government-enforced anti-discrimination legislation and affirmative action (Prasad et al. 1997). Since then, many have critiqued the way diversity has been debated and enacted in organisations. Ahmed and Swan (2006:96) argue that diversity 'individuates difference, conceals inequalities and neutralises histories of antagonism and struggle', also by replacing more radical terms such as 'equal opportunities' and 'anti-racism' (see also Gordon 1995; Melamed 2006). As bell hooks writes,

> The eagerness with which contemporary society does away with racism, replacing this recognition with evocations of pluralism and diversity that further mask reality, is a response to the terror [of whiteness]. It has also become a way to perpetuate the terror by providing a cover, a hiding place. (hooks 1992:176).

Divorced from anti-racist and feminist politics, 'diversity' can become part of the corporate toolkit, even within enduringly unequal work contexts. Accordingly, Ahmed (2012) dissects the everyday ways in which the institutionalisation of diversity not only obscures ongoing structural racism but can become integral to the reproduction of inequalities inasmuch as it becomes 'non-performative' – i.e. organisations do diversity performance instead of bringing about diversity.

Shell's adoption of D&I principles has been described as a top-down, business-oriented approach (Mirvis 2000). That Shell's D&I initiative did indeed stand in the service of business needs is suggested by the 'vision' that the Group 'will benefit from this diversity through better relationships with customers, suppliers, partners, employees, governments and other stakeholders' (Mays et al. 2005:316). Similarly, HR Director Mitchell argued that diversity was 'part of the war for talent' and allowed Shell to 'recruit the people we need', including 'female technical people' (cited in EIU 2009:22, 13, 16). However, the fact that Shell was missing out on this 'talent' had long been noted within Shell. Female Shell employees in locations such as the Netherlands, UK and Canada had actively lobbied for more equal opportunities since at least the 1960s. The Group's Committee of Managing Directors had already declared in 1973 'that more efforts should be made to recruit women' into graduate positions up to top-management levels, and Shell Netherlands hired a woman, M. C. Endert-Baylé, to focus solely on this task in 1971. A 1973 report titled *Career Possibilities for Women in Shell in the Netherlands*, prepared by Endert-Baylé, critiqued the exclusion of women from expatriate positions and noted that 'As many secretaries, nurses, female teachers and programmers served overseas, there is no reason why women graduates could not, except in very isolated locations.'[10] It took social and political pressure that created organisational difficulties to turn gender equality in its upper corporate ranks – at least rhetorically – into a 'business case' for Shell. Moreover, while the 'flexibilisation' of expatriation discussed above was supposed to support women's careers – both the careers of female Shell spouses and Shell employees – its success in doing so is questionable. In 1998, still only 24.6 per cent of international staff recruits were women (Shell 1999:15), and in 2008 women held only 14 per cent of senior leadership positions (Sucher and Beyersdorfer 2010:7).[11] In 2014, 87 per cent of long-term assignments were still headed by male employees (Fenton and Spyra n.d.). As Hindman (2013:134) notes, while talk about flexibility and individualisation was originally touted 'as a family-friendly policy, one that might encourage the promotion of women in business', it 'often further disempowers those already struggling in their desired career' by imposing more mobility demands, more competitiveness and offering less job security.

Shell's 'nationality' diversity target was similarly tied up with 'business-critical' considerations. In 2002, Leslie Mays told the *Houston Chronicle* that the benefits of 'localisation' included reduced costs and increased 'effectiveness in selling across cultures' (*Houston*

Chronicle 2002). Which national diversity became valued in this framework was subject to business priorities, as HR Director Mitchell made clear: 'We need the right talent, of the right profile, in terms of the different environments we are in. There's no point in having lots of Nigerians but no Kazakhs if we're spending $20 billion in Kazakhstan' (cited in EIU 2009:22). The main benefit of promoting the Other was still the strategic use of their 'embodied difference' (see Chapter 3). As a strategic business tool, diversity was put to use in the service of Shell's aim to favourably position itself in fast-growing Asian markets. When Jeroen van der Veer took over as Chairman in 2005, he redefined Shell's business strategy as 'More Upstream, Profitable Downstream' (Shell 2008:2). This meant concentrating investments in 'upstream' oil and gas production, while adjusting its 'downstream' portfolio of refining and marketing to tap into emerging markets, specifically the 'newly developing Asian markets' (Sucher and Corsi 2012:2). As Shell began to target its marketing efforts at Asia, its diversity thrust became oriented towards Asia too. Accordingly, for the 2002 diversity priorities, Asia was identified as 'critically important to feeding the talent pipeline' (*Houston Chronicle* 2002), and in 2005 Shell established an 'Asian Talent Council' to help identify, mentor and promote promising Asian employees (Sucher and Corsi 2012). Between 2005 and 2008, the number of Asian nationals in senior management roles increased from 81 to 112, while the number of expatriates working in Asia dropped from 170 to 119 (Sucher and Corsi 2012). During the 2009 restructure, too, Asians became a special focus. Their numbers in senior management were specially monitored and the new CEO Peter Voser vowed to personally ensure 'that our top 25 Asian talents ... got the right jobs' (Sucher and Beyersdorfer 2010:3). Indeed, Voser's newly appointed 'all-white, male, Swiss, American, and British' executive committee raised eyebrows because it included no women, no Dutch and no Asian members, despite the latter being 'a major thrust of Shell's strategic growth' (Sucher and Corsi 2012:1). What emerges is not so much a 'business case' for diversity, as a case of diversity standing in the service of business.

While embodied difference was strategically useful and used – for example for securing profits in specific markets, by drawing on 'local' cultural knowledge or showcasing embodied corporate belonging in those places – there were clear limits to how much, and which,

Otherness would be accommodated. One limit to diversity and inclusion lay where it threatened existing 'company culture'. HR Director Mitchell thus argued that

> If ... you take Diversity to extremes, you corrupt that cultural model and you end up with a dysfunctional organization, and little can get done. So, for example, in our company there is a focus on doing things in a calm and reasoned and logical way. If you are the type who is highly emotional and given to outbursts and shouting, then you are unlikely to have a great career here (cited in EIU 2009:22).

Mitchell's example has racialised and gendered overtones. It evokes the figure of the rational and reasoned white man, contrasted with the emotional, potentially hysterical and certainly less reasonable woman and 'native'. While Shell's diversity and inclusion campaign was meant to signal inclusion of difference, it did not challenge white Western masculinity as norm and normative. Imagined as embodied Otherness, difference could be selectively integrated in an otherwise unchanged organisation (Ahmed and Swan 2006).

Notably, Shell's nationality target merely measured the number of 'nationals' in the management of their regional and national companies. It did not measure national diversity of the core international staff. That the international staff was far from diverse was well known to central management, and in 1991 an external evaluator hired by Shell to assess its International Graduate Recruitment Programme found that, 'without explicit or malicious discriminatory intentions, [the Programme] excluded many suitable candidates' and 'minority groups and women had fewer chances of being selected because of Shell's narrow definition of a person with high potential' (Sluyterman 2007:260). The fact that Shell's official corporate history concludes that 'Whether any specific action followed, however, is not clear' (Sluyterman 2007:260) might suggest very little specific action. In effect, Blair's 1959 'logical conclusion of the philosophy of staff integration', namely the recruitment of 'local' staff into 'continuous expatriate service' and thereby into higher group management, seemed not only unfulfilled but forgotten (Kunz 2020b). In this regard, the diversity targets of the 1990s were arguably less ambitious than those of the 1950s. However, even those less ambitious targets seem to have been missed. In 1998 international staff recruits were 56.3 per cent Anglo/Dutch (Shell 1999:15), in 2001 expatriates were

63 per cent Anglo/Dutch (Sluyterman and Wubs 2010:811) and in 2008 only 37 per cent of countries had majority national senior leadership teams (Sucher and Beyersdorfer 2010:7). While Shell's *conditions* of expatriation diversified in the 1990s and early 2000s, its expatriates did not become a significantly more diverse group.

Diversity implied the addition of racialised and gendered embodied Otherness, in managed quantities and strategically useful positions, into an otherwise largely unchanged organisation. The limits of Shell's diversity agenda are arguably foreshadowed in its very definition, cited above, of diversity as 'all the ways we differ'. In the context of a multinational business built on a key natural resource, which Shell first extracted in colonised territories within an industry constituted by conquest, violence and exploitation, this 'diversity' and its constitutive notion of 'difference' do not acknowledge the inequity and injustice foundational to the business and its management. That is, the inequity and injustice which necessitated a 'diversity and inclusion' programme in the first place are neither acknowledged nor overcome by it. At stake is not simply a swapping of staff. Divorced from history and power, diversity implied performative modification in the service of conservation. As Fields and Fields (2014:146) note, those guilty of reproducing 'race' today include those whose 'most radical goal ... remains the reallocation of unemployment, poverty, and injustice rather than their abolition'. Shell's diversity programme did not achieve the long-overdue decolonisation of management, which would have meant acknowledging and redressing historical discrimination and exploitation but also reforming uneven and undemocratic organisational structures. Indeed, 'diversity management' might have become 'strategically important' to corporations like Shell not because it corrected historical injustices but because it allowed them *not* to do so (Ahmed 2012). In the oil and gas industry, correcting these injustices would have anyway introduced more fundamental challenges to conceptualisations of 'natural resources' and their right(ful) use, which to this day remain deeply indebted to colonial and racialised knowledges (Wilson 2012). Instead, diversity became a neoliberal 'marketing device' (Ahmed and Swan 2006) that allowed capitalising on a whitewashed notion of difference. From this process, the category expatriate emerged, just as it had in the 1950s, 'diversified' in a way that did not fundamentally redress its constitutive inequalities. Still racialised and gendered, and hence still constituted in inequality, the process of incorporating Others implied, as Ahmed (2000:189) puts it, a transformation of the expatriate that did not question its 'already white constitution'.

Taking charge of their stories: from Shell wife to global expat

The Shell Ladies' Project: claiming expatriate status

In the 1990s, the Group transformed its expatriate from the loyal 'Shell man' who spent his career migrating within a nuclear family unit, into an individualised and 'flexible' elite worker circulating within professional global labour markets. With the neoliberal emphasis on the 'autonomous, entrepreneurial self' (Fortier 2013:67), an all-encompassing Shell identity built through corporate socialisation lost its strategic importance. The divorce of individual careers from Shell, and the greater diversity in terms and conditions, encouraged an individualised self-identification as, simply, 'expatriate'. The memory work of Shell spouses reflects how expatriate became a migrant identity largely uncoupled from its Shell umbrella. In 1990, a group of 'Shell wives' posted in The Hague initiated the 'Shell Ladies' Project' (SLP) to document the lives of the migrant families administering Shell's worldwide enterprise.[12] According to its founding members, the project resulted from a dinner conversation among wives of senior Shell managers who discussed the Royal Dutch centenary celebrations and found they left out the stories of the families of the workers being posted abroad. The women decided it was high time that their contributions and sacrifices were recognised as integral to the business, and took matters into their own hands. They collected writings from Shell spouses and children all over the world and published them in two anthologies for the 'Shell community': *Life on the Move* (SLP 1993) documented Shell wives' experiences since the 1920s, and *Life Now* (SLP 1996) focused on their lives there and then.[13] The women behind the SLP were aware of and had themselves experienced the fundamental changes taking place in the early 1990s, a recognition that inspired them to archive their own Shell history, but which also led to their gradual decoupling from the corporate patriarch and their self-definition as expatriates independent of the 'Shell world'.

The women's initial plan to publish a call for contributions in an internal Shell magazine was declined by Shell who feared the potential sensitivity of the project. Instead, they sent out the call with their personal Christmas cards and relied on word of mouth. Yet the SLP initiators neither wanted to upset their husbands nor did they see their project as a challenge to the company. They therefore invited Shell public affairs to sign off the first book, and with the official approval

> it was magic … doors opened all down the corridor … And when we did the second book, I mean we did the first book on yellow paper, everything was very unprovocative unless you knew where to look. And the second one was much bolder. (interview, 2016)

Once the two anthologies had been published, the hundreds of contributions remained 'in limbo' until the idea to set up an archive and expand the collection emerged in the early 2000s. As founding member Dewey White noted, 'there were all kinds of commercial archives, but for the social history of these societies that form all over the world around the oil business, and other international business, no history collecting was going on' (Chow et al. 2017:318).[14] With White as its first director, the *Shell Outpost Family Archive Centre* was established in 2001 under the umbrella of Outpost. To gather donations from the Shell community, the Archive Centre ran workshops, advertised in the Shell magazine and at Outpost events.[15] In 2003, Shell decided to bring Outpost in-house, much to the regret of the archive founders, who understood this move as an infringement of their new independence, identity and influence as spouses. Moreover, some worried that the archival collections, which belonged to the 'community of wives', would 'disappear into the Shell archive' never to be seen again.[16] To prevent this, the *Outpost Shell Family Archive Centre* was transformed into a foundation separate from but still funded by what was now *Shell Global Outpost Services* in 2005. The archive was still 'only serving Shell families' and seeking 'Shell family reminiscences'.[17] This liminal position seems to have proved untenable. Three years later, in 2008, the archive more fully decoupled from Shell. Shedding Shell from name and mission, it became the *Expatriate Archive Centre* with the broadened remit to document the social history of all expatriates.

For Shell, the expatriate was a category tied to elite, normatively male labour, yet with the Shell Ladies' Project, spouses appropriated this category and filled it with the realities of *their* lives. They not only claimed their place in the oil business and established their agency vis-à-vis the company but thereby helped further stretch the category expatriate from a staff into an identity category. In this tightly networked 'despatialized community' (Hindman 2013:12), women's lives were simultaneously cosmopolitan and parochial, tightly circumscribed by a set of strong social norms and prescriptions, inter-reliant yet often lonely. The community depended on wives' labour and sacrifice, yet they felt rendered invisible unless they were 'troublesome' (Kunz 2020b). It is out of this shared experience that the SLP arose. 'Shell wives' identified with the corporation, as their adopted title clearly shows. Somewhat begrudgingly, they saw themselves as 'partners in a *ménage à trois* in which we shared our husband with the oil industry' (SLP 1996:260). These 'Shell wives' thus generally accepted the gendered role that Shell's model of incorporated migration assigned them, and the imperial capitalist project that this migration advanced. What they asked for was recognition of their work *in that role*.

As the spouses of senior Shell managers, the SLP initiators were aware of the gendered challenges to expatriation that the corporation faced at the time. The postscript to *Life Now* thus declares that 'The 1990s have seen the end of a Shell era' and recognises a disappearing 'earlier, less flexible, international community' (SLP 1996:261). Whereas in 1959, Shell's Head of Recruitment Division, Blair, was still able to ignore spouses in his history of Shell expatriation, the company now recognised expatriation as a family project, and spouses as individuals with agency (Kunz 2020b). Accordingly, the *Life Now* postscript enthusiastically states:

> Now into the field, all over the world, comes a new creature! She may be the breadwinner, she can control her fertility, she expects to be recognised as an individual, she expects to contribute to the history of the world on her own terms, and she expects to be given credit for it. In Shell the recognition of this person was sealed in 1993 when the upstream management sent out a mobility questionnaire separately to husband and wife, of many nationalities. (SLP 1996:260)

Yet, ultimately, Shell did not acknowledge spouses until forced to do so by societal changes that destabilised its model of corporate control and coordination. One former Shell spouse notes: 'What drove it [the survey] was not our welfare, no, it was what held the engineers and upstream people back from being mobile. One thing was their wives' (interview, 2016). Shell's recognition of spouses was ultimately driven by younger women's refusal to take on this role: 'it was the effect of when you came back to your own country and your mates, your previous school and university friends were no longer impressed with your exciting life. They thought you were being exploited' (interview, 2016). Although the SLP pointed a critical spotlight on Shell's gendered labour regime, it did not fundamentally challenge it. Tellingly, the SLP remains silent on the fact that women contributed to Shell's business not only as spouses, but also as salaried workers and in 1993, Shell's recognition of its women employees worldwide was anything but 'sealed'. In fact, the SLP was only one of several women's initiatives within Shell at the time. As the *Life Now* postscript mentions, 'In the early nineties there were several women's initiatives in Shell Central Offices and around the world that faded or failed, some of which were exciting but ahead of their time' (SLP 1996:261).[18] These other projects remain unnamed in the SLP anthologies. 'Shell wives' strove for their own recognition as expatriates, but their project did not fundamentally challenge the category's gendered constitution.

The category expatriate's development out of corporate family migration reverberates today in the central role of the family in many conceptualisations of the expatriate. The Expatriate Archive Centre (EAC 2018)[19] still stated that

> We collect material from expatriates and their families during and after their stay abroad. Our definition of 'expatriate' is anyone who lives temporarily in a country other than their 'home' country.

This contains a telling tension. While the first sentence distinguishes between expatriates and their families, the definition offered thereafter posits these families as expatriates too – rendering some doubly expatriate and others more precariously included. This incongruity is not accidental but reveals its origins in the experiences of 'Shell wives', who struggled for emancipation from being 'just' dependents of expatriates to being recognised as expatriates in their own right, if not in full equality. This gendered tension is not just a historical 'leftover' but actively reproduced in current migration regimes and uses of the category expatriate. In a study of expatriates in the Netherlands, van Bochove et al. (2011:8, 9) describe their research sample:

> In The Hague, 14 female respondents are partners and 5 are expats themselves. In this report, the term 'expat' is used both for respondents who came to the Netherlands because of their own job and for respondents who came because of their partner's job …

Again, the authors first differentiate between expats and their partners, then position both as expats. This contradiction bears the traces of the expatriate's evolution from denoting normatively male migrant labour constituted within a heterosexual family unit, to a more generalised migrant category. Yet it also reveals the ongoing gendered inequalities structuring professional labour markets, where 'skill' remains normatively associated with male labour (Leonard 2010ab).

From 'Shell families' to 'global expats'

The Shell Ladies' Project's transformation into the Expatriate Archive Centre reflects a broader evolution: Studying the memory documents of 'Shell families' *in the archive*, as well as their changing curation *by the archive*, allows us to trace the gradual transmutation of the 'Shell wife' into the individualised 'expatriate', a figure decoupled from corporate context and history that is intensely political precisely in its decontextualisation. Whereas expatriate had long been a staff category for Shell, it was not always a prime identity category. A strong corporate identity seems to have discouraged a Shell-independent identity of expatriate. As discussed, Shell's post-war management model relied on the primary identification of expatriates with each other and with the corporation, as 'Shell men' and 'Shell wives'.[20] While some individual SLP contributions contain the category expatriate, the anthologies do not centrally rely on the term. Instead, the collected stories are introduced as experiences of 'families "on the move" with Shell' (SLP 1993) and as 'relating the insights of and experiences around the world of women married to Shell men' (SLP 1996). One contribution to *Life on the Move* positions 'Shell as a way of life' (SLP 1993:146) and be it the 'Shell family', 'Shell wife' or 'Shell men', the 'Shell umbrella' or 'Shell world', the SLP narrates a clear sense of belonging to Shell. In contrast, the category expatriate plays a secondary role in the SLP. While Shell is fore-grounded in editorial framing and individual stories, expatriate is explained in the 'glossary of some special or unusual words' as 'a person living semi-permanently out of his or her home country' (SLP 1993:185). The term's very inclusion in such a glossary is indicative of the secondary status of 'expatriate' in these women's narrations of their lives and identities (SLP 1993:185).

In 2008, the Outpost Shell Family Archive Centre transformed itself into the Expatriate Archive Centre. This involved a generalisation from 'Shell families' to 'expatriates' that assumed that 'the experiences and challenges faced by these families will resonate with expatriates everywhere'.[21] Coinciding with its decoupling from Shell, the archive published a third compilation of Shell-related sources, titled *The Source Book, An Expatriate Social History, 1927–2007*, with the subtitle *Shell Lives Unshelved* (Outpost Archive Centre 2008). As Chow et al. (2017:319) write,

> During the process of compiling and publishing this third book, the founders of the EAC further developed their ideas of what type of social history they were documenting and how it fit into a larger historical narrative.

While this *Source Book* contains Shell-related sources just like the two earlier anthologies, it differs in curational framing. The two initial SLP anthologies addressed the 'Shell community' and situated their stories as particular and special experiences, of significance for the 'Shell community' and Shell corporate history. In contrast, the *Source Book*'s title frames its materials as expatriate social history first and foremost, with Shell relegated to the subtitle. As Shell spouses came to de-emphasise their relationship with Shell, they looked for new ways of framing their materials and establishing the archive's relevance, and looked for new audiences for their work. In doing so, they reimagined the Shell man and wife as the global expat, a subject at the heart of globalisation. Chow et al. (2017:319) describe how

> White and her colleagues effectively transformed themselves and their constituency from Shell wives into world citizens at the vanguard of globalization in the early twenty-first century. In turn, this expanded the audience for the archive and its collection.

In her foreword to the *Source Book*, archive co-founder Judy Moody-Stuart accordingly describes how she 'watched the Archive gradually develop into a history of globalization in the century of oil'. Elsewhere she argues that 'What we are chronicling with this, are the roots of globalization because we, our families, are the people who made (it) possible' (cited in Chow et al. 2017:327). A few pages on, in the introduction to the *Source Book*, archive director White speaks of life in the 'global village', and elsewhere in the book Shell families are described as 'global nomads' and 'global citizens' (Outpost Archive Centre 2008:vii, 30). The expansion of the archive's representational remit from the *Shell world* to the *world* involved the generalisation of *Shell family experiences* into *expatriate experiences*.

Notwithstanding such generalisation, Shell families brought *particular* experiences and perspectives to categories like expatriate and global citizen. Geographies of imperial corporate power shape the life writings of Shell wives and their husbands collected in the expatriate archive. Two interrelated themes central to the Shell Ladies' Project anthologies are living 'on the move' and encounters with 'other cultures' (SLP 1993). Shell families understood themselves as not belonging to any locality of residence but to Shell – they lead a peripatetic life under the 'Shell umbrella'. This geographically unpositioned figure was centrally constituted through (and privileged over) rooted others – those who stayed back home as well as locals in the places visited. Many SLP contributions are concerned with peculiar cultural and national habits, with local cuisine and strange traditions. Other entries provide sociohistorical and sometimes political commentary on the places that expatriates found themselves in. For example, 'The Filipinos adjust easily to misfortune' starts one *Source Book* contribution from 1995. In four brief paragraphs the piece notes 'beautiful beaches' and 'turquoise waters' but also how 'centuries of colonization, followed by years of turmoil, created a "do as you choose" way of life', to conclude that 'true cooperation and a future discard for self-interest will be the only way for the country to prosper' (Outpost Archive Centre 2008:31). The author assumes a non-situated perspective, speaks from nowhere, to claim a privileged and arguably paternalistic understanding of what 'the Filipinos' are like and what they need. Despite the rhetorical nod to colonisation, the suggested solution remains internal to the country, as is, by implication, the problem. The practices of multinationals like Shell and the international political economy, forged through colonisation, that continue to link the Philippines and expatriates' Euro-American home countries disappear from view. Narratives like this thus rely on temporal and spatial disconnects that occlude the imperial relations which were, centrally, constructed by expatriates.

The claim to a superior perspective springing from outsider-status is also expressed in the *Source Book* editorial: 'Many expatriates are stationed in a country which is going through enormous internal development; with the eyes of a stranger we are often better positioned to observe and record these changes' (Outpost Archive Centre 2008:30). It remains unacknowledged that being a white Euro-American migrant associated with an MNC renders this stranger's perspective a particular one. This is the case especially where 'internal developments' were protracted processes of decolonisation in which oil multinationals like Shell played an important role. As Ahmed (2000:85) writes, 'some movements across spaces become a mechanism for the reproduction of social privilege, the granting of particular subjects with the ability to see and to move beyond the confined spaces of a given locality'. Tellingly, this peripatetic expatriate, privileged because of their very outsider-status, is quite unlike how migrant outsider-status is usually read. An imperial geographical imagination also reasserts itself in the account of a Shell marketing and sales executive when he writes that 'Between the two representatives, our territory stretched from the Turkish frontier in the north to Aden and Oman in the south and from Cyprus in the west to Afghanistan's border in the east'.[22] Pratt (2007:59) identifies this figure as the 'white male subject of European landscape discourse – he whose imperial eyes passively look out and possess'. This 'monarch-of-all-I-survey' trope is 'perhaps the ultimate colonial symbol: of superiority made spatial, of being "up above", transcendent of the earth, in proximity to God' (Jackson 2011:357).

Shell journeys and the global visions that sprang from them were steeped in postcolonial power relations. While their husbands managed business, Shell wives managed the domestic and social realms, equally steeped in ideologies of 'whiteness-as-management' (Roediger and Esch 2012). Some stories thus reveal conflict, such as those of Dutch Shell employees who recount the threats and violence they experienced in post-World War II Indonesia as the Dutch tried to reinstate their colonial authority. Yet the SLP editors and most contributors remained silent on the postcolonial dimensions of their lives. Indeed, one Shell wife explicitly positions Shell migrations against colonialism: 'Both the Dutch and the Brits know all about colonies, but this is something else, because of the commercial, the great equality of the whole thing ... That thing which we take for granted in Shell'.[23] The majority of memories in the SLP anthologies thus include innocuous, often humorous encounters with locals, with domestic staff, while shopping or on holiday. These stories perform political work by portraying the expatriate as a harmless figure, detached from socio-political contexts and power relations. In such anecdotes, the Euro-American corporate presence can appear 'absolutely uncontested' (Pratt 2007:59), what Pratt (2007:9) calls 'anti-conquest' as the 'strategies of representation whereby European bourgeois subjects seek to secure their innocence in the same moment as they assert European hegemony'. It was a decidedly particular form of living in mobility under the Shell umbrella that became generalised as *the* normal expatriate experience. Reframing the Shell wife and her Shell man as the global expatriate risks separating their experiences from the postcolonial capitalist projects they were part of, which makes for a social history of expatriation, and globalisation, that does not acknowledge but reproduces its imperial character.

The Shell Ladies' Project redressed gendered gaps in history writing while also reproducing gendered, racialised and classed silences. The SLP aimed to depict the diversity of Shell families' experiences, as evidenced by an 'Information Sheet' calling for contributions from those who had moved within their own country, and offering translation into English for contributions written in Dutch, Spanish or Malay.[24] Accordingly, one archive founder subsequently described the Shell Family Archive as including 'Very diverse content, very diverse contributors, difference of time, age, socioeconomic, I mean every – talk about *diverse*, you know the buzz word of our time – we have a very diverse set of documents and sources with an emphasis on personal stories.'[25] Yet the very inequalities that shaped who became an expatriate for Shell in the first instance also shaped the archive assembled by the SLP. While the anthologies and the *Source Book* contain the occasional account of, for example, a Nigerian spouse, the normative whiteness of Shell's expat is poignantly revealed in an anecdote in which 'a five year old Nigerian Shell boy found himself along Oxford Street London, for the first time. "My word, this place is filled with expatriates" he exclaimed to his parents' (Outpost Archive Centre 2008:67). The West Indians hired to perform manual labour in Venezuela's oil camps (Tinker Salas 2003) or Shell's Indian 'migrant workers' that Menon (2016) writes about were as excluded from Shell's category expatriate as they are from its archive. The SLP expatriate remains a racialised and classed subject, and the SLP depiction of the expatriate as a racially unmarked category ultimately represents white middle-class privilege to position one's experiences as the norm and normative (Frankenberg 1993; Morrison 1992).

The SLP and its subsequent family archive focused on collecting personal memory documents, and thus contains the perspectives of expatriates on their own lives. Collecting donated personal archives necessarily implies a heavily mediated selection of documents on facets that donors are able, interested and willing to document and share; this is compounded by the challenges small archives like the EAC often face in getting and processing donations.[26] While the memories of Shell wives and families are without doubt important historical documents, Shell expatriate memories cannot on their own represent the social history of expatriation, the oil industry or globalisation. Claiming as much would amount to an imperial attitude in itself. Yet, expatriates largely get to describe and characterise their own lives. This was recognised by one archive founder, who noted that

> When historians in the future need to talk about what were expatriates doing, ... what were the roles of these expatriate societies in say the current terrorism environment in which we live [*sic*]. Very hard questions are going to be asked about the way we have lived and if you don't have source material for your point of view, then your history, and by that I mean expatriates living in these societies around the world, your history will be told by other people and their own sources. So, best to have your own record.[27]

Here the struggle over history writing is no longer, as articulated in the earlier SLP anthologies, between Shell wives and male-centric conceptions of Shell's business and the oil industry that wrote out wives' labour and experiences. Instead, the struggle here seems to be between expatriates and 'these societies' in a defence that speaks back at but does not name the 'hard questions' asked about 'the way expatriates have lived'.

The Shell archive assembled here is marked by the structural absence of certain voices. Partiality is an unavoidable but nevertheless political feature of archiving and requires reflection on 'the negotiation of absent, powerful or powerless voices in the archive' (Moore 2010:263). For example, the experiences of local domestic staff working for expatriates are, if at all represented, mediated by expatriates' accounts and selection of sources. From the collected sources we also cannot learn about local workers' experiences of the classed and racialised structural inequalities of life in the oil industry noted in Chapter 3. The Subaltern Studies Collective's project of reading colonial archives 'against their grain' to extract 'subaltern histories' (Guha and Spivak 1988) remains as relevant as ever and extends to corporate archives and the private archives of those managing those corporations. Yet there are topics we cannot learn about from the Shell Family Archive's sources, even if we read them against the grain. There is, as Pratt (2007:5) writes, 'a huge gap in the archive' and ultimately 'the archival, historiographic, disciplinary-critical and, inevitably, interventionist work involved here is indeed a task of "measuring silences"' (Spivak 1988:286).

Conclusion

This chapter has traced the transformation of the Shell expatriate from an organisational into an individualised migrant (figure). The Group had throughout the century been a pioneer in multinational management, and also the 1990s transformation of the Shell expatriate reflects a broader historical conjuncture as IHRM studies' turn to exploring new forms of 'flexible' and 'diversified' global work also indicates (see Chapter 7). In the 1950s, Shell responded to a fast-decolonising world by regionalising its business, devolving some authority to national management and accepting some 'regional staff' of national operating companies into its cadre of expatriates. Shell planners also recognised that the 'logical endpoint' of regionalisation would be a truly multinational group of 'international staff' and thus central management – that is, to share decision-making over the key natural resource of the twentieth century. However, for the time being, Shell responded by internally differentiating the category expatriate and reinstated HQ control, by circulating well-socialised international staff still primarily recruited in Europe and tied to HQ not only by contractual design and constant mobility but also by racialised and classed distinctions. This bipartite expatriate lasted until the 1990s when new social transformations threatened Shell's model of migratory management: women's unwillingness to sacrifice their own careers to become 'trailing spouses' (Tremayne 1984). Shell decided to reform its expatriate, again in the context of a broader overhaul of its business structure, this time within the parameters of neoliberal globalisation that spelled outsourcing, offshoring and flexibilisation but also the centralisation of decision-making and control.

The expatriate survived this restructure but in adapted form. Expatriation terms and conditions diverged. 'Flexibilised' and individualised, former company-rooted 'Shell men' were now given choice when and where to move – and the corporation the choice to 'let them go' or discipline them with variable pay and privileges. Similarly, spouses could now stay behind and were supported as workers if they did decide to move – but the corporation's paternalistic care was scaled back and the warm feeling of the 'Shell family' significantly reduced. While Shell diversified the conditions of expatriation and adopted a diversity discourse, it did not necessarily diversify its expatriates. The number of female expatriates rose only slowly. And having a nationally more diverse international staff – the 'logical endpoint' of regionalisation in the 1950s – was not an explicit diversity target. Indeed, diversity always stood in the service of business needs, and from the early 2000s the focus on promoting 'Asian' managers became part of Shell's strategy to increase its profits in fast-growing Asian economies. Diversity thus implied the addition of embodied Otherness, in managed quantities and strategically useful positions, into an otherwise largely unchanged organisation. Divorced from history, power and social structures, diversity implied performative modification in the service of conservation, not decolonisation as reparation and democratisation.

Whereas the expatriate was a key staff category for Shell from at least the 1950s, a strong corporate identity discouraged Shell men's self-identification as simply expatriates. This changed from the 1990s, with the neoliberal transformation of 'Shell families' into individualised and disembedded global 'expatriates'. Wilson (2012:213) notes 'the tremendous capacity of neoliberal discourses to flexibly incorporate critical ideas', transform and redeploy them in 'legitimising policies of liberalisation, privatisation and outright corporate plunder, and marginalising questions of inequality, oppression and exploitation'. Refashioning the 'company man' into the 'global citizen' by fetishising 'choice' and individual 'empowerment' through the market (Wilson 2012) is a key example. What emerged is the neoliberal ideal-type, the mobile professional roaming globalised labour markets, staying only temporarily, constituted in colour-blind diversity and embracing a performative cosmopolitanism that forgets about material passports in a world of increasingly bifurcated border regimes. As Melamed (2006) notes, neoliberalism perpetuates racial capitalism in ways that do not rely on 'conventional' racial categories. Models of corporate management that wedded white supremacy and patriarchy were reworked by neoliberal reforms that however did not dismantle their logics.

The Shell case also shows that MNCs, alongside nation-states, produce migrants and citizenship, belonging and borders, hierarchies and difference. As Walters (2015) argues, we need to question what we count as migration policy. International HR policies produce, allow, forbid, regulate, mould, discipline, channel and divide movement, and they have legal purchase. This book thus argues for studying international HR policies as migration policy, too, that works 'as a form of police inasmuch as it concerns the ordering of populations, territories, and their bureaucracies' (Walters 2015:14).

The SLP also brings into sharp focus the politics of remembering and archiving, and confirms, as Burton (2005:7) writes, the value of 'talking about the backstage of archives'. Increasingly decoupled from Shell in activity and identity, the Shell Ladies expanded their archive's representational remit from the *Shell family* to *all expatriates*, and from the *Shell world* to the *world*. They framed their new expatriate, now free from its organisational shackles, in the master narrative of globalisation. Yet, claiming a greater representational remit did not necessarily involve a diversification *of* expatriate experiences represented, nor a diversification of perspectives *on* the expatriate. The Shell Ladies' Project and its subsequent archive remained largely silent on the imperial genealogies, functions and effects of the Shell expatriate. Yet the Shell expatriate is an imperial migrant whose constitution, roles and effects cannot be understood without accounting for histories of European imperialism and their accordant racialised and gendered labour hierarchies. Shell's internally differentiated and shifting category expatriate reflects how imperial logics continued to work in postcolonial times, if in adapted and ambiguous ways. This history belies the striking absence of empire, colonialism and 'race' in the Shell Ladies' Project. The emergent 'global' expatriate is thus at least partly constituted through selective remembering as a key strategy of power. Yet it was by haphazard acts of colonial aphasia rather than by grand design that a particular migrant experience became whitewashed and generalised: that the Shell family became seen to represent the experiences of all temporary movers. Gendered and racialised elite corporate migrants thus became positioned as the embodiment of globalisation and, moreover, became known primarily though their own memories. Reading such corporate accounts and the memory documents of corporate elites against and along their grain can enable a better understanding of how power is reproduced and adapts. Yet there remain structural limits to this project that require ongoing reflection on *who*se stories are archived and whose *perspectives* recognised as important.

Notes

1 'Shell and its staff: The evolution of an internationals service', report written by A. P. Blair, 1959 (Blair report). Shell The Hague Archives.
2 SLP 1993:185; EAC 1.0053.
3 Outlook Expatriate Survey: Summary of Findings, November 1993; ATRIA Folder Enquête, in Archief Netwerk Shell Partners 1992–1998, IIAV00000724.
4 Ibid.
5 Outlook Expatriate Survey: Summary of Changes, February 1995; see footnote 3: ATRIA Enquête IIAV00000724.
6 Ibid.
7 Ibid., pp. 3–4.
8 More detail on Royal Dutch Shell's process of implementing diversity and inclusion can be found in Paine 1999ab; Egan and Bendick 2003; Mays et al. 2005; Sucher and Beyersdorfer 2010; Sucher and Corsi 2012.

9   In 2005, Shell also included an 'inclusion' target aimed at improving work culture (Sucher and Corsi 2012).

10 Archief Jasna Esser-Bronic 1975–1993, ATRIA IIAV00000276; for examples of women serving overseas as Shell teachers or secretaries in the early days, see also EAC 1.0053; EAC 1.0058.1.1.01; EAC 1.0032; EAC 1.0076.

11 Although this was still above average. In comparison, women comprised 12.5 per cent of senior management in the majority of UK-based oil and gas organisations in 2012 (Shortland 2012:39).

12 EAC 8.1.3.05.3.

13 A third compilation of Shell sources, the *Source Book*, was published by the newly independent EAC in 2008.

14 The SLP and its archive's founding story are documented in detail in Chow et al. (2017).

15 SLP 1.0005.1.3.23.

16 EAC 1.0016.2.07.

17 Ibid.; see also Chow et al. (2017).

18 See e.g. ATRIA, Archief Esser-Bronic IIAV00000276.

19 This definition has since been amended.

20 This Shell man found 'his' equivalent in the 'organisation men' (Whyte 2013 [1956]) of other companies, as Fieldhouse (1978) discusses for Unilever.

21 EAC 8.2.4.18.4.

22 EAC 1.0086.

23 EAC 1.0016.2.09, p. 21.

24 EAC 8.1.3.05.3.

25 EAC 1.0005.6.34, p. 5.

26 See Chapter 6 for various challenges the EAC has experienced in acquiring, processing and making collections available to researchers.

27 EAC 1.0005.6.34, p. 5.

Part II

The expatriate today

5

Making international expats in Nairobi

We believe there's something unique about expats – a strength and spirit that drives us to move towards the unknown and embrace it. Like the explorers of the past and scientists of today, expats choose to go where things are unfamiliar, where they don't know what to expect. Expats are modern-day pioneers. Nothing symbolizes this pioneering spirit like the albatross. These birds travel long distances around the world, all while maintaining a special connection to their place of birth. Their life is a journey. Constantly on the move, albatrosses use their formidable wingspan to cross oceans and fly for hours without rest. ... By design and spirit, albatrosses are explorers. During their long life, they cover millions of kilometres and see the world from a unique perspective – the perfect symbol for our community.

InterNations (2022b)

In 2016, I spent five months in Nairobi to find out how a category like the expatriate is generated and generative in a particular urban setting. To do so, I ethnographically 'followed' the category in urban space: I explored who used the category and what expatriate meant to different people, who (was) identified as an expat and how it was narrated, embodied and challenged; what forms of belonging, community and social relations the category engendered; and how it was realised sociospatially. I found expatriate to be a performative and embodied category that was inscribed with various meanings and mobilised by diverse actors for different purposes. A key reading of the expatriate inscribed this figure with *internationality*, and a central actor mobilising this expatriate was *InterNations*, a business that provides a social and professional networking platform and advertises itself as 'the largest global expat network'. As I wrote in my fieldnotes:

Two weeks into my fieldwork, on a dark Wednesday evening and in pouring rain, the streets busy with Nairobi's notorious rush hour traffic, I arrive for my first InterNations event. The Uber driver drops me off inside the open-air mall and, although I awkwardly try to stop him, calls over a security guy with an umbrella to escort me inside. We rush to the fancy bar, where the two InterNations ambassadors stand prepared to welcome guests. Tess, InterNations 'ambassador' and, as I'm about to learn, an institution in Nairobi's 'expat scene', welcomes me with a big smile and cheerful hello just to direct me to her left, where Adriano takes over. He checks my name off a list, asks me if I'm German, gives me a wristband, takes my 1,000 Ksh, hands me a drink token and points me to the entrance. Seamlessly, Tess takes charge again to usher me inside. 'Where are you from, oh, Germany, we will introduce you to some German friends, oh, you live in the UK, we will introduce you to some British, too!' She is a whirlwind, loud, confident, smiling. I stand by the bar, on my own again – Tess has rushed off to welcome a new guest – and somewhat intimidated by the chit-chatting crowd around me. Ahead of me, two people are waiting for their drinks and we start talking. He is Canadian, she Kenyan, they are a couple, met in Uganda. She works as a global talent recruiter, he for some German organisation the name of which I don't catch. They happen to live just around the corner from me and seem nice, much less formal than I had dreaded. It is their first time at InterNations Nairobi too. In fact, they only moved here two months ago – Nduku left Kenya when she was only 6 years old. They tell me they have been to a few InterNations meet-ups in Uganda but then stopped going, also because they 'were too involved with each other'. Later, when he is getting them drinks, she tells me they met at an InterNations event. But, she tells me, InterNations in Uganda was mainly businessmen networking, or 'local people trying to meet an expat' or a third type of person that I can't remember now. Then she corrects herself: the second group were 'people trying to meet SOMEONE, not expats, let's make it less divisive'. The conversation is pleasant and turns to Nairobi's urban history, and while I feel I should move on and mingle, it's more comfortable to stay with these two people. I nevertheless lose sight of them not long after, as we're drawn into other conversations, and I don't meet them again after this night. Later in the evening, I'm exhausted and tired of socialising. I want to go home but am hesitant whether I should try to meet more people. I have exchanged numbers with some, not explicitly for research purposes, but I'm cautiously excited, thinking I might be able to take this InterNations thing somewhere and that I finally found a way to grasp the 'expat scene'. It is just before I leave that I exchange numbers with Tess, who says she'll be happy to meet me for a coffee and – I can barely contain my excitement – invites me for drinks at the Canadian High Commission the very next day. In fact, she'll email someone right away to put me on the guest list. (field notes, 18 May 2016)

(Not) finding expats in Nairobi

Nairobi is *the perfect place* to study expats I was told repeatedly and with emphasis during my five months in the city. Yet locating the 'expat' in Nairobi proved trickier than this statement suggests. Arriving in Nairobi, I tried to identify nodal spaces of the city's expatriate scene(s) to study the making of the category in an urban context. In my attempts to *follow the category itself*, I quickly realised that the expatriate is a salient yet elusive category, talked about a lot but hard to locate. Nairobi has several exclusive private members' clubs that were, like elsewhere, narrated as traditional stables of expat socialising (Fechter 2007; Leonard 2010c; Beaverstock 2011; Hindman 2013). These clubs are all located in upmarket neighbourhoods like traditional Muthaiga and Karen, happening Lavington and Westlands, or busy Kilimani (K'Akumu and Olima 2007; Rahbaran and Herz 2014). InterNations' housing advice and Facebook groups like '*Nairobi Expat Housing*' and '*Nairobi Expat Social*' confirmed that expatriates live and socialise primarily in Nairobi's upmarket neighbourhoods. Here I found expatriate socialities stretch across a wide array of public and private, professional and social spaces, private members' clubs and hotel bars, restaurants and nightclubs, flashy malls, and the enclosed compounds of international schools, embassies and organisations. Yet, while plenty of spaces were thus associated with expatriates, these did not officially, or exclusively, promote themselves as expatriate institutions. Even the *American Women's Association of Kenya* promoted itself as 'a diverse group of women who are both newcomers to and long-term residents of Nairobi', and 'with members representing nearly 35 nationalities and a broad range of ages, interests and backgrounds, all women in Kenya are welcome to join AWA' (AWA n.d.). As Hindman (2013:11) suggests of Kathmandu in the early 2000s, 'the clear boundaries of the expatriate community were fading'. Ultimately, I found no place or institution that narrated itself as *explicitly* for expatriates – except InterNations.

InterNations allowed me a grip on the simultaneously pervasive and elusive expat scene in Nairobi, and after my first event I joined the club. This chapter thus explores Nairobi's 'expat community' as assembled and narrated by and around the business InterNations. InterNations was founded in 2007 by three Germans, is headquartered in Munich, and advertises itself as 'the largest global expat network', with 4.4 million members and 'communities in 420 cities worldwide' (InterNations 2022c). InterNations provides information on where to live, eat and socialise in 'destinations' like Nairobi, and a forum where members can chat or organise offline social events. As such, InterNations represents a sort of 'event-based social network', a hybrid platform that intersects the online and offline to create 'a special type of hybrid community where people are connected online to organize themselves for offline gatherings' (Chen et al, 2019:1892). Event-based social networks like InterNations primarily facilitate contact among people in geographical proximity, yet entering and exiting are easy and 'penalty-free'. At the time of research, Nairobi's InterNations community was, according to its ambassadors, the largest in Africa. With its curated online content and through assembling members and organising events, InterNations had an important stake in constructing the category expat and the 'expat community' in Nairobi. Whether one participated in it or not, InterNations was an important institution of Nairobi's expat scene.

I conducted participant observation at InterNations meet-ups and related events, semi-structured interviews with people I met through or talked with about InterNations, and textual analysis of the InterNations website. I also draw on dozens of informal conversations with taxi drivers and staff working at venues. For reasons discussed below, these conversations remained tentative, often 'between doors'. I found that a diverse, shifting and as such ultimately self-contradictory group of individuals self-identify as expats or are thus identified by others. This included people with different professional backgrounds and legal statuses, who came from different countries for a variety of reasons. There was no straightforward 'they', no stable subject to which the term expat referred. As a 'floating signifier', expatriate could take on different meanings and fulfil diverse functions; it emerged as a performative and embodied category that narrated modalities of movement and belonging, and organised social space and the subject positions within it. Crucially, although focused on migrants, the category involved migrants and non-migrants alike. That is, the term 'expatriate' was used by both migrants and non-migrants and summoned both into roles and relationships. Tellingly, even InterNations, although directly aimed at expats, was in fact widely used by Kenyans. Rather than hermetically segregated or nationally circumscribed – if they indeed ever existed in such a form – 'expat communities' are becoming 'international communities' built also on an ethos of openness to (some) 'locals'.

Internationals: settled in mobility

Performing mobility, becoming international

InterNations taps into and actively reproduces a prominent reading of the expatriate as a worldly subject leading a peripatetic international life. On its website, InterNations defines itself as 'the largest international community for people who live and work abroad', 'a place where international people like you meet, connect, and exchange information. A welcoming community of open-minded individuals who share your experiences' (InterNations 2022a). As evidenced by this chapter's opening quote (InterNations 2022b), InterNations produces glorifying images of such international expatriates in its aim to attract members. The expatriate emerges as a subject effortlessly and voluntarily 'settled in mobility' (Morokvasic 2004), someone who chooses a peripatetic life and ultimately comes to inhabit the globe. Interlocutors' narration of expat life similarly revolved around casual international mobility, always on the lookout for the next 'international experience'. Here, migration seemed to be taken up with a carefully planned spontaneity, as individuals seemingly did not want or need to specify what might happen next. At my first InterNations event, I met Jane and Nathan. Jane is Dutch, in her late twenties and had been in Nairobi for two years. She worked for a company owned by her father, who had lived in Kenya for decades. I asked her if she wanted to stay. 'God no', she wanted 'to have a bar in Barbados or something like that'. Nathan had been

in Nairobi for five years and had recently opened a gym. He kept
his options open, saying he might leave if his business did not work
out. I asked if he would consider returning to the UK; he did not
think so, partly because he could never afford his current lifestyle
there (field notes, 18 May 2016).

That same week, I went to see off a friend who was leaving as
her work assignment with the UN had ended. As she packed, I and
her other friends who had come along joked about her excessive
luggage and someone commented, 'you learn that in expat life, not
to over-pack'. My friend exclaimed 'this is my third or fourth expat
experience, and I still do'. The discussion shifted to people's views
on Nairobi: one woman declared 'It's okay after all the shitholes
I've been in' (field notes, 16 May 2016). In such narratives, Nairobi
becomes positioned as a temporary home, a pit stop. The InterNations Nairobi web page similarly welcomes expatriates by already
suggesting the next, imminent departure:

> With InterNations, you never stand alone. Whether you move to
> another city or go on a business trip somewhere – our communities
> around the world are there to make you feel at home wherever you
> are. Feel free to also check out our other vibrant InterNations Com-
> munities like the ones in Dubai or Riyadh. (InterNations 2022g)

Hyperlinked cities suggest a world accessible to expatriates. In such
narrations, the expat never becomes dependent on a particular place.
This focus on openness to potential future mobility echoes Polson's
(2015:1) findings on professional migrants' mobile 'sense of place'
and professed belonging to an 'international community', Fechter's
(2007) findings about expats' claim to an 'international outlook'
and Favell's (2008:104) 'Eurostars' who valued movement as a
'permanent state of mind'. Indeed, flux and transience define the
expatriate experience that InterNations offers. With a simple mouse-
click members can change their city, and thereby their 'community'.
InterNations is always available but does not demand regular
attendance or other commitments. Besides a small core of regulars,
many only attended when they initially arrived in Nairobi; others,
including those who found it difficult to maintain friendships due
to regular work-related travel, attended events sporadically, whenever
they had a lonely evening in town.

The expat not only casually inhabited the international; her migration allowed her to embody the international, the expat *becomes* the international. In his work on 'global citizens', Urry (1999:174) talks about their right to various forms of mobility through which they 'consume' the places and environments they visit en route. Indeed, embodying the international expatriate is centrally achieved through such a performative 'consumption' of places:

> we talk about Michelle's trip to Senegal. Laura asks her if she liked it, and I suspect that she is once again contemplating where to move after her job in Nairobi ends. Michelle says she 'loved' it, although she didn't see much of the country. She had a 'crazy and great holiday'. 'But', someone interjects, 'Dakar might be great, but there is nothing around it'. Many African cities, they discuss, might be great to live in, but then there is nothing else in the country. Kenya is special in this regard, they agree. Michelle says she wants to live in West Africa one day, it's her dream. She talks about feeling claustrophobic every time she goes back to Europe. After a week back in France, she was like 'get me out of here' and went to Barcelona. She says that she likes it 'exotic', gets bored back in Europe. Laura asks her something about Vietnam, where she has apparently lived before. Michelle exclaims, 'I'm an Asia person but Marco isn't.' But anyway, she doesn't want to move back, she always wants to move to a new country, otherwise it would feel like a step back. We compare our experiences in and impressions of various South East Asian countries. Michelle says that Thailand felt like a Club Med. André adds that Phnom Pen has changed so much, the area where all the tourists used to stay has been torn down. Then Michelle talks about her 'crazy trip' up north to Lake Turkana. (field notes, 1 June 2016)

Like luxury commodities or food on a menu, places – cities, countries or continents – are summoned and assessed in the performance of being an expatriate.[1] In often appropriating, even aggressive, language one has 'done' Hong Kong or Kenya – passive places acted upon by the agentive expat. Such a discursive consumption of places in the constitution of the 'international' self is mirrored in InterNations' feature that allows expats to display the flags of countries where they have lived on their online profiles.

Crucially, the expatriate consumes places without ever fully becoming part of those places: without *being consumed* by them, or 'going native' as it used to be called (see Chapter 3). Places are discussed in an appropriating yet detached manner. Hence, moving back to a country where she has lived before felt like 'a step back' to Michelle, as for many others I met. The international expat can 'know', 'love' or 'hate' a place but always from the vantage point of the outsider, the subject settled in mobility. Such consumption of places frequently implies the erasure of the people living in them – tellingly, people do not centrally figure in our conversation above. It also frequently relies on exoticising tropes, as Jackson (2011) has diagnosed of Kenya's production for tourist consumption and wa Thiong'o (2012:35) notes for prevalent imaginations of 'a Kenya of fauna, flora, and slums' that leaves out 'the Kenya of modern highways, cars, trains, and airports'. In our conversation, a 'boring' Europe is constructed against its various 'exotic' Others.[2] The 'exotic' here is not an innocent label but 'a way of thinking and speaking about the non-west that is underpinned by a series of lasting colonial binaries which at once privilege western agency, modernity and mobility over non-western passivity, tradition and rootedness' (Jazeel 2012:9). Michelle distances herself from this Europe in a discursive move that positions her as adventurous and exciting. Yet, as exoticised places become consumable resources for expatriate self-constitution, the expatriate self retains their unmarked position (hooks 1992). Expats/internationals can assimilate difference without ever becoming that difference. As Hindman (2009b:267) puts it, 'The privileged few can take "culture" on and off like an accessory.' For the expatriate, constituted within a neoliberal multicultural framework, difference is celebrated as long as it is commodifiable and consumable within contemporary systems of capital (Hindman 2013).

Mobility privilege as achievement

The category expatriate, constituted in the performative consumption of places, is shaped by uneven international mobility regimes. The international expatriate as albatross evoked by InterNations in the opening quote to this chapter 'travels long distances around the world, all while maintaining a special connection to their place of birth'. This 'connection' is decidedly more material than acknowledged: usually it is their passport which allows relatively unimpeded access to casual global mobility. The idea of a borderless globalised world has been identified as 'folklore' (Yeung 1998), and is an ideological construct inasmuch as it renders invisible how and for whom borders not only persist but have multiplied and hardened. International movement is a social resource distributed unevenly and in interconnected ways, playing a crucial role in the differentiation of global society (Cresswell 2010). Social class, constituted in economic, cultural and social capital, including wealth and educational qualifications, is important in facilitating the itinerant lifestyle that the expatriate narrates (Fechter 2007; Leonard 2010abc). More decisive still, citizenship has become the key 'resource for mobility' today (Shachar 2009), and in particular European and North American citizenships represent 'a crucial form of transnational capital' (Lundström 2014:89) as a transnationally valid embodied and material economic, social and symbolic resource. As discussed in Chapter 1, a growing body of scholarship traces the unevenness of the current international border regime, and its colonial and imperial fashioning. Citizenship, possibly the single most important factor determining ease of international movement, is 'racially differentiated' (Achiume 2019:1530). Mau et al. (2015:1192) find 'a clear bifurcation in mobility rights' since 1969, as citizens of rich countries have gained in mobility rights while those of other regions, especially African countries, have 'stagnated' or 'diminished', a trend that has been 'accelerated and driven by the processes of globalization' (Mau 2010:339). As Achiume (2022:46–47) argues, international borders are 'racial borders', that 'disparately curtail' mobility and political membership 'on a racial basis' to 'sustain international migration and mobility as racial privileges, especially privileges of Whiteness'. Inasmuch as the internationalism of the expatriate remains predicated on 'free movement', its implicit normative core remains the 'white West'.

The importance of citizenship to their lifestyle was often recognised when I asked interlocutors whether they considered taking up Kenyan citizenship. As Michaela, a British woman who intended to stay in Kenya for good, told me,

> Couldn't possibly give up British citizenship, just from a travelling point of view. My job involves so much travelling and you can just like walk in anywhere. When I see my colleagues, the pain and suffering they go through applying for visas and stuff. It's ridiculous.

Yet, when I did not ask about it, citizenship usually went unmentioned in accounts of international expat lives, at least in the accounts of those who held a privileged citizenship. Laura, originally from the UK, had recently quit her job as a school teacher in Nairobi, where she had lived and worked for several years. She wanted a change of career and scenery, as she told me:

> *Laura*: I have been looking at Jordan because I heard – people tell me that Amman is a really fun place. ... it has got really nice excursions, you've got Petra, you've got the Red Sea. I like the Middle East but – so, for example, Oman, but I don't know if I'll be able to find a job there that is not in teaching. So – and Asia, I used to really, really like Asia but now I got accustomed to this quite rural, you know like – have a lot of trees, grass and I can drive around the city. In Asia, all the cities are like so busy, you know. ... African cities are just so much smaller and more like – so, maybe not Asia but I don't know, I think I might go travelling a bit and just work it out. ... I would love to live in Dar es Salaam actually, but the visas have got really difficult now.
>
> *SK*: how?
>
> *Laura*: There is a new government, and they are trying – they said that foreigners are taking Tanzanians' jobs. And therefore they have cut the visas hugely for all foreigners, African and European. So I think it is unlikely, but I have been considering going to Dar es Salaam and just hanging out and asking around and seeing if it is possible. I know people in Nairobi who do not have a work visa and who work here. Even for big NGOs, it is really crazy, yeah. It is quite surprising how many don't get work visas, that is probably something I shouldn't say.

Laura eventually found a job in West Africa, before moving on to Central America. Her legal status as a British citizen and her embodied white Britishness crucially conditioned her ability to casually cross international borders for visits or settlement and her capacity to 'bend' or break immigration regulations relatively effortlessly, and thereby proved crucial for her expat life. While Euro-American passports are not the sole, nor a sufficient condition for inhabiting international mobility, the expatriate as a subject casually and willingly settled in mobility positions a 'privileged passport' as norm and normative, and thereby a priori excludes a majority of the world's population from this category. As a migratory subject, the expatriate is ultimately predicated on uneven global power geometries and mobility inequalities.

While structural privilege often remains unacknowledged in narrations of the international expat life, casual mobility becomes positioned as normal, desirable and, eventually, as an achievement. That is, privileged access to mobility is not only a taken-for-granted entitlement, but its exercise is frequently asserted as an accomplishment. If Achiume (2019:1521) conceptualises working-class migration from the Third to the First World as acts of resistance that enact 'an entitlement of neocolonial imperial membership on grounds of political equality', then the expatriate as here constructed achieves the opposite. The chapter's opening quotation, evoking a heroic image of the albatross, exemplifies par excellence how the rhetorical constitution of the expatriate not only presumes an entitlement to international migration but imbues it with value. By association with the albatross, expats become strong, driven and restless, qualities which, literally and figuratively, elevate them above the world and seem to explain their implicit right *to the world*. The very inclination of the expat to embrace the unknown justifies them doing so – their desire becomes their right. As Mimi Sheller (2018:40) writes, 'the iconic masculinist figures of the explorer, the entrepreneur, and the frontiersman require implicit "others" who do not exercise autonomous self-directed mobility: women, children, slaves, servants, bonded workers, lazy poor, and wild natives'. InterNations is rag-picking in the ruins of empire to create its expatriate. It recycles imperial racialised and gendered tropes in creating a flattering identity which it offers – or rather sells – to privileged migrants with the ultimate aim of attracting members, selling its product and making a profit. While the figure of the explorer came to rationalise European imperial expansion – his 'embrace' ultimately being a euphemism for dispossession and exploitation – InterNations' expatriate rationalises unequal postcolonial migration regimes by transforming mobility privileges into achievement. This expatriate reproduces the normativity of the idealised male, classed, white subject: unattached and unrestrained, physically and mentally strong, driven and capable. Laura's account evidences the often unquestioned normativity of such a peripatetic lifestyle. When I asked her what she planned to do next, she answered that she was not sure: 'I keep on saying I'm staying in Africa but it's only because I'm comfortable here, when I should really get out of the comfort zone and go elsewhere.' Laura felt comfortable in Nairobi but she also felt compelled to 'get out of her comfort zone' – not by anyone in particular but rather by an unspecified cultural norm.

The 'expat' can be so eulogised only after a prior act of detachment from the social relationships and institutions that structurally enable it. That is, movement can be claimed as entitlement and achievement only once conceptualised as springing from individual choice and action. Accordingly, as a self-driven and agentive subject, the 'expat' moves, rather than being moved (Leinonen 2012). The expatriate is represented as an individual that *chooses* mobility, free from sociostructural constraints, whether economic crisis and unemployment, gendered expectations and family commitments, cultural norms and discourses – all factors that in actual fact mattered very much for my interlocutors' decisions to migrate, despite their relatively privileged position on the migratory spectrum. Yet these constraints hardly figure in celebratory evocations of the idealised figure of the international expat. This expat depends on structural inequalities as much as on their occlusion through discursive strategies of individualisation, decontextualisation and reification. Exercising the *privilege* of casual migration thus allows the expatriate to appropriate the international, and so privilege turns into its own justification and becomes the means of its own perpetuation.

Unequal labour in the international community

Producing the 'international community'

The 'international talk' discussed above creates community among those that can partake in it, and talking about places one has visited is a habitual way of introduction and topic of conversation at 'expat events'. As Scott (2006:1123) notes, 'Mobility … is now a dominant feature of middle-class reproduction' as 'where we go to outside the UK and what we do there are now key elements in middle-class "talk"' which 'offer the middle class a routeway towards distinction'.

In Nairobi, a discursive performance of migration enables recognition and bonding and thereby helps create the 'international community', as well as police its boundaries. As such, individuals depend on each other for the performance of their 'internationality' in a sort of shared social ritual that can include Kenyans who have previously lived or travelled abroad. In the current globalised economy, 'international' carries cultural capital (Polson 2016; Bauder et al. 2017), and the international capital attached to the category expatriate was key to its mobilisation by both migrant and non-migrant actors as a strategic tool to secure social and economic gain. The category expatriate too thereby became a form of cultural capital, a resource that could bestow status and distinction upon migrants and non-migrants, who benefitted symbolically and materially from association with it – as Crang et al. (2003:450) write, identity can be a resource 'mobilized for economic gain'. The InterNations business model is a prime example. The business had successfully commodified the ubiquitous idea of the 'expat community'. Yet InterNations was not the only business venture built around the category expatriate. InterNations was part of a bigger 'migration industry' (Gammeltoft-Hansen and Nyberg Sørensen 2013) including Kenyan businesses and entrepreneurs that capitalised on the term expatriate and in turn shaped the sociospatial realisation, cultural imagination and lived experience of migration in Nairobi.

Indeed, the 'business' InterNations was far from a homogeneous entity. It was made up of the largely invisible headquarters (InterNations, after all, sells itself as a community not as a business), as well as Nairobi-based volunteer ambassadors and consuls who organised online groups and offline events. InterNations communities are usually managed by one or two 'ambassadors' who act as 'middleperson' between members and headquarters, organise large monthly events and 'create a welcoming community' – in return, they 'receive a free membership upgrade' (InterNations 2022e). In Nairobi, InterNations ambassadors organised official events in varying locales on at least three Wednesday evenings a month. I met three ambassadors: Tess, a Kenyan event organiser and 'socialite' who had acted as Nairobi's ambassador for many years, Adriano from Belgium, who ended up leaving Nairobi while I was there, and Thomas from Germany, who replaced him. One step down from ambassadors are the consuls, who 'host regular activities at least once a month and inspire other members to get involved' (InterNations 2022f). Consuls, too, receive a free membership upgrade. In Nairobi, consuls organised picnics, hikes, yoga, club nights or even weekends away. InterNations' classed terminology of 'ambassadors' and 'consuls' and its choice of upmarket venues signalled and reinforced the high status of the expat it catered to. Yet much of the actual work that goes into maintaining InterNations' international community is thus done by volunteers, a euphemistic (mis)use of the term to denote unpaid labour for a profit-oriented business.

InterNations depended on Kenyans to participate in this com-modification of the expatriate, even if they did so from uneven positions of power. Prominently, the InterNations ambassador Tess had established herself as a powerful intermediary. She seemed to know every expat in town and had started organising her own weekly drinks event, called *Monday Revival*, at an upmarket hotel bar. Similar to the event organisers Polson (2016) observed in Paris and Singapore, Tess's work was largely built on her access to a privileged customer group, expats, which she could mobilise for various events at Nairobi's many bars and restaurants. Seemingly, enough people, including both privileged foreigners and Kenyans, were willing to pay for this service. InterNations not only sold various services and a social life, but also identity, access to networks and thus a chance to accrue social and cultural international capital and, for some, a rationalisation of their privileged yet often lonely migratory lifestyle. Possibly most of all, InterNations sold access to networks, which it assembled via the category expat, presumably consisting of high-powered migrants. InterNations thus protected its brand and commodity, centrally including its membership base, when it selected which Kenyans could join. While InterNations markets itself as being for expats, membership is open to all 'global minds', and the citizens of any location, including Kenyans in Nairobi, may thus join InterNations – yet 'To ensure the quality of the network, InterNations membership is by approval only' (InterNations 2022a). In Nairobi, ambassadors told me that headquarters unofficially capped local membership at one third. Ultimately, it proved ironic that InterNations' most long-standing and successful ambassador, Tess, and many of its consuls were Kenyan. In an organisation for expats, predicated on the desirability of expats, where the number of Kenyan members is carefully managed, relatively well off migrants therefore attend events organised for them by Kenyans who are not only not paid for this service, but who are deemed to gain from meeting expats. All this takes place within the framework of a profit-oriented business headquartered in Germany, which migrants presumably join largely because it promises to connect them with other migrants. Also, in the commodification of the category expatriate, postcolonial inequalities are reproduced. Lifestyles and identities conditional on these inequalities are reified and sold as desirable, including to those Othered, excluded or marginalised in the first place.

By constructing a particular lifestyle as desirable, the category expatriate does work disciplining migrant and non-migrant workers for a neoliberal global economy. Also, privileged migrants are arguably compelled to perform and reproduce the international expatriate. Lundström (2014:171) similarly notes that 'expat' self-segregation can also be a means 'to uphold and increase privileges', and Hindman (2007:158) suggests that for assigned workers, 'going native' would be 'obviating their value as an expatriate'. InterNations' representations allowed migrants to feel closer to the global jet set, (almost) part of that exclusive elite inhabiting a transnational space of privilege. Facilitating this self-imagination is one service InterNations offers. Ultimately, as Polson (2011:14) highlights, social networks like InterNations that create identity and community around the 'international' support the needs of MNCs by helping to produce

> a force of flexible, mobile, culturally nimble managers who consider as a matter of pride that they no longer demand the security of home, stability, and certainty that was the provenance of corporate life in the industrial welfare state. (Polson 2011:160)

She further notes that 'although any comparison to the global majority would rightly brand these global lifestyles as elite', they can also be understood as new form of 'precarious labor', in which case 'the cosmopolitanism driving them' reveals itself as a 'technology of power' (Polson 2011). Indeed, many migrants I met had foregone the social connection and security that a more settled lifestyle might have allowed. Instead, they settled for sometimes more lucrative but often also more precarious 'international careers' and the social life offered by InterNations, which not a few described as ultimately superficial, soulless and 'just all a bit fake' (Robert). After my first InterNations event I tried to capture the atmosphere in my field diary:

this atmosphere of semi-forced joviality that always surrounds networking and socialising with people one doesn't know, has potentially
nothing in common with and yet needs to constantly smile at. Show
one's most pleasant self, be entertaining and funny but not too quirky,
show personality but don't be too different, collect numbers and
connect ... It is this kind of event where you can meet nice people
and actually have an interesting conversation, and be positively
surprised, or where you leave feeling alone, empty, resentful, disap-
pointed with the world. I feel luckily that I'm here for research purposes
and so my expectations and goals are slightly different, or so I think.

Ultimately, the category expatriate, like the migrant, is a tool to
govern both those included and excluded by it.

Valuable labour: internationals come to give

While those who joined InterNations in Nairobi are undoubtedly
privileged in the Kenyan context, they included many middle-class
migrants on the broader spectrum of international mobility (Favell
et al. 2007; Polson 2011). InterNations members worked for a living
rather than having their accumulated wealth reproduce 'itself' with
the help of a growing set of professional intermediaries specialised
in doing precisely that (Harrington 2016). They ranged from diplomats and CEOs, to English teachers, humanitarian volunteers,
yoga teachers and unpaid interns further down the socio-economic
ladder. Polson (2011:145) diagnoses the discursive production of a
global middle class that is 'fundamental, economically and culturally,
to expanding processes of neoliberal globalization'. The expatriate
is a valued 'international' worker in this context of neoliberal
globalisation: driven, determined, skilled. In Nairobi, this fantasy
and desire was also constructed vis-à-vis imaginations of the parochial
and traditional local, the poor, stagnant and immobilised: the slum,
the refugee camp, the village, the orphanage. The expat could enter
and (positively) intervene in these spaces but their international
belonging was ultimately constructed against them. The category is
taken to denote labour associated with progress and development,
and expatriates are frequently imagined as possessing specific skills
or experience that render them vital for such projects, so that their
labour 'adds value' to the host country which in turn justifies higher
salaries and privileged status. As Khushi, an Indian American scientist
tells me, when she lived back in the States,

I always put them ['expats'] like in a higher social class and a higher economic class, because I felt like they are in a country because of their advanced technical skills and they are getting like highly compensated for giving back in that technical area and then once they are done they will go back to their country.

In Nairobi today, it was particularly staff of international development and humanitarian organisations and diplomatic staff who were positioned as typical expats. Especially in its association with the developmental and humanitarian sector, the expatriate was frequently imagined as having come to Kenya to fix problems – rather than being recognised as part of the political and economic structures that helped produce poverty and inequality, uneven access to high-powered 'international' jobs and the uneven valuation of skills, degrees and qualifications (Liu-Farrer et al. 2021; Le Renard 2021). As Jaji (2019:46) puts it, 'North–South mobility ostensibly proclaims diffusion of benefits of affluence in contrast to South–North migration, which seemingly signifies transplantation of poverty, dependency, and the social ills correlated to material deprivation.' The label expatriate helps construct certain migrations as desirable, imbuing them with purpose and value within the logic of capitalism.

Yet, expatriate was in actual fact a label claimed by individuals with diverse professional qualifications and trajectories. I did not come across the expatriate as a defined staff category. Even where multinational companies and organisations distinguished a form of 'international staff' or 'direct hires' from those on 'local' contracts, these employment categories did not neatly map onto self- or other identifications as expatriates. For example, the United Nations, possibly the biggest employer of expats in Nairobi, differentiated between two types of professional staff, those in the 'professional and higher categories' and 'national professional officers'. 'Qualifications for National Professional Officers are the same as for the Professional category', but while the former 'are normally locally recruited' and 'are nationals of the country in which they are serving and their functions must have a national context' the latter 'are normally internationally recruited and are expected to serve at different duty stations' (UN 2022).[3] Expat might be a colloquially used term to talk about staff on 'international contracts', but in practice the expats I met included those on international staff contracts – also dual Kenyan citizens on 'international contracts' – as well as foreign nationals on 'local contracts', besides others like self-employed workers or home-making spouses. There were also expats who were informally (self-)employed while on 'visitor's passes', thus in breach of immigration regulations and technically irregular and deportable (Anderson and Ruhs 2010).

The migrations designated as expat were also not necessarily purposeful and driven by carefully weighted professional considerations. Neither were they necessarily well compensated or responding to skills shortages in Kenya, as evidenced by the fierce competition between Kenyan and 'expat' yoga teachers. Jessica had been in Nairobi for a year with her husband and young daughter when I met her, and was deeply unhappy with her 'expat life'. Originally from the US, she had met her husband in Dubai and they had moved to Nairobi, where he had found a job. Knowing little about the city, they had hoped to find a quieter and more relaxed life. But Nairobi had turned out to be more hectic and expensive than they had anticipated. Jessica felt lonely and isolated. As she could barely afford taxi rides (public transport did not appear an option) to attend social events or meet acquaintances, she found it hard to make friends. While Jessica was in Kenya on a dependant's pass, she had started working as a yoga instructor, technically in breach of her visa status. However, given the over-supply of yoga teachers in Nairobi she found it difficult to find clients and they still struggled financially. Like Jessica, many of those labelled expats recounted messy stories revealing multiple, enmeshed migration motives. Some lived luxurious lives while others barely made ends meet, and yet others relied on support from families 'back home'. Some younger Euro-American migrants came to Nairobi because finding fulfilling employment at home was difficult in the context of economic crises and stagnating labour markets; others migrated to pursue promotion opportunities not as easily available to them at home. For others, employment was simply a means to an end, with the ultimate goal being to live in Kenya for personal or family reasons. Yet others just seemed to have arrived here by chance:

> At the InterNations women's brunch, the Kenyan women repeatedly refer to us as 'expats'. I look at myself, then Ellen. She left the Netherlands after breaking up with her long-term boyfriend, travelled around South East Asia, then worked in South Africa for some months, before coming to Nairobi. She works for someone she met travelling, in a British Kenyan company, she says. She has been doing unpaid

work for several months – the company 'needed to find out whether they need her services'. Now, she finally gets a salary, but I wonder how high it is given that she came all the way from Karen by Matatu and not for reasons of principle or enjoyment, I believe. (field notes, 12 June 2016)

While the migrants that the term expatriate assembled did not conform to a specific type of (labour) migrant, the category expatriate had retained an association with skill and status. As such, the label expatriate did not simply describe skilled and valuable migration but participated in constructing and identifying it, often in implicitly racialised terms. In many formerly colonised contexts whiteness continues to signal wealth and status, echoing Fanon's (1967:32) diagnosis of European colonialism where 'the economic substructure is also a superstructure. The cause is the consequence; you are rich because you are white, you are white because you are rich.' What Fanon (1967) highlights reverberates in Nairobi, as even in the absence of personal wealth or elevated professional status, whiteness still confers class status on migrants like Ellen and myself. In this context, the label expatriate possibly shields 'economic migrants' with substantially less individual economic, social and cultural capital than assumed, who make skilful use of the vast international differences in cost of living (Hayes 2014).

Jaji (2019:120, 36) too points to 'ideologies that perpetuate equivalence between whiteness on the one hand and competence, merit, and achievement on the other hand' and notes the 'mundane reference to migrants from the North as expatriates regardless of their reasons for migration'. Miranda was from the US and had been living in Nairobi for some time with her Kenyan partner. Although the two lived in a better-off neighbourhood, Miranda, like Jessica, struggled to support herself as a yoga teacher in Nairobi's saturated market, and her partner also did not earn much. Miranda hardly conformed to the dominant imagination of the socio-economically privileged expat. Accordingly, she told me:

Expats that I do connect with really well are the ones that live a bit more like Kenyans. They have a Kenyan salary, they live like in their means, and that's challenging, it's challenging for us as well. It would be really nice if one of us had an expat salary. Because expats get paid like four times as much. And that's why I feel like I do call it expat community here, because it's very different, like if you are an expat you can live like a nice lifestyle, like you would in any other country, like where you come from. I don't feel like they are really connected to what real Kenya is.

Mirroring her own precarious self-identification as an expat, Miranda mobilised multiple and contradictory meanings of expat, first including as expats those on a 'Kenyan salary' (like herself) then suggesting that expats had a higher salary and privileged lifestyle. Consistently, however, Kenya and Kenyan came to stand for lower socio-economic status and wages. The binary thus constructed of expatriate and Kenyan as fixed hierarchical labour positions resuscitates the logics of racialised capitalism, especially as the expatriate continued to be imagined as normatively white and Western. As Melamed (2006:14) writes, 'a racial-economic schema continues to associate white bodies and national populations with wealth and nonwhite bodies and national populations with want, naturalizing a system of capital accumulation that grossly favors the global North over the global South'.

The racialised and classed everyday ordering of the international

International bodies: intersections of race, class and gender

The international claims the grand, the wide and the open; it evokes a map of the world criss-crossed by nation-state borders, or the sterile spaces of airport lobbies traversed by busy people. Yet a spatial imaginary like the international is produced through particular institutional structures, legal frameworks, relations of production and consumption, cultural representations and, counter to its grand projections, it is realised in situated instances of the most intimate and everyday social encounters. The international is fashioned rhetorically on the InterNations website, is realised as an imagined community in its chat forums and inscribed on bodies as they move in and out of event spaces, crossing physical as much as social borders. In this reading, the international is also realised in the social relations and spaces assembled under its heading. InterNations events are occasions where people of many nationalities mingle under the banner of a worldly, cosmopolitan and diverse expatriate community. Literature has noted growing diversity in international business and aid work, and I met Robert and Laura from the UK, Amina from Pakistan, Elisa from Cameroon and Thomas from Germany. There were Dutch–Brazilian and Canadian–Kenyan couples. InterNations events were also attended by many Kenyans, some of whom had previously lived abroad, like Nina in Hong Kong or Danielle in Nigeria. But the international is not a level space: it is marked by power asymmetries, silent normativism and unsavoury rules of inclusion and exclusion. Despite the diversity of who considers themselves, and becomes considered, an expatriate today, migrants inhabit the category expatriate differently based on intersections of racialisation, citizenship, gender and class. A particular embodied subject becomes normalised as an international expat.

Nairobi's 'diverse' international community was narrated as relatively new. Arabella, an upper middle-class Kenyan in her early thirties, told me that 'when someone tells me expatriate I never pin it to race. I just think "oh I wonder what country you are from"'. However, she also told me that she remembers how in her childhood most expats were British or American, working at embassies or for NGOs. Yet, despite the noted diversification, the ongoing normative whiteness of the expatriate revealed itself when respondents unwittingly gave answers about whiteness to questions about expats, or when I was told that it was interesting that I researched expats, because I was 'of the same ethnicity' and usually ethnography studied Others (field notes, 21 May 2016). The whiteness of the expat is structurally reproduced by the racialised unequal access to international mobility discussed above, which privileges those with European and North American citizenships. Yet it is also produced in the everyday construction of 'international space' that takes place through organising racialised, classed and gendered bodies in that space. Sheller (2018:57) writes that all racialisation is 'deeply contingent on differential mobilities' and Ahmed (2007:24) notes that

> racism is an ongoing and unfinished history [that] works as a way of orientating bodies in specific directions, thereby affecting how they 'take up' space. We 'become' racialized in how we occupy space, just as space is, as it were, already occupied as an effect of racialization.

Messy movements within and across the city, and fleeting encounters at InterNations events were important moments in the production of the expatriate – and evidenced its ongoing classed, racialised and gendered nature. While Nairobi's expatriate continued to privilege Western whiteness as norm and normative, this does not mean that expatriate is a category reserved for 'white people'. Instead, white privilege is nowadays also reproduced in more indirect and insidious ways, under the cover of a diverse and international expat community.

The urban geography of InterNations events locates the expatriate in upmarket neighbourhoods. Not everyone will be looked at or treated the same in these neighbourhoods, not everyone will (be made to) feel they belong here. Designated 'expat spaces' were spaces where white people knew there would be other white people, where they might momentarily form a majority and even if they remained a racial minority this passed politely unnoted as whiteness *still felt like* the silent norm. They were spaces where white people could recover, if temporarily, a racially unmarked position (Morrison 1992; Frankenberg 1993). Into such expat spaces, past askaris[4] and doormen, white bodies crossed class boundaries easily (see also Fechter 2005). Rooted in colonial history, whiteness is *already* classed in Nairobi (Kennedy 1987). As Jaji (2019:123) notes for the Zimbabwean context, 'tied to the legacy of the historically racialized political economy ... whiteness, for many low-income Zimbabweans, is not a neutral skin color. It has both political and socioeconomic meanings.' The association of whiteness with (relative) wealth meant that white people frequently complained about being overcharged or not being seen for who they 'really are'. On the other hand, the classed nature of whiteness meant more courteous service and being allowed largely unobstructed movement into Nairobi's most upmarket hotel bars and restaurants. Here, people read as white did not have to justify their presence. They were assumed to be and made to feel in place. In everyday life, whiteness opened exactly those doors that the discourse of the expatriate narrated as open.

In and around spaces positioned as expat spaces, whiteness functioned as a shorthand to locate expatriates. Here, social encounters were organised by micro-instances of racialised ordering and bodies read as non-white had to do extra work to perform their expatriate foreignness:

> Thursday evening at Brew Bistro is 'Salsa Night' – which usually means there are even more white people around. There are four of

us, friends of friends, two white women, one Latina and a black man from southern Africa … we sit at the bar, engaged in a conversation when two young men start chatting to us. Although they stand right next to our male friend, they ignore him and talk across him to ask me where I'm from. Then they ask the other women. Fabian jokingly comments that they did not ask him where he is from. One of the guys replies 'Oh I assumed you were just from here.' 'Just' Fabian repeats, noting the (subtle?) condescension in the man's tone of voice and body language. Later, Fabian points out that the guys, who were ethnically Indian, had immediately mentioned that they were from the US. (field notes, 16 June 2016)

The men presumably mobilised their US citizenship to disambiguate themselves from Kenyan Asians and draw us into a shared community of Western foreignness. This shared Western foreignness was possibly seen to add legitimacy to their advances, or at least it was assumed to be a good conversation opener. At the same time, Fabian was overlooked – excluded – because of his (male) blackness. His blackness positioned him as 'just' local, and as a black Kenyan man he was apparently not only less interesting to talk to, but also easily interpreted as the well-rehearsed stereotype of the local man pursuing white women at Salsa Night. Such racial politics of foreignness structured expatriate events more generally, yet they were rarely overt or even conscious, and as such they hardly violated norms of supposedly colour-blind diversity.

The making of international social space also enlisted racial regimes that did not rely on the terminology expatriate. Bodies also moved into or failed to enter expat hangouts as a result of the decisions of Kenyan doormen who did not use, or even know, the term expat – but who were very aware of the ongoing tethering of whiteness and wealth. So, I learned, when doormen were instructed to use guest lists selectively, they let white women pass but stopped and questioned young black women who arrived unaccompanied (by men), reading them as potential sex workers looking for rich foreigners (see also Smiley 2010). These doormen did not need to be familiar with the term expat to do their job. It is precisely because the expatriate is not defined by an explicit set of rules of differentiation that it needs to – or can – rely on other systems of differentiation to enact racial and gendered discipline in diverse and ostensibly cosmopolitan expat spaces.

One African American interlocutor had moved to Kenya partly to afford his children an upbringing away from the violent anti-black racism structuring US society. Much in the tradition of early twentieth century African American artists and writers that left the Jim Crow US for Europe (Lloyd 2006; Diakite 2021), and the African American intellectuals and political activists that Gaines (2006) writes about, who left the US for Ghana in the civil rights era, migration was here a consciously personal and political project shaped by interlocking experiences of racialised oppression and relative socio-economic and citizenship privileges. The potentially growing relevance of such a 'Pan-Africanist' migratory phenomenon is also noted by Jaji (2019:20), who further highlights its political encouragement, as when the Ghanaian president launched the 2019 Year of Return 'inviting Africans in the diaspora to "return home"'. In Nairobi, being a black US citizen implied new experiences of blackness, within wider Kenyan society as much as within the 'expat community', that demand further study. While experiences differed significantly based on citizenship, gender, socio-economic position and their racialisation, those privileged migrants not read as white repeatedly expressed a feeling of having to 'qualify' as expatriate, to make up for their 'lack' of whiteness:

Sarah: The last question I have is around whiteness in Nairobi. Do you think it still carries certain privileges?

Aadesh: Yes, of course. It's a big thing. Like, if you're just fairer skin you don't even have to call yourself an expat, you're a de facto expat.

Not being white, as Aadesh and others told me, meant you had to 'call yourself an expatriate', hail yourself into position and prove that you could fill it. This claiming of the label expat meant claiming the status and privileged treatment associated with being middle class and professional; yet sometimes, it also meant distinguishing oneself from other less well treated groups of migrants, refugees and minorities. The label expatriate might be increasingly scoffed at by many middle- and upper-class Kenyans, but migrants that can claim the title are still treated better than many other categories of migrants, as Jones and Last (2021) similarly find for contemporary South Africa.

Not all expatriates are white, but whiteness thus arguably remains the expatriate norm, and culturalist distinctions are made about what counts as 'familiar (assimilable, touchable)' Otherness (Ahmed 2000:100). Accordingly, Laura self-consciously admitted that she imagined expatriates to be of 'European origin', however she then corrected herself: 'my friend, her husband is Filipino but he is completely Western, so he is still an expat in my mind, but he is not of European origin'. As Korpela (2010) observes in Varanasi, and Le Renard (2021) for Dubai, in Nairobi 'Western' was a habitually used and infrequently questioned identity category closely associated with the expatriate. Western is a contextually formed sociocultural category and being Western could mean hailing from North America or Europe, being white or being sufficiently fluent in what were deemed Western habits, tastes and discourses. As such, 'Westernness' emerged as a condition for non-white migrants to qualify as expatriate. For those not from the rich Global North, this almost certainly implied socio-economic privilege and echoed imperial contexts, where 'assimilation to the colonizer's cultural world becomes essential for any colonized subject who hopes for any social or material advancement' (Lopez 2005:17–18). Yet, unsurprisingly, Western proved an unreliable signifier. When I asked Laura to specify what she meant by 'Western culture', she struggled to define it and ultimately settled with 'Someone who just has a similar understanding to my own. Not necessarily sort of the same points of view or same agreements, but yeah ....' The flexibility of the construct Western, like that of the international, proves crucial for fashioning exclusionary social categories. It allows, for instance, the production of 'contingent insiders', whose positioning as 'integrated' not only means 'they are always at risk of becoming constituted as a threatening "them"' (Erel et al. 2016:1348) but also reproduces the normativity of the social position which does not need to be integrated in the first place, which provides the benchmark against which integration is judged.

The expatriate's work to define (and discipline) non-whiteness that could be assimilated into the Western project of capitalist globalisation against that which could not was further suggested by the category's opposition to the figure of 'the Chinese'. The relatively recent arrival of larger numbers of Chinese migrants over the last two decades – itself a highly diverse diaspora (Sullivan and Cheng 2018; Park 2022) – was viewed with suspicion or outright racism by some interlocutors. Often homogenised, 'the Chinese' were positioned as only temporary labour migrants, as not belonging, as self-segregating and as racist (see also Yan, Sautman, and Lu 2019; Park 2022). All of these were claims interlocutors also made about expats. Yet Chinese migrants were hardly ever labelled expats and I spotted only a few at InterNations events. Tellingly, an online InterNations guide to 'Working in Nairobi' positions its expat-to-be audience in opposition to 'Chinese business':

> all these [construction] plans could be a convenient chance for foreign experts who are interested in working in Nairobi. However, you should take into account that such mega projects are mostly tackled in cooperation with Chinese businesses, which are currently making inroads into the African market. (InterNations 2022d)

Similarly, Arabella laughingly told me:

> Aaah, we don't consider them expats, they are just Chinese coming to build the roads. They are contractors, actually. I think of them as contractors, cause the government has hired them to come and do a job. I don't know, I think there could be that perception that I am seeing you in a hard hat and work boots, building the road: you are here to build a road!

The figure of expatriate here revealed its ongoing association with white-collar work and professional social status, but also its racialisation by excluding a nationally circumscribed homogenised category of people, 'the Chinese'. Ultimately, this contextually formulated and possibly relatively new expatriate Other appeared responsive to geopolitical and economic developments. 'The Chinese' as a category of foreigners decidedly not expats seemed to draw on 'a longstanding, global Yellow Peril discourse' (Yan et al. 2019:20) to negotiate newer anxieties, whether over Chinese challenges to Western economic and geopolitical influence, or the creation of new relations of 'dependency' between African countries and China (Carmody 2011; Taylor and Zajontz 2020).

The expatriate emerges as an adaptable racially bordered and ordered category, that can include 'contingent insiders' (Erel et al. 2016) while reproducing whiteness as normative and norm. Crucially, what counts as white is itself circumstantial, unstable and fuzzy around the edges, and does not always translate across contexts. Although white people are arguably still privileged in most settings, the meaning, role and experience of whiteness differs, and whiteness is an internally differentiated and changing construct (Lundström 2014; Hayes 2018). Accordingly, I met interlocutors, for instance from Turkey or Albania, who were racialised as white and called expatriates in Nairobi, whereas they suggested this would not be the case in Europe. The flexibility in racial categorisation was also exemplified by the story of Khushi, who troubled local categories of Asianness and whiteness:

> When I am talking to them [Kenyan colleagues] I talk like an Indian Indian [imitates Indian accent], and they really understand me. But if I start talking like this [American accent] it is like 'oh wow, what is she' and you should have seen their reaction, they start calling me 'Mzungu' when I talk like this, and they are like 'what is this Mzungu' and 'here this Mzungu goes again'. But then two minutes later the same Mzungu starts talking like this [Indian accent] and then I'm a Mhindi [laughs].[5]

Khushi's status proved flexible and unclear: was she Asian because of her skin colour or white because of her citizenship and professional status? The accent was taken to decide. Racial ideology has always had to draw on more than physical markers (Stoler 2009, 2016) and language, tastes and cultural repertoires have been summoned to establish the expatriate's racial boundaries in Nairobi.

In all these instances of delimiting the expat, whiteness remained at the normative centre of the category: it became the privileged marker and benchmark. Yet expat was not a category reserved for 'white people'. Indeed, in order for InterNations to be able to sell a worldly cosmopolitan identity and community to its members, at least some people that were not racialised as white had to embrace the label expatriate. Rather, the expatriate positioned Euro-American whiteness as the norm and ideal, regulated its meanings and differentiated which non-white bodies could be assimilated into the expatriate category and spaces. The category is thus 'transformed by the process of incorporating non-white others, but a transformation that does not question the already white constitution' (Ahmed 2000:189). This expatriate was part of Nairobi's wider racial landscape, shaping and in turn shaped by it, entangled and articulated within a densely racialised context, marked by the enduring hold of colonial social taxonomies alongside newer divisions and inequalities. As a racialised category it does not work on its own, so to speak, especially insofar as the category expatriate does not matter – or even exist – for many of Nairobi's residents.

Unstable whiteness and competing categories: Kenyan Cowboy, expat or mzungu?

Whiteness also exceeded the category expatriate in ways that further caution against a simple equation of the two. This was evidenced by the question of whether white Kenyans were expats too, which came up sometimes:

> A discussion about different types of expats ensues. Rowan says, 'for example, the white Kenyans are very interesting, who have been here even up to three generations.' Laura replies: 'But would you call them expats? I would not!' Rowan seems unsure now, she tentatively replies: 'For me colonials are colonials, but still …,' she concludes, she 'would see them as expats.' Laura disagrees. She explains that for her they are not expats, also because they don't mix enough, they aren't international enough, they stay in their bubble …. (field notes, 21 May 2016)

For Rowan, white Kenyan descendants of colonial settlers seemed to remain essentially foreign to Kenya and hence expats. Laura disagreed – notably, not because she perceived them to be Kenyan, but because they did not integrate sufficiently into the 'international community'. Ultimately, the very question whether white Kenyan citizens, sometimes settled in Kenya for generations, are expats evidenced how central whiteness remained to the expatriate, especially in the Kenyan context, where national identity and belonging had historically been established against white supremacist colonialism (see Chapter 2). However, this exchange also demonstrates that some white self-identified expats engaged a form of what Dickinson (2016) calls 'time work' by positioning today's expat against yesterday's colonials. In such readings, white Kenyans are constituted as an Other whiteness, which is associated with the colonial past and onto which expats can project 'all things white' that prove uncomfortable. Jones and Last (2021) similarly note the 'privileged exceptionalism' that white immigrants in South Africa enjoy vis-à-vis white South Africans, inasmuch as they are not 'burdened' with 'culpability' for the apartheid regime. Hence, migrant interlocutors frequently pointed to the racism, 'colonial attitudes' and nostalgia of 'Kenyan Cowboys', a label used somewhat disparagingly by both black Kenyans and expats that evoked the vast stretches of land white Kenyans still own, but also suggests their unsophisticated provinciality. In such constructs, white Kenyans are not only the descendants of *colonialists* but the heirs of *colonialism* – while expats emerged as cosmopolitan and modern. Those white Kenyans, in turn, projected foreignness onto 'temporary' expats to establish their belonging in Kenya (McIntosh 2016). In both processes, what arguably disappears from view are shared privileges of whiteness.

Mzungu, in turn, cuts across such white distinctions carefully maintained by some. The categories expat and mzungu are both frequently used to denote white people in Kenya, yet the terms differ in their history, connotations and in who uses them:[6]

> The Uber driver, Michael, studies business in his fourth year, and asks me what I do. I tell him that 'I do research for my PhD, on expatriates'. 'Expats?' There is a pause, and I ask if he knows the term. He doesn't, so I say 'wazungu'. 'White people' is his answer. When I ask him about it, he says that the term includes both 'local and foreign whites'. He then tells me, 'We Kenyans have an inferiority complex, you know, we think you are better, but we need to realise that that's not true.' (field notes, 7 September 2016)

The 1955 *Standard Swahili-English Dictionary* owned by one of my older interlocutors similarly translated 'European' as 'mzungu' and thus confirmed the racialised history of the term's usage. Yet, mzungu, like the expatriate, is a flexible category that exemplifies the historical fastening of foreignness, whiteness and socio-economic privilege in Kenya, as well as its fuzzy boundaries and instability. Some interlocutors, like Khushi quoted above, who might not pass as white, especially in expat circles, but whose dress, speech and bearing identified them as well off and foreign, also recounted being called mzungu. Indeed, there exists a potent history of using mzungu for people who 'act white', as a heated debate in the *Kenya*

Legislative Council from 25 June 1964 suggests.[7] In the debate about the resignation of a Dr Y. Otsyula from the Kenyan Medical Service – a problem given the serious shortage of medical officers – the Parliamentary Secretary for Health and Housing, Argwings Kodhek, explained that Dr Otsyula had in 1961 been promoted to 'inducement terms of service'. When it was later decided that 'local' officers like him who had been induced should obtain 'accelerated promotion' under the country's Africanisation programme but lose their 'overseas privileges', Dr Otsyula 'did not wish to lose the overseas privileges which he considered more beneficial to him. He therefore refused promotion and retired.' As Kodhek exclaims, 'If this person wanted to go after all the persuasion on our part, he had to go, and he not only shirked his responsibilities, he dodged and he refused to take promotion. He wanted to be a *Msungu* [*sic*]'. That Dr Otsyula refused to give up greatly privileged employment terms which were generally reserved for white British officers (see Chapter 2) earned him the title 'Msungu', that is, the accusation of 'acting white'.

Knowing and caring about the term expatriate, or the distinctions between Kenyan Cowboy, mzungu and expat, itself appears racialised and classed (Uusihakala 1999). Learning to use the terminology *of* the expat seems part of migrants' socialisation *as* expats, the social process by which foreigners become socially positioned in Nairobi. Upper- and middle-class Kenyans, too, engaged the term expat, whereas many service staff I spoke to did not know the term. In contrast, while some whites appropriate mzungu to refer to themselves,[8] the term more often brings unwelcome attention, being singled out by one's whiteness – as when a child randomly called me mzungu in passing in the supermarket. It is thus often met with irritation, implying assessment on terms that are not one's own, and being identified by one's whiteness when one would like to pass unmarked (Fechter 2005; Lundström 2014; Hayes 2018). While expat and mzungu can thus denote the same person, the terms differ in their connotations and in who uses them for what purpose. A fellow PhD student in Kenya therefore suggested I should 'cast my net further' to catch categories related to the expat: 'Mzungu', she said, 'means exactly the same thing in some contexts.' And she rightly noted that by focusing on the expat, I was already delimiting whose views and experiences are heard in my research (field notes,

18 August 2016). Pratt (2007:7) suggests, with similar intent, that 'If one studies only what the Europeans saw and said, one reproduces the monopoly on knowledge and interpretation that the imperial enterprise sought.' This remains relevant and, to some extent, unresolved in this research. A danger of 'studying up' is to not only study the 'culture of power' (Nader 1972) but prioritise the voices of the powerful.

One's embodied positioning matters in this context. Being white German certainly facilitated getting to know and gaining the trust of many of the relatively privileged migrants I encountered in Nairobi. It affected what was said around me, as when some respondents casually complained about immigration to Europe, or made racist jokes about 'locals', assuming I shared or at least tolerated their sentiments. Yet being white also made it more difficult to get at the views and knowledges of some interlocutors and, importantly, many 'unrealised' interlocutors who I did not manage to speak to in any systematic way. Most obviously, this included the many working-class Kenyans employed as domestic staff by privileged foreigners or as service staff at the venues I frequented. They surely had a lot to say about those positioned as expat or mzungu, yet intersecting classed and racialised boundaries meant that these things were rarely said to me. I did attempt to talk to some doormen, security guards and domestic staff, but unless I felt they reacted with interest to my conversation openers, I usually did not pursue a conversation, being aware of the power relations structuring our interactions and my interruption of their work. Maybe unsurprisingly, I found that the many Uber drivers I talked to during often long drives across town in rush-hour traffic proved more talkative and frank than other service staff. Uber drivers were not as financially reliant on me, or on someone whose house I visited, and talking to me did not interfere with their work. Sometimes we talked about expats but more often about 'wazungu'. This terminological distinction thus brings into sharp relief the importance of considering *who* gets to speak on expatriates – indeed, who even knows the terminology and is therefore able to intervene in the conversation. It also shows the need to ensure that 'studying up' does not further amplify already powerful voices or render invisible already under-documented instances of marginalisation and violence (Anderson-Levy 2010; Stich and Colyar 2015).

Conclusion

This chapter has examined how InterNations, privileged migrants and upper/middle-class Kenyans produced and used the category expatriate in Nairobi. It explored how the expatriate is mobilised to perform identity (as an expat or against it), assemble social groups, create social and professional hierarchies, organise space and negotiate the role of migrants and migration in Kenya. I encountered a variety of understandings of the expatriate in Nairobi, with one prominent reading positioning the expatriate as an 'international' person engaged in an itinerant lifestyle characterised by flux, choice and a worldly cosmopolitan orientation. In this reading, the expatriate comes to inhabit and embody the international: expats are 'internationally mobile', classified as 'international staff', make up the 'international community' and have an 'international outlook', eat 'international food': in short, they become 'the international'. InterNations has seized on this reading for creating its business and brand and has become an active transnational actor shaping the borders and meaning of the category expatriate and its community.

But *what* international? The chapter discusses the international enunciated by the expatriate, its sociostructural foundations and political effects. It considers how an individual becomes international through the performative consumption of places and casual international mobility, which in the context of uneven border regimes involves the reinterpretation of privilege as achievement. While many self-proclaimed expats, as well as those who reject the category, thus aim to perform an embodied internationalism constructed in progressive opposition to a supposedly parochial local and backward nationalism, the 'material reality of the national order' (Dzenovska 2013) is precisely what allows them to do so. In this sense, the international expatriate arguably has the markers of a tragic figure, possibly well intentioned but hubristic, caught up in the unrecognised self-contradiction of its social position. This 'international' ideal-type of neoliberal globalisation comes to discipline both those it privileges and its imagined Others, who it is peddled to as desire and aspiration. In everyday life, this international is realised centrally through the uneven social relations and unequally valued labour that reproduce InterNations' community and business, and in the ordering and orientation of racialised, gendered and classed bodies that make up Nairobi's international community.

The expatriate's international is that of neoliberal globalisation, an imaginary that idealises flux and mobility across a space that remains intensely bordered and ordered along ascribed gendered, classed and racialised schemata. The normative ideal at the heart of this international expat remains whiteness – spatialised as 'Western' – even if the category is diversified in line with broader shifts in local and global power. The spatial imaginary 'international' that the expatriate is articulated through, which it embodies and helps construct is thus a *particular* international – different from, for instance, the successive 'internationals' organised by nineteenth and twentieth century socialist, communist and anarchist groups and parties the 'New International Economic Order' (Getachew 2019) aspired to by anti-colonialists or the internationalism of African literature discussed by wa Thiong'o (2012). As Walters (2015) notes, thinking beyond the spatial imaginations made 'obvious' to us holds political opportunities. Ultimately, this international, like its expatriate, is contextually co-constituted. Despite all their rejection of the local and grounded, these are locally realised events. Crucially, while the expatriate is reproduced as normatively white, what whiteness means and where its borders lie is renegotiated every day and was shaped by Kenya's specific historically formed racial hierarchies. The international expatriate is thus an event, realised as everyday reality through a set of material resources, embodied characteristics, discourses and performances that change and are always contested.

Notes

1 Being 'international' is similarly performed through the consumption of food, material objects and cultural practices, as evocatively shown by Fechter (2007) and Hindman (2009ab, 2013).

2 Michelle's narrative also shows that imagined powerful entities such as 'Europe' and 'the West' have their own internal hierarchies, normative centres and peripheries.

3 Note the similarities with Shell's mobility policies and the need to study these organisations, and their mobility practices, as produced by the same histories.

4 In the past, askari designated an African soldier fighting in the army of a European colonial power. Today it is used to refer to police or private security guards, e.g. those guarding housing compounds in Nairobi.

5 See further below; mzungu is often used to denote a white person, while muhindi is the Kiswahili designation for Asian Kenyans.

6 See Jaji (2019:121) for the use of murungu to denote white people in Zimbabwe, and Hayes (2018:92) for a similar usage of 'gringo' in Ecuador as an implicitly racialised terminological alternative to 'expat'.

7 LegCo, 25 June 1964.

8 Although often using the anglicised plural 'mzungus' instead of the grammatically correct 'wazungu' (Uusihakala 1999).

6

Archiving the temporary expatriate

I don't use the word [expat], **I try** *not to use it, because sometimes you have to use it. It's a bit like, you know, I'm sure if I went into the municipality and there was a doorman there and I say I'm Moroccan and I want to talk about my BSN [citizen service number], he will send me to a normal Balie [counter]. If I say 'expat', he will send me to the International Centre.*

Ed, British citizen living in The Hague, interview, 2021

The *Expatriate Archive Centre* (EAC) is centrally located in The Hague's Archipelbuurt neighbourhood, with its wide avenues and beautiful late nineteenth-century buildings. Here, down a quiet side street and through a door flanked by roses, visitors are led into the bright and welcoming front room of the archive. This archetypically Dutch facade harbours a trove of materials, including many documenting the lives of those migrating in the service of Royal Dutch Shell. Founded by 'Shell wives', the EAC decoupled from Shell in 2008, and broadened its remit to the social history of *all* expatriates. The EAC's explicit focus on expatriates makes it a unique archival project and significant stakeholder in producing the expatriate. This chapter traces the expatriate that emerges from the Expatriate Archive Centre's work, from the personal stories of staff and volunteers, and from the EAC's 2015 exhibition, '*Expat Impressions of The Hague*'. The chapter also explores the broader stakes of this expatriate by interrogating its interaction with the migration politics of The Hague and the Netherlands.

The EAC website welcomes visitors with an enticing image of pale blue archival folders amidst scattered old papers. Clicking through to the page 'Collection', the visitor reads that 'We collect material from expatriates and their families during and after their stay abroad. Our definition of "expatriate" is anyone who lives temporarily in a country other than their "home" country' (EAC 2018). Temporariness is a common criterion for defining the expatriate, as discussed throughout this book, and the tensions and politics of the EAC's temporary expatriate have broader relevance. The chapter argues that the temporary expatriate is neither a category that derives self-evidently from past migration, nor is it a category easily operationalised for the task of assembling an archive of such. In practice, the expatriate in the archival space simultaneously falls short of and exceeds its definition as the 'temporary migrant'. Other readings of the expatriate, including the category's association with racialised and classed privilege, silently mould the supposedly universal expatriate: they work within and beyond temporariness to assemble a decidedly more situated expatriate history.

Defining the temporary expatriate

Tracing a genealogy of the temporary expatriate to the Shell Ladies' Project

The genealogy of the EAC's temporary expatriate leads back to the Shell Ladies' Project (SLP). As argued in Chapter 4, the transformation of the SLP into a *Shell Family Archive*, and finally an archive of *all* of expatriate social history, required a changed framing and *raison d'être*. It also necessitated specifying who was an expatriate. The Shell spouses who set up the archive thus came to define expatriates as those who reside abroad temporarily. Yet their own personal experience of being 'on the move' with Shell actually proved temporally more complex. The Shell Ladies' Project's first anthology, *Life on the Move*, defines the expatriate in its glossary as 'a person living semi-permanently out of his or her home country' (SLP 1993:185). This emphasises the experience of extended emigration. Similarly, the introduction to the third compilation of Shell sources, *The Source Book*, describes expatriates as 'people living permanently on a temporary basis in a distant location dictated by their source of income' (Outpost Archive Centre 2008:vii). A former Shell spouse involved in the SLP describes that

> expatriate definitely means someone who keeps moving, not someone who is out from home, but who is on the move. We have argued about what an expatriate is, you can imagine. So in my view an expatriate is someone who leaves their home – happily – but is constantly leaving which is so much more painful than settling in. And we get quite good at settling in. And it's always interesting, but leaving is painful. (Cornelia)[1]

For Shell spouses like Cornelia, being an expatriate was defined by being repeatedly torn away from what was or might have become home. It is the potentially endless repetition of temporary residence that mattered. For her, the expatriate was not really someone living abroad just to return home after a few years.

The permanent temporariness associated with being international staff described by Shell spouses was not random, but built into Royal Dutch Shell's model of postcolonial corporate management, as discussed in Chapter 4 (see also Kunz 2020b). The SLP's definition of the expatriate as 'permanently temporary', however, also engendered exclusions. Frequent rotation of international staff certainly became the norm after Shell's regionalisation in the 1950s, and will have defined the lives of the Shell Ladies' Project founders. However, at the same time, expatriation of Shell's regional staff could very well be a one-off affair. Regional staff were usually moved abroad for one or two postings before returning to their base operating company. For the Shell Ladies at least, this regional staff seem to have not quite fully counted as expatriates. The Shell Ladies' conceptualisation of the expatriate thus suggests hierarchies among Shell expatriate staff, and the secondary positioning of regional staff expatriates within Shell. This testifies to the ongoing relevance of historical inequalities based on origin within Royal Dutch Shell well into the 1990s (Chapter 4), and within multinational business more generally (as Chapters 3 and 7 suggest). Moreover, before Shell had to regionalise its business in the era of decolonisation, and before the advent of cheaper travel, Shell's expatriate postings had not necessarily been temporary at all. In 1959, Blair described how Shell was keeping some expatriates in one 'cultural region' for the greater part of their career and, indeed, that most British staff in Burmah-Shell India served out their career in India. Here, it is not temporality but being dispatched abroad in an administrative function that makes expatriates, just like it made colonial administrators and now makes many development and corporate expatriates. Even in the Shell context, the temporality associated with the expatriate has thus always been more complex than the notion of temporary residence abroad suggests.

Whether 'semi-permanent', 'semi-permanently temporary' or 'temporary', temporality as such was a decidedly partial story of what made expatriates within Shell. Dewey White accordingly noted that expatriates' move was 'dictated by their source of income' and mentions the 'prosperous way of life' associated with expatriates (Outpost Archive Centre 2008:vii). Temporality can only partially explain the socio-economic privilege marking Shell lives, and its racialised, gendered and classed features. Instead, as a sociostructurally 'disembedded' criterion, temporariness effectively conceals the criteria that really produced expatriates. A sole focus on temporality arguably produces distinctions that do not matter while it 'misses' those that do (Stoler 2016). Ultimately, Shell's expatriate emerges as a category of labour migration that organised corporate power and institu-tionalised postcolonial inequality. As argued in Chapter 4, the Shell Ladies' Project constructs an image of expatriate life largely cleansed of its imperial dimensions and functions. Relying on temporality as the main definitional criterion is part of this process, and helped construct an individualised figure of mobility disconnected from the imperial corporate project this migrant moved in, was enabled by and which it served. The EAC inherited this individualised concep-tualisation of the expatriate as defined by the temporality of their move, even if the notion of temporality was now broadened to also include those who returned after a stint abroad. Yet the occluded social context of this temporality continues to haunt the temporary expatriate.

Temporariness and 'problematic connotations'

Since 2008, the EAC has proactively worked to expand and diversify the personal collections it holds, for instance by seeking personal collections by those who did not move as corporate assignees or within family units. In doing so, the EAC faced various challenges in acquiring, processing and making the collections available to researchers. These have included limited staff and budget, and the legal status of personal collections, but also the fact that many migrants have not produced written materials or might not be easily convinced that these are worth preserving and making publicly available. Among the intersecting challenges and opportunities of archiving the social history of migration with a focus on personal documents, the category expatriate itself is a central factor.

To make the category expatriate, and the archive assembled with it, as inclusive as possible, the EAC relies on the broad definition of 'temporariness'. The EAC does not distinguish expatriates from other migrants by origin, profession, role or skill level, cause or manner of move: its core objectives include 'documenting the experiences of expatriates of all nationalities and backgrounds' (EAC 2022a) and it states that:

> Our collection includes letters, diaries, blogs, photos, videos, and other documents which together give a complete picture of everyday life abroad, from the late 19th century to the present day. (EAC 2022c)

This historically and geographically unbound notion of the temporary expatriate has universal ambitions, inasmuch as anyone anywhere can theoretically become an expatriate. In practice, however, the criterion of temporariness introduces challenges for archival work, such as the acquisition of collections.

Temporary is a vague notion and can, technically, refer to time spans ranging from a couple of weeks to several years, even decades. So, when does one start *living* somewhere, rather than being a tourist or guest? This is a relevant question in the case of one personal collection the EAC holds of a young man who spent time in Berlin between December 2009 and April 2010, and in that period travelled to several other countries. What renders this person an expatriate *living* abroad rather than a tourist on an extended trip? Similarly, after how much time does temporary stop and permanent begin? Ultimately, temporariness can only be determined in retrospect. Accordingly, Alina, who has been at the EAC for some years, tells me that 'the intention to eventually return' is decisive for the EAC and that, in practice, it looks at someone's *intention* to stay temporarily rather than trying to assess what actually happens.

A 2016 publication by EAC staff and volunteers similarly notes that 'the expatriates to whom we refer are migrants of a particular sort, who maintain strong ties to home and *think of themselves* as temporary in their foreign residences, even while building homes and lives for themselves abroad' (Chow et al. 2017:314; emphasis added). They argue that the (anticipated) temporary nature of one's stay matters because it means that 'the concept of "home" becomes a complex construction incorporating a variety of tensions between present location, origin, daily life, national identity, extended family, friends, and more' (Chow et al. 2017:314).

Yet an intention to return can similarly blur temporariness and permanence, and is a poor predictor of actual behaviour. It can be upheld for decades or until death, as amply demonstrated in the 'myth of return' or 'return fantasy' (Bolognani 2016), or across family generations as the case of Palestinian refugees demonstrates. In all such cases, 'the possibility of return, independent of its feasibility and likelihood' can become an integral part of migrant lives and 'orientate much of their everyday thinking' (Bolognani 2016:197). In other cases, intentions can change, sometimes daily, or people simply do not want to decide what might happen in the future. In general, maintaining a return option is a growing phenomenon, with international migration increasingly characterised not by permanent moves but by movements that are 'transient and complex, ridden with disruptions, detours and multiple destinations' (Dickinson 2016:737; Griffiths et al. 2013). Temporalities of migration, both planned and actual, are complex, often muddled, even self-contradictory, and frequently interrupt the assumed linearity that notions like 'temporary' or 'permanent' migration rely on (Bivand Erdal 2017; Page et al. 2017). In any case, focusing on a decontextualised intention to return risks sidelining the specific social contexts and power relations that always shape notions of home and often underwrite the intended temporality of migration. Temporary migration is not a unified experience and temporality a tricky tool for archival selection.

Temporality is not the only criterion that shapes the expatriate history documented by the EAC, as Chow et al. (2017:313) acknowledge: 'One challenge that the EAC has faced is confronting the sometimes problematic connotations of the word expatriate.' Chow et al. (2017:313) recognise that 'the term can be contentious', quoting a *Guardian* commentary by Matanle (2011) which argues that it connotes 'outdated attitudes inappropriate for 21st-century global living'. However, Chow et al. (2017) do not specify the term's 'problematic connotations' or quote Matanle's (2011) explanation of *why* the term is outdated – namely, because it is 'too redolent of the days of empire'. Imperialism and coloniality become evaded in the act of their acknowledgement. Not being named, the 'problematic connotations' continue to be highly productive in fashioning the term expatriate and the histories assembled under its rubric. This becomes evident as Chow et al. (2017:313) go on to explain that while the EAC considered alternatives, it 'has not found a better term to describe the source community for its collection' and has therefore retained the term 'but according to a specific definition', that of the temporary expatriate. Yet, on the very next page, the authors abandon their inclusive definition to specify that

> The expatriates to whom we refer are migrants of a particular sort, who maintain strong ties to home and think of themselves as temporary in their foreign residences, even while building homes and lives for themselves abroad. The French Algerians described in chapter 7 may be considered expatriates.[2] Expatriates and their families go abroad for work, yet they differ from what is considered a guest or foreign worker in that they occupy specialized or higher echelons in their companies and often receive visas on that basis. Whereas an international corporation might find it less expensive to hire a manual laborer on site, these expatriates and their families are sent abroad because their employers could not find someone with equivalent skills or relevant knowledge there. (Chow et al. 2017:314)

First, the expatriate is defined as the temporary migrant. Then an example is given of former French settlers in Algeria, also known as pieds-noirs, who returned to metropolitan France following Algerian independence (Sims 2017). It is not clarified how these former colonisers qualify as temporary migrants: arguably, European colonisers did not typically conceive of themselves as temporary, or as migrants, and once forced to return to France they might have continued to yearn for their lost colonial home yet likely did not harbour illusions of return to a re-colonised Algeria. Then Chow et al. (2017) explain the expatriate to be a higher echelon corporate worker and specifically disambiguate expatriates from 'guest workers', a term often associated with working-class Turkish and Moroccan nationals invited *temporarily* to perform industrial labour in the post-war Netherlands (see below). Only a few lines further on, the category expatriate is stretched yet again:

> the focus of the EAC's collection has expanded to include not only expatriates transferred for work, but also those who move to a new country for diplomatic, intergovernmental, academic, lifestyle, NGO, religious, sport, cultural, military, or other reasons, as well as repatriates and 'Third Culture Kids'. (Chow et al. 2017:314)[3]

While the guest worker is excluded, returning European colonisers are included, and many of the other examples of movers carry middle- and upper-class connotations that reinforce the category's association with privilege. As the list of examples grows, the temporality of the expatriate retreats into the background, and seems less rather than more relevant, while its 'problematic connotations' become more rather than less influential. Specific categories of movers are included and excluded by logics other than temporality, logics that silently recuperate the term's problematic connotations. Or rather, the term's problematic connotations continue to work in the space of ambiguity opened up by a practically unworkable definition of the expatriate as a temporary resident abroad. The expatriate emerges from these texts as implicitly reconfirmed in its association with white and middle-class privileged migration. The next section examines the political effects of such inadvertent recuperation.

Expat impressions of The Hague: the city, the nation and its temporary migrants

Curating expatriate history: Expat impressions of The Hague

Since it decoupled from Shell in 2008, the EAC has engaged in activities and collaborations to expand its collections, and to increase the visibility of and encourage research into expatriate social history. It held an academic symposium on *The Expatriate Experience: Past and Present* in 2013, co-organised and curated the *Saudade* expatriate art exhibition and book in 2018 and began archiving expatriate blogs to create a digital collection of expatriate life in 2019. This section discusses one of these activities, the multilingual Dutch–English exhibition *Expat Impressions of The Hague*, or *Den Haag door de ogen van expats*, which the EAC co-organised with ACCESS and The Hague Municipal Archives (EAC 2014), and exhibited in the atrium of The Hague City Hall in autumn 2015.[4] The exhibition is instructive as it argues for an inclusive conception of the expatriate, but reveals the challenges of defining the category solely along lines of temporality by indirectly and unwittingly reproducing the classed and racialised readings of the expatriate it hopes to dismantle. The exhibition also reveals broader political effects of this temporary expatriate by showing its role in constructing particular imaginations of the city and nation as welcoming and 'international'. Such imaginations, in turn, sanctify the city and country's unequal treatment of its residents, which centrally relies on their framing as different categories of migrants.

While the EAC takes a global approach in its collections, activities and collaborations, it is also a locally embedded institution, and an integral part of the network of organisations that cater to expatriates in The Hague. As one archive founder argued, The Hague is 'an excellent place' for an Expatriate Archive Centre because it is 'such an expatriate sort of place'.[5] Accordingly, the EAC held its 2008 launch in the City Hall, with the ceremonies led by the mayor, and also showcased its 2015 exhibition there. The Hague City Hall is located on the Spui, right between the main railway station and the city's central shopping district. Opened in 1995, the striking all-white building has the largest atrium in the Netherlands, an expansive space flooded with natural light streaming in through its glass roof and facades. The City Hall atrium hosts many exhibitions, and the EAC's exhibition was placed right by the entrance, with a constant stream of visitors filtering through on their way to appointments or popping in to have a look while warming up from the chilly November weather outside. It featured quotes and short anecdotes about expatriate life in the city, covering the time period from the 1950s to the 2010s, alongside which ran historical and contemporary photographs of The Hague, contributed mostly by the municipal archives.

As described by the online Archive News, the aim of the exhibition was to 'reveal the history of The Hague as seen through expatriate eyes' and to provide 'a rich picture of what it has been like to live in The Hague as an expatriate during the past several decades' (EAC 2015b). The exhibition was organised along the themes of *Housing*,

Nature, Shopping & Interaction with the Locals, Transport, Customs and Socialising, Food and Drink and *The Beach*. The featured anecdotes and quotes were generally upbeat, sometimes nostalgic and often humorous. They provided snapshots of life in the city at different times, showing expats enjoying The Hague's beautiful beach, its tree-lined avenues, cafes and restaurants. Other quotes expressed surprise, delight or confusion at what was experienced as particularly Dutch, or took a gentle poke at one curious Dutch habit or another. The central panel of the exhibition offered an introduction:

> In the past, the term expatriate has often been relegated to a certain type of international resident – especially those with high-paying jobs at multinational companies ... [The exhibition] aims to expand the concept of expatriate to include many who are excluded by the narrow definition, such as the self-employed, students, 'love-pats', diplomats, NGO employees, and anyone else who calls Den Haag home for a season.

The Archive News from 26 October 2015 expanded on this theme:

> 'Expatriate' has sometimes been used as a narrow term that encompasses only a certain class of people who are transferred to another country by large multinational companies and live stereotypically privileged lives in the infamous 'expat bubble', reserving terms like 'internationals', 'migrants', or 'knowledge migrants' for other groups. However, in a post-colonial world where globalisation happens in all directions, old distinctions like these are both outdated and objectionable. (EAC 2015e)

Both texts explicitly address how class matters to the term expatriate in that it has historically been associated with socio-economically privileged forms of mobility. In comparison, while the online Archive News references a 'post-colonial world', it does not specify how postcolonialism or multidirectional globalisation might matter.

While objectionable uses of expatriate are primarily positioned in a past which the exhibition helps overcome, postcolonial politics permeate the exhibition's expatriate, figuring in and working through it. Indicatively, the exhibition's project of expanding the category expatriate assumes that inclusion in the expatriate is desirable for those newly included. Such a positioning of the expatriate as a desirable label arguably relies on the very kind of hierarchies of mobility that historically associate expatriate with power and privilege, which the exhibition hopes to overcome. The expatriate further gains in symbolic value through its positioning in more current hierarchies like the 'expatriate'/'migrant' distinction evoked in the news item. This hierarchy is rightly problematised but not overcome. Instead, the classed and racialised distribution of value it creates are partially reproduced by the very suggestion that those usually labelled migrant might want to be recognised as expatriates.

The exhibition does not differentiate the migratory experiences it showcases under the label expatriate from those of other temporary residents of The Hague. Following on from the above cited introduction, the central exhibition board states:

> The exhibition offers new perspectives on local history, sometimes showing parallel circuits (such as expats having their own clubs and schools), but at other times close cooperation and integration (for example in the areas of food and culture). Viewed from this angle, expats are not that different from other immigrants, really.

Indeed, temporary as well as permanent migrants have to adjust to cultural novelty and social mores, and may do so with more or less enthusiasm and support. Both – like Dutch nationals for that matter – may enjoy The Hague's serene neighbourhoods and pretty beach. What goes uncommented on is that, unlike many other migrants and Dutch nationals, those featured in the exhibition can, as far as the visitor gets to see, experience daily life in The Hague from a position of relative comfort. The vast majority of exhibited quotes are attributed to expatriates from the US or the UK. Others are from Australia, New Zealand, Germany, Nigeria and 'India/the US'. This is unsurprising given that, as one organiser recalls, repeated calls for contributions and for people to join the organising team (see e.g. EAC 2014, 2015ac) got few responses. The exhibition consequently relied heavily on textual sources held by the EAC, with further additions from the British School and the American Women's Club archives, and to a lesser extent from the *Expat Journal*, the *Haagsche Courant* and *Shell Destinations* magazine, The Hague University of Applied Sciences and the International Institute of Social Studies (EAC 2015d). This might go some way in explaining the exhibition's contented upper middle-class feel. One engineer recalls painting on the stormy beach in his time off. Another contributor recalls, with 'Proustian intensity', a taxi ride through The Hague's 'exclusive' and 'tree-lined' streets with 'huge and splendid houses'. A 1964 contribution describes nightclubs where 'dinner jackets were not worn except to formal dinner dances, but for women long evening dresses were in favour'. The expatriate in the exhibition curates a history that will be more easily identified with by some – namely those who share a similar upper/middle-class experience today, who get to enjoy The Hague's splendid houses and exclusive establishments.

Besides the classed character of the experiences represented, the absence of challenging and negative experiences or hardship is similarly revealing. Jo, one of the exhibition organisers recalls,

> People liked the exhibition. I think the most negative, in a way, feedback was, and I can see that to a certain extent and I think I probably agree with it to a certain extent, that it's kind of warm and fuzzy ... Nothing was really critical.

Jo goes on to conclude that they 'wouldn't have minded a more, let's say critical result' but explains that the exhibition's positive feel did reflect the materials they could find, with most negative comments directed at particular institutions or people, and hence not usable. The exhibition itself comments that

> although the memories of the former expats in Den Haag tend toward the nostalgic, there are also complaints about the traffic, the Dutch cuisine and the trouble with learning to speak Dutch (if everyone around you speaks English!).

Again, complaints about traffic and Dutch cuisine might come from temporary as well as permanent migrants, as much as from the Dutch themselves. Tellingly, however, the exhibition here not only positions expatriates as English speakers but suggests that their Dutch counterparts were happy to accommodate their lack of Dutch – certainly not the experience of all (temporary) migrants. Potential barriers or even discrimination due to lack of *both* Dutch and English, hardship and poverty, experiences of navigating a confusing and potentially hostile (immigration) bureaucracy, of everyday racism and structural discrimination in the labour market or educational system – issues frequently associated with both temporary and permanent migration to the Netherlands (see below) – remain absent from the exhibition. An inclusive definition does not on its own guarantee a diverse perspective, and the exhibition re-inscribes a classed and to some extent white experience in universal guise. The exhibition thus produces a generalised temporary migrant that silently reclaims its classed and racialised privileged position.

Sanctioned occlusions: The Hague's other temporary migrants

Seen 'through the eyes of expats', the exhibition produces a particular representation of The Hague and its place in the world. In an entry advertising the upcoming exhibition, the online Archive News writes that 'As one of the quintessential international cities in the world, Den Haag has always welcomed those from other countries who come to stay, whether for one year, ten years, or more' (EAC 2015d). In this way, the exhibition repeatedly stresses The Hague's internationality and suggests its welcoming and cosmopolitan character as 'the international city of peace and justice' (EAC 2015e). This image concurs with The Hague's self-portrayal. Since the late nineteenth century, Dutch governments have intended The Hague to develop into the 'Legal Capital of the World' (Luo 2011), and the city now hosts central institutions of international law, alongside international organisations and multinational corporate headquarters. As such, The Hague's image plays into the Dutch national self-imagination as a tolerant, cosmopolitan and world-oriented country.

In its portrayal of The Hague as welcoming and friendly, the exhibition confirms the city's self-portrayal but eclipses crucial aspects of its complex relationship with its (temporary) migrants. It effectively excludes from the expatriate experience those temporary residents who might have had a less warm welcome. The Hague became a 'quintessential international city' also through its historic location at the heart of Dutch imperial administrative and business networks. The Royal Court and the Ministry of the Colonies were based in The Hague, and many merchant enterprises accordingly established headquarters in the city, including Royal Dutch which was originally founded to exploit oil reserves in the Dutch East Indies (Jonker and van Zanden 2007). Since the nineteenth century, well-to-do colonial civil servants and merchants used to spend their leave or retirement in The Hague (Furnee 2012). The upper middle-class Archipelbuurt neighbourhood, where the EAC is located, was built for these returning colonial officers, and its street names are evocative of Dutch colonialism. One can find the EAC in Paramaribostraat, turning right via Surinamestraat from Javastraat. The EAC's location in the Archipelbuurt reflects its own links with Dutch imperial capitalist history. The EAC's premises were donated by Lady Judy Moody-Stuart, founding member of the Shell Ladies' Project and archive, and her husband Sir Mark Moody-Stuart, former chairman of Royal Dutch Shell's highest organ, the Committee of Managing Directors. The Archipelbuurt is still a coveted area, pleasantly laid out, a short tram ride from the beach and within walking distance of the city centre and Shell headquarters, which likely explains why the Moody-Stuarts chose to reside here.

Throughout the existence of the Dutch colonial empire, The Hague hosted temporary migrants, and following the decolonisation of the Dutch East Indies, almost 300,000 Dutch citizens – so-called 'repatriaten' ('returnees') – arrived from what is now Indonesia. Until the late 1950s, the Dutch government actively tried to minimise their numbers despite their legal right to settle in the Netherlands. This attitude was especially marked with respect to those described as 'Oriental Dutch' – 'Eurasian' descendants of 'mixed ancestry' (Buettner 2016:218–219). The Eurasian population thus faced hostility and discrimination, and some stayed only temporarily before migrating further, for instance to California (van Amersfoort and van Niekerk 2006). Many of those who stayed settled in The Hague, which is still nicknamed 'the widow of the Indies' ('weduwe van indie') (Dragojlovic 2016). The city has also been (temporary) home to many Surinamese. The Surinamese colonial upper and middle classes partook in extensive migration circuits, for instance for educational purposes, with Creole and white elites sending their children to the Netherlands for schooling (van Amersfoort and van Niekerk 2006; Bosma 2012). By the 1970s, political instability in Suriname, then still a Dutch colony, increased migration to the Netherlands and 'the mounting anxiety about West Indian (particularly Afro-Surinamese) settlement' was a main reason why growing numbers of Dutch favoured Caribbean independence (Buettner 2016:102). Suriname's 1975 independence was supposed to reduce migration but had the opposite effect, and again the Dutch government initially 'stubbornly maintained the idea that ... the Surinamese were soon to return' to Suriname (van Amersfoort and van Niekerk 2006:336).

Nationalistic Surinamese also propagated a 'myth of return', partly due to disappointment given the racial discrimination that especially black Surinamese experienced (Buettner 2016). Eventually, many Surinamese, especially Indo-Surinamese, settled in The Hague, which further cemented the city's status as the Dutch 'centre of Asian culture' and earned it the nickname 'Dollywood', 'a meeting of Den Haag and Bollywood' (Bal 2012; Schrover 2013; Buettner 2016:279, 383).

The exhibition's expatriate also eclipses another set of The Hague's (intended) temporary residents. In the 1960s, the Netherlands started recruiting guest workers, initially from Italy, Spain, Portugal and Greece, and later from Turkey and Morocco. Guest workers arrived under the assumption that they would return home; ties with origin countries were encouraged, and many did return (Castles 1986; Schrover 2013). However, in particular Turks and Moroccans were recruited in the last years of the guest worker regime just shortly before the industries in which they worked collapsed:

> The bleak prospects in these industries were already known at the time of their recruitment. However, they were recruited to make the closure of these industries simpler: they had fewer rights as workers and were less well organized, and as a result there were fewer protests against layoffs. (Schrover 2013:3)

Laid-off workers could choose between returning home or staying, and despite Dutch efforts at their repatriation many guest workers decided to stay and bring their families (Oostindie 2011). Yet again, 'until 1983 they were officially regarded as residing only temporarily in the Netherlands' (van Amersfoort and van Niekerk 2006:343). Guest workers too should thus be quintessential expatriates.

The city of The Hague usually associated with guest workers, repatriaten and Surinamese is a different one from the elegant city portrayed in the exhibition. Many settled in the working-class Schilderswijk district. More recently, Schilderswijk has hosted yet another group of temporary and often irregular migrants. Prior to the 2007 European Union (EU) enlargement, Engbersen et al. (2006:213) found that irregular 'Bulgarian seasonal labourers come to the Netherlands during the summer months where they primarily work in market gardening'. Dragojlovic (2016:95–96) reports estimates that around 150,000 people from more than 200 countries live undocumented in the Netherlands, in indefinite legal limbo, always potentially 'temporary', providing a low-cost and vulnerable source of flexible 'reserve labour' in a labour market increasingly fashioned 'to favour temporary, insecure forms of employment'. Schilderswijk is now one of the Netherlands' most multicultural areas, but also often associated with poverty, unemployment and crime (Mota 2019).

Of the Netherlands' four largest cities, The Hague has the greatest housing segregation for 'non-Western allochtonen' – a contested category, with 'allochtoon' defined as someone born abroad or with at least one parent born outside the Netherlands, yet in public and political debate often reserved for those seen as 'non-Western' (HWWI 2007:2).[6] Indeed, all the temporary migrants discussed in this section are, in Dutch parlance, more likely to be positioned as allochtonen than as expatriates. Indicatively, current usage of 'allochtoon' is traced to a 1971 sociological report prepared for the Dutch government, in which allochtoon was used to refer to: 'repatriates, Ambonese, Surinamese, Antilleans, foreign labourers (guest workers), Chinese, refugees, and foreign students (from "Third World" countries)' (Yanow and van der Haar 2013:234). This smorgasbord of groups of people arguably does not share much besides their positioning as Other to the (white) Dutch nation – and their unlikelihood to be considered expatriates. Yanow and van der Haar (2013:229) thus argue that 'the Netherlands's allochtoon/autochtoon integration discourse is, in all but name, a racial discourse – one perhaps all the more powerful for being carried out in disguise'.

While The Hague might be a profoundly international place, it is thus not always a welcoming one. The city also showed its less-than-welcoming side when, on an explicitly anti-immigrant and Islamophobic platform, Geert Wilders's populist right-wing 'Party for Freedom' (PVV) became the city parliament's second-largest party in 2010 and remained so in 2014 (Koch 2014). The city government then defied EU and central government regulations in 2013, announcing it would deny Romanian and Bulgarian nationals registration numbers unless they met stringent checks that they have 'honest employment and are not living in overcrowded accommodation' (Waterfield 2013). Nevertheless, in its self-marketing, The Hague mobilises its 'multicultural diversity', as Hendriks and van Niekerk (2014:96) write: despite the city's 'tough new realistic discourse towards immigrants', its 'local government has an extremely positive discourse on branding the non-Western culture in ethnic neighbour-hoods as an economic product in the tourist industry'. The presence and cultural activities of past immigrants, often met with a less warm welcome if not outright hostility, are now commodified to attract tourists, and expats.

The unintended result of a privileged expatriate in universal guise is the eclipsing of experiences of not so privileged temporary migrants and the obfuscation of the city's more exclusionary pasts and presents. Many of The Hague's past and present residents would technically fit the exhibition's designation of the expatriate, yet their experiences would probably diverge from its portrayal of expat The Hague. Claiming that the city has always welcomed those from other countries and positioning the exhibition as representing the experience of its temporary residents per se contributes to whitewashing the city's internationality. This is not to say that the international The Hague portrayed by the exhibition is any less true than those just outlined. It means that the exhibition's unacknowledged classed and racialised expatriate offers a decidedly particular experience of The Hague that betrays its attempted inclusiveness and, ironically, reconfirms exactly the 'narrow term that encompasses only a certain class of people' (EAC 2015e). And there is more at stake than The Hague's representation as the welcoming and cosmopolitan 'international city of peace and justice'. The exhibition's image of a content expatriate is useful not only for the city's self-marketing but also for the Netherlands' increasingly Janus-faced immigration politics.

Attracting 'talent' through temporal governance

The expatriate as the universal temporary migrant risks producing whitewashed imaginations of The Hague and the Netherlands that have political effects beyond expatriate social history. A growing scholarship thematises the Netherlands' troubled (mis)remembrance of its colonial empire and involvement in the transatlantic slave trade, and empire's frequent dissociation from the imagined national project. Bosma (2012:193) sees 'no sense of continuity with the colonial past' and Dragojlovic (2016:138–139) argues that the 'Dutch national memory project' represents the Dutch 'as humanitarians involved in international human rights affairs (e.g. as hosts of the

International Criminal Court and the International Court of Justice in The Hague)'. Wekker (2016:1) finds Dutch self-imagination of the Netherlands as 'a place of extraordinary hospitality and tolerance toward the racialized/ethnicized other' to be steeped in postcolonial 'repression' that produces a 'strong paradox ... at the heart of the nation', which remains structured by racism. Bijl (2012:451) draws on Stoler's (2011) notion of colonial aphasia to argue that 'the Dutch aphasiac condition produces an inability to see the nation as the former metropolis of a colonial empire and to acknowledge the lasting racial hierarchies stemming from this past, leading to a structural inhibition of the memorability of colonial violence'. 'Colonial aphasia' (Stoler 2011, 2016) thus enables the seemingly paradoxical situation that the Dutch put considerable effort into representing themselves as a tolerant and worldly nation, while simultaneously embracing racist and ethnonationalist politics. This is reflected in increasingly bifurcated migration politics that rhetorically oscillate between the 'global war for talent' and 'invasions of illegal immigrants'. In this context, the figure of the expatriate plays a useful role, with temporality emerging as a technology of governance that allows a differentiation of Others that quietly reproduces racialised and classed hierarchies of the good/bad migrant.

Despite positive net immigration since the early 1960s, successive Dutch governments have officially considered immigration 'a temporary phenomenon' (Meeteren et al. 2013:118). This denial required various symbolic and rhetorical measures, like replacing the word 'immigrant' with terminology such as 'repatriate' and 'allochtoon' (Amersfoort and van Niekerk 2006; Yanow and van der Haar 2013). The term expatriate can be seen to fulfil a similar function. After Dutch politicians finally began to acknowledge immigration, it was not long until the topic

> topped political and policy agendas in the Netherlands with racist discourses among politicians, media and the public stipulating that 'the Netherlands are being flooded (through "mass immigration") by desperate immigrants from non-western societies ("fortune seekers") and that their integration into Dutch society has not worked ("the multi-cultural society has failed")'. (Bal 2012:3)

Immigration and failed integration became positioned as the source of social evils, a rhetoric that resulted in increasingly punitive migration and naturalisation policies introduced by parties across the political spectrum, and the growing popularity of populist right-wing parties like the PVV (Bal 2012; Roggeband and van der Haar 2018). At the same time, the Netherlands began to actively position itself in the global 'knowledge economy' and the 'global race for talent' (Shachar 2006; de Haas et al. 2018). Following a broader trend (de Haas et al. 2018), increasingly selective immigration policies were supposed to facilitate entry of only the highly skilled – in practice, the highly paid, called 'knowledge migrants' and 'expats' in Dutch debate.[7] In 2004, the Netherlands introduced the *kennismigrant* ('knowledge migrant') visa route. Those that come under this route do not require work permits, are granted longer residence permits that more easily bring them up to the threshold for permanent residence, receive speedier service, can bring partners, who are moreover entitled to work, and benefit from an 'expat tax break', the so-called '30 per cent rule' where they are taxed on only 70 per cent of their Dutch salary for five years (Meeteren et al. 2013; Kirk and Bal 2020).[8] Van Bochove et al. (2011:6) note that in marked contrast to other migrants, 'expats experience an enabling policy environment, rather than a restrictive one'.

The rhetorical construction of expatriates as temporary labour has political uses in a debate that marries an increasingly ethnonationalist vision for the Netherlands with neoliberal notions of competing for talent in the global knowledge economy. The Netherlands' increasingly bifurcated migration politics is racialised and classed, yet, in an officially meritocratic and colour-blind context, racism and classism are enacted on proxy grounds and by indirect measures. Temporality is one of them. In Dutch political discourse and policymaking, 'highly skilled migrants' are 'desirable migrants' and are 'normally conceptualized as temporary' (Kirk and Bal 2020:5). In reality, Dutch policy today renders all migration, at least initially, de facto temporary (Reslow 2018), and while 'knowledge migrants' are constructed as highly mobile skilled itinerants, the route in fact offers a comparatively straightforward path to permanent residence: 'the most used tool for permanent labour migration in the Netherlands is currently the *kennismigranten*-scheme' (De Lange et al. 2019:35). As a result, many 'temporary expatriates' turn out to be longer-term, even permanent immigrants (van Bochove et al. 2011; Kirk and Bal 2020). This inconsistent expatriate is at least partly the result of policymaking that engages temporality to negotiate – and obscure – political matters of power and privilege. *Framing* some migrants as temporary enables governments to facilitate their entry and stay while continuing to foster a debate where permanent immigration is used as a scapegoat for social evils.[9] This echoes other enactments of migration governance by temporality. Yeoh (2006:26) argues that Singapore's building of a globalised nation deploys bifurcated labour migration policies enacted via a 'transience/permanence divide'. The 'structural (non)incorporation' of highly exploitable 'contract workers' contrasts with policies aimed to 'entice foreign talent' while, ultimately, both sets of migrants are legally and discursively moulded into pliable 'flexible' workers. Similarly, Le Renard (2021) finds that Dubai weds racial exclusivism and neoliberal development in large measure through temporal governance that prescribes differential belonging and rights along racialised and gendered lines. Really, it is not the middle-class expatriates who represent the quintessential temporary labour migrant today but their working-class counterparts. And yet, in political debate and academic literature, 'the notion of an "immobile highly skilled migrant" is nearly oxymoronic' (Babar et al. 2019:1553).

Temporality is engaged at least partly to enact intertwined racialised and classed distinctions. Bonjour and Duyvendak (2018:882) argue that despite the heavy rhetorical reliance on education and skills, Dutch 'political constructions of migrants as wanted or unwanted are barely, if at all, driven by economic instrumentality' and the 'recent trend towards selective immigration policies is based on the racialization of certain categories of migrants into irretrievably unassimilable Others'. The Dutch self-imagination as middle-class, hardworking – and white – relies on imagined Others, like the 'Moroccan youngsters' positioned as products of a culturally reproduced socio-economic underclass (Roggeband and van der Haar 2018). Expatriates, or 'global talent', in contrast, are imagined to be 'like us' in the ways that matter: 'the expat, imagined white, male and upper class, is the ultimate insider' (Bonjour and Block 2016:790). As a neoliberal ideal-type, this expatriate subject is skilled, adaptable and international – as opposed to parochial, rooted and backward – and hence by default at least potentially temporary, and in any case a relatively desirable addition to the imagined Dutch nation. The construct of the temporary expatriate thus performs diverse functions for Dutch public debate and policymaking, and helps implement an approach to migration that is furtively bifurcated along intertwined racialised and classed lines. That is, imaginations of the temporary expatriate help rhetorically justify and legally enact increasingly bifurcated migration policies that marry neoliberal capitalist logics with racist and ethnonationalist politics.

Further evidencing the tensions arising from this racialised governance dressed in the cloak of temporality is the fact that while expatriates are conceptualised as temporary, Dutch national and city governments expend a good deal of effort to help them 'integrate', in this case more positively framed as 'feeling at home'. Knowledge migrants are not encouraged to imagine themselves as permanent residents, and are exempted from civic integration and Dutch language requirements. They are assumed not only to find employment easily, but also to share core values and practices of the host society (Bonjour and Duyvendak 2018), and are 'not asked to make the same social, economic and political commitments to the country/city' as other migrants (Kirk and Bal 2020:4). Indeed, the roles have arguably been reversed as national and urban economic strategies are focused on *attracting* expats. Several Dutch cities have services specifically for expatriates, including 'expat desks' aiming to give expats a 'red carpet welcome' and 'to make them feel at home in the city' (van Bochove et al. 2011:6). At the forefront is The Hague, often called 'the ultimate expat city of the Netherlands' (van Bochove et al. 2011:7), whose International Centre, formerly called 'Xpat desk', was initiated around 20 years ago and is located prominently on the ground floor of the City Hall – just a short stroll from the exhibition. The office helps expats with bureaucratic matters, provides English-language information about housing, healthcare and education, and runs regular welcome events aimed at expats. In neoliberal fashion, desirable 'knowledge migrants' have become customers who the country and cities cater to (Kirk and Bal 2020). This courteous treatment of 'expats' stands in marked contrast to that of 'migrants'. Yet the imagined racialised and classed differences between expats and migrants reveal themselves as shaky in the lived experiences of some knowledge migrants, as indicated by Ed's account cited in the opening excerpt to this chapter. When I ask Ed, a British citizen living in The Hague, about the temporal intentions of expats, he answers my question on temporality with a half-joke about how he usually avoids the terminology expat but does rely on it, for example, to escape classification as Moroccan and receive better treatment in the municipality. Indeed, many who enter through the *kennismigranten* route become read as racialised minorities, or 'migrants', in everyday life. Indicatively, among Reslow's (2018:201) non-white 'knowledge migrants', 'Almost all migrants were able to tell a story about discrimination, prejudice or stereotyping that they had experienced in the Netherlands, for instance, being laughed at, spat at or sworn at in the street.' Those who are officially courted as 'expats' thus do not always escape everyday hostilities towards 'migrants'.

Dissenting identifications, sanctioned occlusions and progressive potential

The tensions and politics of the temporary expatriate discussed so far become apparent also in the personal experiences of archive staff and volunteers. By providing volunteering opportunities, the EAC offers a way to belong and participate in the city for a diverse group of people, including Dutch citizens and non-citizens, students, non-working spouses, unemployed or retired people. To all of them, the archive provides a welcoming space that fulfils a variety of professional, social and emotional needs. Volunteers, in turn, help run a small archive and bring their own experiences of migration and their readings of the expatriate to their work. This matters. Archives are living spaces, institutions always in flux, shaped not simply by straightforward or neutral collection policies, but by the experiences, priorities and understandings of those who work in the archives, and those that (do not) engage with them. As Walter Benjamin (1968) recognised, although the past might appear over, or closed, it never is as struggles which began in the past can be fought in the present and may be decided in the future. Such an open-ended interpretation of active history making recognises the importance of how we interpret and narrate the past. Archives have an important stake in this matter, and it is in this context that the stories and perspectives of the people that make the archive work on a day-to-day basis, that donate to them or research in them, emerge as not merely minor topics but as significant to a broader space of political negotiation. In this section, I engage individual relationships to the terminology expatriate to understand broader challenges and opportunities that archiving the expatriate as the temporary migrant encounters.

Personal accounts of (not) being expatriates, the various meanings associated with the term and the connotations ascribed to it reflected the broader politics of the expatriate and revealed diverse emotional journeys and temporalities. For some at the EAC, especially North Americans, expatriate retained an association with a more permanent residence abroad. In Australia, I was told, the term expatriate was not as popular, possibly because of its connotations of class privilege which run counter to the national self-imagination of being down to earth and rugged. In much of the Netherlands and Germany, expat was still unknown terminology. Almost guiltily, Lily told me in our interview that she still self-identified as an expat, although she intended to stay in the Netherlands for good. Lyn on the other hand admitted that she did not identify with the label despite fitting the EAC definition, and despite others having called her expat. Alina recalled how she came to see herself as an expatriate as an adult, not having known the term in her youth despite having lived abroad. For some, the expatriate was unable to shed its classed connotations and for others the term's association with 'white privilege' was even more troubling. Some professed a positive attachment to the label – despite critically noting its colonial history – because the term had accompanied them through their life and become intimately relevant to who they were. These examples evidence complex emotional relationships with the category expatriate and reveal readings of the term that cut across any technical positioning of expatriates as temporary residents abroad. The living archive with its staff and volunteers thus breathes the tensions and politics of the expatriate. It also shows that even when people are given a specific definition, other readings of the expatriate are not fully displaced but coexist and trouble, even oust the official definition, revealing a restless and multiple expatriate.

In this context, translation is key for turning the expatriate into an archival tool. To make the expatriate work relies on translation not only between languages, but between cultures and contexts. Such translation also involves the resignification and reframing of identities, biographies and emotive states of being in the world.

Chow et al. (2017) recognise that expatriate does not have an equivalent in many languages, and many archive staff and volunteers similarly noted that in the non-anglophone world expatriate does not necessarily translate easily. For example,

> It's very much an English word. In my home country it still doesn't exist. I have an extremely hard time explaining what I do when I go back, what the archive does, in the first place, because it's not the mindset, it's not the culture. I can draw parallels and explain in different ways but the word as such I cannot really use. (Alina)

Some interlocutors related how they discovered the expatriate, like Diana: 'Well, before working at the archive, I didn't know very much about them. So, it is still a strange concept for many people. ... And I learned, along the way, that expats are just migrants [laughs].'

This is more than a matter of literal translation. The development of different languages is tied up with different historical experiences. In any language, the available words, labels, figures and cultural tropes of mobility also differ because of different histories of migration and closely related different historical and recent positions in international economic, political and sociocultural hierarchies. Today, expatriate is arguably most well known as an English term, and while increasingly used beyond anglophone contexts, any usage of this expatriate ties into Anglo-American social and cultural narratives, histories and geographies. The very fact that the expatriate has become 'globalised' is tied up with histories of Anglo-American imperialist supremacy that made English a global lingua franca, a 'global language with a high social status' (Leinonen 2012: 217). The term's increasing usage in turn reinforces the sway of the English language. Tellingly, while there was great mobility and circulation of workers in the former Soviet Union, we have not inherited a globalised Russian figure of the mobile worker. While expat has been increasingly adopted by non-native speakers, who cross sociolinguistic and by extension cultural and political boundaries by using the term in their self-identification, the category, though not unaffected by the encounter, has retained its anglophone character and situatedness. It is not without consequence when experiences which used to be made sense of in other languages and categories become subsumed under the term expatriate and incorporated into an expatriate archive with its particular constitutive narratives, priorities and silences.

Because of the noted issues of translation, because of the term expatriate's 'problematic connotations' and for many other reasons, countless people who live abroad temporarily do not self-identify as expatriates. Such seemingly private matters of identification have material consequences for individuals, but they also have implications for building an expatriate archive or curating a diverse exhibition of expatriate life in The Hague. One person I met in The Hague, who was originally from East Asia but had lived in Europe for some years, recalled hesitating to apply for housing advertised as for expats, because they did not know if they qualified as an expat. The issue of self-identification also came up in relation to the EAC's ongoing ambition to expand its collections to be more inclusive of experiences beyond those of privileged workers posted by multinational corporations (MNCs). It probably also played into the muted response to the EAC's repeated calls for contributions to its exhibition on expat life in The Hague. Some saw the issue as especially significant for 'non-Western' migrants because, as Lily explained, 'a lot of people who are not Western don't really embrace this term of expat and so if we want to reach out to them we might even need to do some re-branding'. It was suggested that 'Asians' in particular prefer alternative terms such as 'knowledge migrant' and sometimes it was specified that this was the case, because for them expatriate evoked Western imperialism. This, it was assumed, might be a reason why not many Asians had donated collections so far. While an astute observation, the emphasis on 'Asians' also revealed assumptions about who – other than Euro-Americans – might legitimately qualify as expatriate. 'Imperialism' and 'white privilege', 'guest workers' and 'refugees': such topics and competing categories linger and work, silently, to shape the expatriate archive. Many staff and volunteers enthusiastically embraced the archive's ongoing ambition and activities to diversify its collections. Yet there are limits to any project hoping to represent temporary migration, not least its arguably immeasurable scope. As Siddiqi (2020:742) notes in relation to Gopal's (2019) book *Insurgent Empire*,

> Decolonisation for Gopal does not lie in writing 'better' or more 'inclusive' histories. Rather, she seeks to undo the hold of imperial

archives on the structuring of popular and academic discourse, in the stories we tell ourselves about who we are, our relationship to past and present, our horizons of possibility.

Siddiqi's suggested way forward is not simply an inclusion of previously excluded subaltern experiences and perspectives, but a transformation of the epistemic frameworks and categories within which we understand these hitherto silenced stories, as well as their more readily told privileged counterparts.

As Stoler (2016) argues when she urges us to read colonial archives 'along the grain', working through the violent histories that have produced the current conjuncture and its figures of migration requires a critical analysis of documents of power. One hurdle to doing so is the unavailability of many documents that would allow us to 'read along the grain'. This includes papers held in corporate archives and the personal documents of those working these corporate machines, which might be stacked in attics or old suitcases. The Expatriate Archive Centre helps address this gap. As one staff member suggested, the EAC brings documents into the public domain that would otherwise very likely not have become public, and it might very well be the case that it is able to do so precisely by condoning certain silences. Importantly, the power relations spun by the temporary expatriate are not only silencing, obscuring and inhibiting, they are also enabling and productive (Obgorn 2003). The archive's positioning as an expatriate archive shapes the donations acquired. As argued, the expatriate as a decontextualised temporary resident abroad is not a self-evident understanding emerging from migration history, but a lens brought to it that engenders particular interpretations, makes visible certain connections, while obstructing others. A figure like the expatriate, with its particular racialised and classed connotations, might deter some potential donors but will entice others, whose documents can become important resources for critical research into power and privilege. Crucially, those willing to donate materials to an archive of expatriation might not be equally tempted to donate to an archive of (temporary) migration. Ultimately, the effects and possibilities of assembling historical documents around a figure like the temporary expatriate remain undetermined and depend as much on the documents themselves as on the analytical frameworks and strategies brought to them. That is, the realisation of the progressive potential of bringing into the public realm documents of privilege and power depends also on the perspectives, tools and skills we bring to the archive. The possibilities provided by an expatriate archive thus remain undecided, ambivalent, even paradoxical.

Conclusion

What emerges from institutional narratives and practices, collections and collaborations, and the stories and lived realities of staff and volunteers is not an expatriate defined solely by temporariness. In her work on 'colonial aphasia', Stoler (2016:163) speaks about 'categorical errors that produced distinctions that did not matter as they missed those that did'. Colonial aphasia does not necessarily involve a purposeful or conscious concealing, nor is it helpful to think in binary terms between preservation and silencing. As Bijl (2015:12) argues, something might be present but 'not meaningful within established frameworks'. In this chapter as throughout the book, temporality thus plays a key role in making the expatriate, but not necessarily in the ways expected or professed. Temporality on its own cannot account for the category expatriate. Yet, in its seemingly apolitical and technical innocuousness, temporality is nevertheless central to the work achieved with the expatriate. It is maybe not so much that temporality is an unworkable criterion as that it performs unstated work: providing an individualising and decontextualised framework that seems inoffensive but prescribes political blind spots; focusing on some distinctions while obscuring others; rendering colonial categories irrelevant, while recuperating their logics; offering particular interpretations and framings of past and present mobility and its governance. Expatriate emerges as an unruly category. The expatriate as the temporary migrant eclipses, but does not erase other meanings, which continue to taint it. The polysemic space that stretches beyond temporal definitions is intensely political: in the unacknowledged space of polysemy, sheltered by the temporal designation of the expatriate, postcolonial politics are at work as racialised, classed and gendered distinctions are enacted.

If the expatriate in the archival space does not adhere to its designation as the 'temporary resident abroad' it is highly productive as such, with paradoxical outcomes. On the one hand, it facilitates the collection and public availability of documents that allow 'studying up' (Nader 1972) to advance our understanding of the working of power and privilege. That is, the expatriate archive enables research into power, potentially partly through its very silence on the topic. Yet the temporary expatriate also has effects that run counter to the EAC's inclusive aims. A racialised and classed expatriate in universal guise occludes past and present structural inequalities, and risks 'sanitising' past and present migrations of their more unsavoury genealogies, functions and effects. This figure of the temporary expatriate is also central to The Hague's neoliberal marketisation as an international city, and becomes co-opted into the highly unequal immigration policies that the Netherlands have adopted, which both rely on the occlusion of imperial and colonial histories.

Making categories of migration is often seen as a state project. Over the past few decades, many countries have implemented 'hostile environments' and fortified their borders, while some forms of migration are being facilitated and idealised. The enacted distinctions might rest partly on labour needs and desired skills but they are also racialised, gendered and classed. In this context, the figure of the expatriate plays a useful role and reveals some of the ways in which temporality is one ground on which less meritocratic distinctions are enacted. Temporality here is much more than it seems. It is imbued with moral meaning and value judgement, and emerges as a technology of governance that allows the ordering and hierarchisation of populations and the reproduction of racialised and classed imaginations of good/bad migration on supposedly neutral ground. This category expatriate is not only made by state or municipal bureaucracies but always entwined with the making of individual stories and identities, with cultural projects and products, with the working of organisations ranging from MNCs to small archives. States are not the only relevant actors in the categorisation of migration, nor in the making and enactment of migration policies, or the social governance of and through migration.

Notes

1   All names and some personal details in this chapter have been changed to ensure anonymity. Unless stated otherwise, all interviews were conducted in 2016.

2 This refers to Sims (2017), published as chapter 7 of the same edited volume as Chow et al. (2017).

3 See also the EAC's collecting policy (EAC 2022b).

4 ACCESS was established in 1986 as a volunteer grassroots initiative of the members of the international community in the Netherlands, and serves the needs of the international community.

5 EAC 1.0016.2.09.

6 In 2016, Statistics Netherlands (CBS) replaced the term 'allochtoon' with 'person with a migration background'. In 2021, it announced plans to drop the Western/non-Western distinction, see www.cbs.nl/nl-nl/faq/specifiek/wat-is-het-verschil-tussen-een-westerse-en-niet-westerse-allochtoon- and www.cbs.nl/nl-nl/uitgelicht/het-gebruik-van-westers-niet-westers-door-het-cbs [Accessed 1 March 2022].

7 Under the *kennismigranten* scheme, 'skill' is measured by salary, with exceptions for those working in research institutions.

8 Shortened from originally eight years in 2019; see www.government.nl/topics/income-tax/shortening-30-percent-ruling [Accessed 31 January 2022].

9 Although, arguably, the 'knowledge migration' scheme legislates neither temporary nor permanent migration, it grants some migrants the right to decide for themselves on the temporality of their stay. The questions become: who gets assigned a temporality and who gets to imagine their own temporality, gets to have options, and on what grounds?

7

Studying expatriates: academic divisions of (skilled) labour

Since the late 1990s, IHRM literature has noted a diversification of international work and identified a range of alternatives to the 'traditional expatriate'. Among them, 'self-initiated expatriates' are the most widely studied, while 'inpatriates' are distinguished from expatriates by their opposite directionality of movement (from subsidiary to headquarters), and debate has arisen over whether (self-initiated) expatriates are 'migrants' or not. This chapter interrogates these new categories of IHRM literature and the debates about them, and finds that in its rush to serve multinational business, IHRM literature still helps normalise asymmetrical corporate power relations and geographies.

A few years before IHRM began noting the new international work, migration studies discovered expatriates – and at least initially followed IHRM's lead by studying expatriates as corporate assignees from the Global North. Chapter 1 critically examined this focus and the equation of the expatriate with the 'highly skilled migrant'. This chapter follows on from that discussion by focusing on the fact that the now burgeoning scholarship on expatriates highlights privileged migrants' invisibility in much mainstream migration research and theory. The chapter revisits well-known disciplinary self-critiques – focused on scholarship's methodological nationalism, its sedentary and marginality biases and ethnic lens of analysis – to discuss how migration studies helps reproduce popular imaginations of migrants as the global racialised poor and thus actively participates in the postcolonial governance through migration.

Finally, the chapter examines the relationship between IHRM literature and migration studies, which for the most part takes the form of mutual disregard. Despite the fields' many differences, the chapter argues, both are traditionally marked by a colonial aphasia that not only underwrites shared silences on coloniality and racism but also their very academic division of labour. That means that colonial aphasia is at work in the very constitution of the two fields as *separate fields*.

Beyond the 'traditional expatriate': the new international work in IHRM

Around two decades ago, IHRM scholars began to study what they called alternative types of 'international work'. Baruch et al. (2013) present no fewer than 20 types of 'international work', including 'globetrotting', 'ex-host country nationals' and 'sabbaticals'. A 2017 issue of the *Journal of Global Mobility*, the self-proclaimed '*Home of Expatriate Management Research*', includes articles on 'religious expatriates', 'talented young footballers' and 'professional sailors' spouses'. It is against this plethora of new forms of international work understood to result from intensifying globalisation that the 'traditional expatriate', Chapter 3's privileged intracompany assignee, is positioned as the historical norm. This chapter focuses on three now central categories of IHRM literature – the inpatriate, the selfinitiated expatriate and the migrant – and discusses how they redraw or resignify the conceptual boundaries of the expatriate and with what effects.

The inpatriate: culturally bound uses

The terminology of inpatriate was introduced in the early 1990s by Harvey (1993) and is defined as a move where 'host country nationals are transferred to the home country of the MNC on a permanent or semi-permanent basis' (Collings et al. 2007:205). Some authors include the inpatriate as a type of expatriate (Tung 1998; Shaffer et al. 1999) but most scholarship conceptualises inpatriates as 'a complementary model of global staffing' (Harvey 1993, 1997; Harvey et al. 1999b:459; 2000, 2005; Moeller et al. 2010; Williams et al. 2010). As Reiche (2006:1586) argues, 'expatriates and inpatriates differ along several dimensions and, therefore, have to be treated as distinct subsets of international staff'. Particular geographies underlie the assumedly abstract staffing category inpatriate, as reflected in Harvey et al.'s (1999b:459–464) 'model of inpatriation', where

> Many of these emerging markets (e.g., China, Russia, India, Indonesia, Thailand, Malaysia, Turkey, Philippines and several Eastern European countries, as identified by the World Bank) represent difficult relocation assignments for expatriate managers. The economic level of development is different, the cultural distance from Europe and the United States is significant.

Therefore,

> inpatriate managers would be located in the headquarters' organizational structure but would make frequent trips to the developing country subsidiaries ... By locating the inpatriate managers in the home country, top management would not experience the loss of control generally felt and partially exercised when using host-country nationals located in their own country.

Here as elsewhere, expatriates are identified as Euro-American, while inpatriates hail from 'culturally distant' and 'developing countries' (Harvey 1993, 1997; Harvey et al. 2005; Moeller et al. 2010). Such assumptions about the 'normal' geography of corporate labour mobilities seem so deep-seated that even when Reiche (2006:1578, 1572) finds a 'high share' of US inpatriates at a German multinational corporation (MNC), their article's framing narrative remains one about mastering challenges resulting from Western MNCs 'expanding their activities to culturally and institutionally more distant ... less developed economies'.

IHRM literature notes the unequal treatment of inpatriates, but instead of naming power, inequality and racism, its accounts more often normalise and sanction them. Harvey (1993:794) finds that inpatriates 'did not receive significant adjustments in salary or fringe benefits when being transferred to the United States'. Moeller et al. (2010:173) agree and further note that their 'level of influence in daily operating procedures is relatively low', which is explained with the 'necessity to learn the corporate culture' first. Reiche (2006:1585) explains the experiences of inpatriates from countries 'at the MNC periphery' at headquarters by arguing that 'individuals entering a new environment frequently become minorities which negatively impacts on their ability to exert social influence'. However, as ample research on the influence of parent country national (PCN) expatriates suggests, it is not 'minority status' that disempowers but uneven geopolitical and economic relationships. Indeed, mobilising the term 'minority' here skilfully deploys its 'quantitative and invidious' double meaning which (mis)represents sociohistorically produced racialised inequalities as an assumedly natural fact resulting from numbers (Fields and Fields 2014:27).

It is useful to remember what Fields and Fields (2014:95) call the 'race-racism evasion', 'through which immoral acts of discrimination disappear, and then reappear camouflaged as the victim's alleged difference' when reading Harvey et al.'s (2005) paper on inpatriate managers' potential 'liability of foreignness' and 'stigmatization' at headquarters. They describe a 'phenomenon of "collective reservation"', where,

> influenced by additional security concerns, home-country nationals tend to develop a checklist of questions relative to the incoming foreign managers ... And the one central concern relative to the 'invasion' of foreigners is: 'When are they going back home?' (Harvey et al. 2005:267–268)

Racism and xenophobia are presented as normal and maybe even rational reactions to the 'invasion' of foreign inpatriates. The authors then suggest solutions that accommodate rather than challenge this 'collective reservation', for instance helping organisations 'to determine which countries to recruit inpatriate managers from based upon the probability of acceptance by home-country managers' (Harvey et al. 2005:274). As the authors stipulate, home country nationals will believe that inpatriate managers of similar origin are 'largely homogenous' and they will judge them by 'the quality of nations from which inpatriates originate', so that 'For example, inpatriates from the United Kingdom may be perceived as quality managers. Conversely, inpatriates from Zimbabwe may be perceived as lower quality managers than home-country managers' (Harvey et al. 2005:273). (Aptly, it is Jaji's (2019) work on migration from the Global North to Zimbabwe which shows that the projection of racist notions about 'nations' onto citizens of that nation, which is here sanctified as legitimate management practice, also operates in migration studies' categorisation of migration.) Harvey et al. (2005:275) further leave racism/'stigmatisation' unchallenged when the responsibility for handling it is assigned to its victim in a patronising 'inpatriate program' that 'should allow inpatriates to both cope as well as empower them by recognizing that overcoming their potential stigmatization is not a depleting process but rather a replenishing and enriching process'. Additionally, such an inpatriate programme must help the US domestic manager 'better understand why another "special interest" group has crowded the ranks for advancement and key management positions' (Harvey and Buckley 1997:47). While the inpatriate emerges as a racialised foreign Other, the US home country manager is reconfirmed, vis-à-vis all those special interest groups that crowd 'his' space, as the familiar Anglo-Saxon white man.

IHRM literature fails to analyse the sociogeographical power relations that its category inpatriate codifies. Instead, it theoretically sanctifies racialised hierarchies in management also in its articulation of an essentialised and reified 'culture' that becomes simultaneously the key reason for, and biggest challenge in employing inpatriates. Feely and Harzing (2003:48) outline the key advantages of deploying inpatriates: 'They inject cultural diversity into the HQ operations, they provide communication links to the operations and institutions of countries from which they came and they offer a cost-effective alternative to situations where expatriates are less likely to succeed'. Moeller et al. (2010:175–176) concur that the 'primary rationale for employing an inpatriate is to provide multicultural diversity', and Harvey et al. (1999a:40) suggests that inpatriates 'infuse knowledge of the host country throughout the global organization and provide a means to enrich the management team by adding a multicultural perspective or cognitive diversity to global strategy development'. Inpatriates become overdetermined by their culture, even reduced to cultural exhibits or ethnographic objects of study when 'the actions of the inpatriate may provide valuable insight into how the inpatriate's home culture works as a whole, which could assist in entering the overseas market' (Williams et al. 2010:75).

Yet the key challenge for employing inpatriates is also their 'cultural distance', which means they need to be 'assimilated', 'integrated', 'trained', 'developed' and 'socialized' into the home organization (Harvey 1993, 1997; Harvey et al. 1999ab, 2000, 2005; Reiche 2006; Moeller et al. 2010; Williams et al. 2010). This represents a problem as their assimilation into HQ 'may necessitate extinguishing their unique insights and social, tacit knowledge of their home countries' (Harvey 1997:159) and 'the need to assimilate may override the cultural dimensions of the inpatriates and in essence they may become Westernized, thereby losing their value to the global organization' (Moeller et al. 2010:176). This not only confirms inpatriates as culturally overdetermined; this project of potentially obliterating assimilation stands in marked contrast to the expectation (put in equally violent terms) that expatriates will carry '"the corporate culture flag" into the global subsidiary organization' (Harvey et al. 1999b:461) and 'impose attributes of the HQ corporate culture onto the subsidiary organization' (Reiche 2006:1576). 'Culture' here encodes and theoretically sanctifies the postcolonial power relations defining multinational business. These power relations are exposed by such violent language as 'extinguishing' and 'imposing' and by the recuperation of colonial tropes like the 'native informant', the 'ethnographic gaze' and the 'civilising mission' for modern management. Again, an essentialised notion of culture fulfils rhetorical functions justifying inequality once accomplished by 'race'.

The self-initiated expatriate and the 'competition for talent'

Self-initiated expatriates (SIE) are probably the most widely studied of the new international workers. SIEs are associated with 'boundaryless careers', seen to move according to their own motivations, independent of employers. The phenomenon is said to have been first identified by Inkson et al. (1997:355), who suggest that

> the activities and knowledge-building of travelling entrepreneurs, small-company salespeople, plus the many people who travel Overseas when young to 'see the world' ... are ignored. In short, the expatriate experience covered in mainstream accounts of EA [expatriate assignments] represents only a small and limited sample of experience imported from overseas.

Many articles since have been dedicated to defining SIEs. However, the category remains debated. Cerdin and Selmer (2014:1290) suggest four conceptual criteria: '(a) self-initiated international relocation (b) regular employment (intentions) (c) intentions of a temporary stay, and (d) skilled/professional qualifications'. All four criteria are contested. Some authors critique that SIEs are unduly homogenised by being cast as (highly) skilled, as they 'may range from those at the margins of the labor market who travel abroad to work in low-level jobs to those at the higher end of the labor market' (Collings et al. 2007:204). Howe-Walsh and Schyns (2010) similarly lament the homogenisation of SIEs yet distinguish between those that leave 'to pursue a career' and those who leave for non-work reasons altogether, including romance or interest in a country. As discussed below, and in Chapter 6, 'temporariness' is notoriously difficult to define. Finally, it is also hard to define what counts as a *self-initiated* relocation, and therefore the very distinction between 'expatriates' and 'self-initiated expatriates' remains shaky. Some authors stress the need to 'conceptually and empirically separate these expatriate categories' (de Araujo et al. 2014:2501). Others instead argue that 'self-initiated' and 'assigned expatriates' are driven by essentially the same motivations (Cerdin and Pargneux 2010), and conceptual boundaries are blurred by constructs such as 'global self-initiated corporate expatriate' (Altman and Baruch 2012) and 'self-initiated organization expatriates' (Farndale et al. 2014). Ultimately, 'despite the growing interest in SIE [self-initiated expatriation] …, it remains unclear how it is theorized in management studies compared to other forms of mobility' (Al Ariss and Crowley-Henry 2013:79).

Despite such substantial disagreements, the literature also shows consistencies. It has been primarily white citizens from the Global North who have been studied as SIEs (Al Ariss and Crowley-Henry 2013). The category was coined with regard to New Zealanders (Inkson et al. 1997), developed further in a study on Finns (Suutari and Brewster 2000) and overall 'a great deal of research focuses on the careers of persons from developed countries' (Al Ariss 2010:342). Accordingly, Al Ariss and Crowley-Henry (2013:87) note that 'female or minority-group SIEs' constitute 'second class SIEs' and among the little research on SIEs from these groups, 'the focus is on White women SIEs from developed countries'. Even their poignant critique, by using 'ethnic minority' to refer to non-white women in a global analysis unwittingly reproduces IHRM's entrenched Eurocentric perspective. Designating the world's non-white majority as ethnic minority implicitly reproduces the white subject as norm and universalises white-majority countries as normal contexts for global analyses. Such geographical, gendered and racialised assumptions about SIEs shape research priorities. There is little if any research on SIE's workplace discrimination due to origin, racialisation or gender. Similarly, the lack of literature on topics such as immigration legislation and border struggles, including visa requirements, work permits and recognition of qualifications, evidences assumptions about where SIEs originate. As Al Ariss (2010:354) notes, SIEs are largely 'described as free agents who can cross organizational and national borders'. Not only SIEs' access to, but also their entitlement to unhindered movement is generally assumed. SIEs have been largely framed as an unproblematic, high-potential and desirable form of international movement, as 'valuable international human resources that benefit organizations and economies' (Al Ariss and Crowley-Henry 2013:79). Hence, research on SIEs is viewed as relevant for understanding 'global talent management' and the 'competition for talent', and contributes to 'careers literature' and 'careers theory' (Doherty et al. 2013; Farndale et al. 2014; Vaiman et al. 2015). Even when SIEs are positioned as 'a challenge to HRM strategy, policy and practice' and potentially 'difficult to manage', this is because of ultimately valued character traits associated with leadership and modernity: 'SIEs are individualistic and nonconformist, self-reliant, self-directed and proactive, operating with a high degree of personal agency and giving personal motives precedence in determining their psychological and physical mobility' (Doherty 2013:451).

The discovery of migrants

More recently, debate has arisen about the migrant status of self-initiated expatriates. Despite substantial efforts to delimit the relationship between these categories, there remains 'an ambiguity in the literature regarding the connection between SIE and migration' (Al Ariss and Crowley-Henry 2013:80). Some authors use 'migrant' and 'self-initiated expatriate' interchangeably (Howe-Walsh and Schyns 2010; Yijälä et al. 2012). Collings and Doherty (2011:368) count not only SIEs but even 'assigned expatriates' as migrants, noting that 'international assignees represent an important cohort of global migrants who enjoy a relatively privileged position in the labor market'. Other scholarship is more ambiguous. Van den Bergh and du Plessis (2012:142) define the category migrant in a way that includes self-initiated expatriates, but then consistently distinguish between 'migrants' and 'SIEs'. Similarly, Al Ariss (2010) explicitly labels his research participants 'migrants', whereas Al Ariss and Özbilgin (2010:275–276) refer to the same sample as 'skilled self-initiated expatriates' and as 'immigrants who self-initiated their expatriation on a permanent basis'. Crucially, given all these terms' multiple and overlapping definitions, all outlined decisions are possible and the choice thus emerges as a largely political one.[1]

Tellingly, most intellectual effort seems to have been expended on disambiguating SIEs from migrants (e.g. Baruch et al. 2013; Doherty et al. 2013; Andresen et al. 2014; Cerdin and Selmer 2014). Different elements are mobilised for distinguishing self-initiated expatriates from migrants, but 'temporariness' is generally taken as a 'key boundary-defining element' (Doherty et al. 2013:102). Indeed, the terminology SIE was coined in explicit opposition to the term immigrant, when an 'informal caucus' at the 2009 *Academy of Management Conference* decided on the term SIE to unify research that had previously used a variety of labels (Doherty et al. 2013). Here, researchers also decided that within the construct of SIE, the element '"expatriate" would distinguish between those who were leaving their home country on a temporary basis and those who were leaving on a permanent basis, i.e. immigrants – a related but qualitatively different group' (Doherty et al. 2013:99). Cerdin and Selmer (2014:1289–1290) thus argue that 'SIEs are expatriates. They are neither immigrants nor short-term travellers (sojourners).' Temporality, it is speculated, matters because immigrants 'could be motivated towards assimilation and integration, attempting to adopt new cultural values and norms' while expatriates 'may only adjust their behaviour, temporarily adopting new social skills to more easily get by in the foreign location, keeping their basic values and norms more or less intact' (Cerdin and Selmer 2014:1290). Yet the same authors acknowledge that temporariness cannot act as a clear-cut criterion. Cerdin and Selmer (2014:1289–1290) note that the intended temporary nature of expatriation 'is an inherently subjective criterion' and Doherty et al. (2013:99, 102) admit that plans 'may change over time' and temporariness 'may even be outside the consciousness of the individual at any given point-in-time, let alone within the gift of the researcher's knowledge'.

A criterion, temporariness, that is impossible to operationalise creates ambiguity that allows for other factors to come into play. The interpretative space opened up is filled with racialised and classed imaginations of migrants and with normative expectations and judgements about different mobilities. Texts silently shift between different meanings of terms and fill the ambiguity with potent examples and subtexts. The conceptual effort to separate SIEs from migrants emerges as primarily a boundary-marking exercise against an imagined Other. Accordingly, Doherty et al. (2013:103) acknowledge that in management scholarship 'SIEs are mainly portrayed as a privileged group' and 'migrants tend to be viewed as unskilled individuals or somewhat inferior'. That the distinction drawn between SIEs and migrants thus often adheres to logics other than those professed, is exemplified by Baruch et al. (2013). The article sets out to discuss the 'wide and growing array of different modes of international work configurations' (Baruch et al. 2013:2369) and distinguishes in total 20 types, among them (1) '"Traditional" corporate expatriation', (2) 'Self-initiated foreign work', (3) 'Immigration – legal, illegal and asylum cross-border moves' and (4) 'Temporary immigration'. The authors suggest that 'The time horizon for both legal and illegal immigrants is typically long term. In fact, the distinction between permanent immigration and expatriation may be considered legally in terms of the rights to permanent residency' (Baruch et al. 2013:2383). Yet immigration is here taken to include documented and undocumented, voluntary and forced movements that in actual fact vary widely in rights to permanent residence – which renders the authors' distinction between immigration and expatriation effectively meaningless. Moreover, given this definition of immigration, it is unclear how their fourth type of international work – *temporary* immigration – which includes those who 'do not necessarily take this step aiming for a permanent change of citizenship' (Baruch et al. 2013:2383) qualifies as immigration; or how it differs from 'self-initiated foreign work', including those 'who decided to move and work in another country for a limited time period' (Baruch et al. 2013:2377).

The authors write:

> Immigration is an age-old phenomenon and economic migration is already mentioned in the Bible (Jacob and his family migrate to Egypt). The motivations typically include push/pull factors (Baruch 1995), often coupled with the belief that immigration would enable one to gain a well-paid job. ... Other key motivations for moving abroad include security and survival. The UN world migration reports have consistently outlined that much migration in Africa happens due to the need to secure food or to leave areas in which one is persecuted.

... Some decide to move without entry visa or work permit, aided by illegal trafficking, which exploits the dire needs of desperate persons. (Baruch et al. 2013:2382–2383)

Highlighting the desire for a 'well-paid job' as a key motivation for migration suggests immigrants' lower socio-economic positioning in their country of origin. The wording 'belief' hints at potentially unfounded hopes, constructing immigrants as potentially naive and in need of guidance, possibly even threats to themselves and host societies. Providing an example from 'Africa' discursively racialises immigrants as black (reinforced further by the pointer below to immigrants' 'stigmatisation'), and highlighting hunger and persecution in Africa mobilises a colonially rooted imagination of a 'troubled continent' that feeds into a politically powerful 'apocalyptic image of a wave or "exodus" of "desperate" Africans fleeing poverty at home in search of the European "el Dorado"' (de Haas 2008:1305).

Further, although the authors write that all types of international work can be done legally or illegally, they explicitly associate immigration with illegality in its label and throughout the article. This not only contradicts the authors' claim that immigration is characterised by the right to permanent residence; more than anything, the repeated mention of 'legal issues' in relation to immigration works to discursively link immigration and illegality. Accordingly, Baruch et al. (2013:2383) write:

The major challenges for employing immigrants are to do with both legal issues, and the need to train the employees and help them adjust to the local culture and rules/regulations. Underemployment and social undermining, even stigmatization, may also pose problems.

That training immigrants is a major challenge suggests they lack skills, reinforcing their suggested lower socio-economic positioning; and to highlight that helping immigrants adjust to the local culture is a special challenge seems ironic given that expatriates' cultural adjustment has motivated decades of scholarly and commercial interventions. In effect, immigrants emerge as a particular Other: unskilled, poor, African. The text alternates between positioning this immigrant as potentially illegal/threatening and desperate/helpless, a dualistic figure that resonates with the colonial trope of the noble versus ignoble savage (Hall 1993). Ultimately, immigrants need either rescuing or controlling, but in any case they need 'managing'. And while SIEs are rational individuals with agency and potential, immigrants, from Jacob and his whole family to the evoked masses of refugees, come in multitudes driven by forces beyond their control (see also Leinonen 2012).

All in all, this account differs greatly from the celebration of SIEs as 'talent' and 'resource', and it appears that the main function of the figure of the immigrant is to discursively reinforce the value and desirability of expatriates. Tellingly, the term immigrant also slips into scholarship on inpatriates, further demoting them in IHRM's hierarchy of labour migration. In their above discussed work on the 'stigmatization' of inpatriates, Harvey et al. (2005:269) alternatively label inpatriates as 'immigrant managers' and 'ethnic/national immigrants'. Similarly, Harvey et al. (2002:1063, 1061) specifically mention 'high-potential immigrants from African countries', arguing that companies should 'allow the talented individuals from African markets to evolve into inpatriate managers in MNCs'. As Al Ariss and Crowley-Henry (2013:80) astutely observe, 'With few exceptions ..., when expatriates come from less-developed countries they are most frequently labelled as 'migrants' or 'immigrants'. No rational theoretical or methodological foundation is given to explain such terminology.' Yet, even critical literature slips into this conceptual separation. Despite all their conceptual boundary-pushing, Al Ariss and Crowley-Henry (2013:87) then note 'linkages and commonalities between migrants and SIEs', which tacitly assumes that migrants and SIEs indeed *are* separate groups.

Selective flexibility: new categories, old power relations?

IHRM scholarship suggests that international work itself rather than IHRM's focus is diversifying, when Moeller et al. (2010:174) designate inpatriation 'a comparatively new phenomenon' and Cerdin and Pargneux (2010:288) find that 'another form of international experience has emerged, known as self-initiated expatriation'. Farndale et al. (2010:163) even include 'immigrants' among MNCs' 'growing number of more flexible forms of global staffing'. This supposed novelty is as questionable as the positioning of the 'traditional expatriate' as ancient norm (see Chapter 3): both appear as temporal strategies of historical and sociostructural dissociation. Presenting self-initiated expatriation as new further disambiguates it from often negatively framed older *migration*, as when Cerdin and Selmer (2014:1281) introduce their paper on SIEs by contrasting 'international movement of workers in the past', which 'were often a result of political conflict and strife' or 'economic calamity and failure', with today's 'knowledge economy' where the 'worldwide demand for human talent seems limitless with well-educated people transferring between countries and contributing to the world economy'. Against the troubled movements of the poor and persecuted, leftover from a presumably pre-modern past, SIE mobility emerges as modern, necessary and beneficial for the global 'knowledge economy'. This temporal dissociation of SIEs from migrants is further reinforced by ignoring a wealth of relevant migration studies literature to claim that there exists a 'dearth of data and analysis' on SIEs (Peiperl et al. 2014:60) or that 'the research on self-initiated foreign work experiences (SFEs) is almost non-existent ... The research among such groups has just started' (Brewster and Suutari 2005:12).

Similarly, claiming the recent emergence of inpatriation obscures more complicated histories and has political effects. Management literature documented 'inpatriation' as early as the 1960s – however, inpatriates were then often labelled expatriates (see Borrmann 1968; Lesher and Griffith 1968; Franko 1973; Perlmutter and Heenan 1974). Rather than new, the inpatriate seems a new 'category invention' to differentiate and devalue South-North movements, possibly precisely because they present a growing challenge to the inherited institutionalised inequality of corporate management. Indeed, in 1959 Blair already documents subsidiary-to-headquarters transfers within Shell, while Holland (1976) and Zeira (1976:37) not only find such transfers 'a common practice' but both describe inpatriate roles that do not significantly differ from those outlined by Baruch et al. (2013) and experiences at HQ that resonate with Harvey et al. (2000, 2005; Williams et al. 2010). Zeira's (1976) discussion of the political nature of inpatriation (see Chapter 3) parallels Peterson's (2003:57) account of 'increased political pressure on the large MNCs to provide career opportunities, as well as a voice at the boardroom level, for their citizens from either the second or third level developing countries'. Seemingly unaware of this history, recent IHRM accounts link the supposedly novel phenomenon of inpatriation to Western MNCs' supposedly novel movement into less developed economies: 'by extending their operations to less developed economies, MNCs encounter unprecedented social, cultural and institutional gaps that complicate market entry' (Reiche 2006:1572). Inpatriates are required nowadays, Reiche (2006:1572) argues, because of 'the greater cultural distance along with poor business infrastructure related to these assignment destinations'. Such explanations have forgotten all about corporations in the earlier age of globalisation. In fact, as argued in Chapter 3, terms and conditions for 'traditional expatriates' were established in exactly those 'less developed economies'. While inpatriate is a new label and the practice might be gaining in significance, designating the phenomenon as *new* is a form of colonial aphasia that again dehistoricises and depoliticises postcolonial power relations.

Claims about novelty and tradition have political effects, contributing to a pervasive colonial aphasia that is central to IHRM literature's normalisation of the power asymmetries shaping labour migration. The category expatriate has exhibited a 'selective flexibility' – a very partial ability to stretch and accommodate certain new subjects, while consistently excluding others. The category inpatriate excludes and demotes what was previously understood to be a type of expatriation – just as such South-North migration might be gaining in importance – while SIE significantly broadens the category to bestow expatriate status – including connotations of skill and purpose, leadership and legitimacy – onto what are primarily Northern migrants. The figure of the immigrant, in turn, is newly mobilised as a potent Other, implying unskilled, disorderly, threatening mobility that thus reinforces the legitimacy, even necessity, of expatriate mobility. A significant element of IHRM scholarship thus engages in acrobatic conceptual manoeuvres to position expatriates not just as *not* migrants but *against* migrants. Mamdani (1996:7–8) has identified European colonialism in Africa as a 'regime of differentiation', variously called 'indirect rule', 'institutional segregation' or 'apartheid'. This is instructive for understanding MNCs' system of social categories, which can be understood as just such a regime, in constant flux yet with predictable outcomes. IHRM continues to sanctify highly unequal power geometries by reproducing what Pratt (2007:37) calls a 'Eurocentered planetary consciousness' rooted in the teleology and spatiality of Eurocentric modernity. Tellingly, when Harvey et al. (1999a:41) visualise their 'Model of Global Management' in a schematic diagram, the 'Globalization Process' is pictured as an arrow pointing from the 'Home Country Organization' towards 'Developing Economies'. Still, 'global management' implies head-quarters' access to and control over the globe, with HQ power and control personified in the movement of expatriates to 'local' host countries that – still – appear as static and bounded 'distant cultures', a passive elsewhere subsumed by the expatriate into an already ordered global.

Expatriates in migration studies: beyond the 'traditional migrant'

What migrant?

Some years before IHRM noted the 'new international work', migration studies began studying expatriates and, like IHRM litera-ture, it primarily studied corporate assignees as expatriates. Despite a shared interest in corporate assignees, conversations between migration studies and IHRM have been limited (cf. Findlay and Cranston 2015). As discussed in Chapter 1, migration scholarship adopted a more critical and macrostructural perspective than IHRM and situated corporate migration in the context of expanding capital-ism and, earlier on, the 'new international division of labour' (Salt 1988; Findlay and Cranston 2015). At the same time, especially earlier migration research reproduced IHRM literature's assumptions and gaps by framing and at times equating expatriates with highly skilled migrants, without addressing the colonial and imperial genealogies of this corporate migration and of its constitutive 'skill'. Today, expatriates are as likely to be framed 'global talent' as 'skilled migrants' (Beaverstock 2018), and Knowles and Harper's (2009:7) critique remains relevant for some research that continues to uncriti-cally frame expatriates as drivers of cross-border knowledge and skills transfers: a 'small, invisible, adaptable uncontroversial segment of migration'. Moreover, expatriate research participates in the whitening of the expatriate inasmuch as literature has employed the label expatriate primarily to frame examinations of white middle-class migration and thus arguably reinforced the notion that expatriates are normally that. Still today, there are plenty of historical and current 'expatriates' (both ascribed and self-defined) that are not studied *as expatriates* in migration studies and whose experiences thus do not inform our understanding of *expatriates* – ranging from Kenya's 'Asian civil servants' to Menon's (2016) Indian Shell workers, and the Kenyan women I met who had lived and worked in Uganda, Hong Kong or Nigeria as dentists or in advertising. The category expatriate that emerges from migration studies is still normally white and Western, regularly framed as skilled and moving temporarily, and thus resembles that of IHRM. It thereby stands in marked contrast to the 'typical migrant' of migration studies.

A growing body of literature documents how the figure of the 'migrant' is racialised and classed in media, public and political discourse and used in ways that defy legal or statistical definitions.[2] This raises the question of how migration scholarship has problematised this central category of research. Frequently, it has not done so at all. For example, Blinder (2015:82) finds that much research on attitudes to immigration 'tacitly assumes that "immigrants" comprise a coherent, agreed-upon attitude object, toward which individuals can express opinions'. Surveys thus typically do not define the term immigrant, or do so in ways that contradict official legal or statistical definitions. This is despite the fact that it has been argued since at least the 1980s that the public's immigrant is decidedly racialised and classed, and distinct from the statistical immigrant (Gilroy 1987). Wimmer (2009:255) too critiques that migration theories have ignored the historicity 'of the immigrant–national distinction' and 'take it as a given feature of the social world too obvious to need any explanation'. In scholarly debates, the category (im)migrant is thus often taken as self-evident rather than studied as a product of social and political struggles – struggles in which scholarship participates (Dahinden 2016). In this self-reflective void, a figure of the migrant emerges indirectly and aggregately, though never unanimously: from situated subjects at the heart of unsituated theory, from the framing of those researched, and from the uneven densities of research priorities and the gaps that mark the field. In the following, I discuss some ways in which studies of migration collectively, though not uniformly, produce a figure migrant. I do so by drawing on post/decolonial and critical race perspectives to reread the well-established disciplinary self-critique of 'methodological nationalism', as centrally articulated by Wimmer and Glick-Schiller (2002, 2003). This critique has had a profound impact on the field, exposing how migration studies are 'a child of the postwar era', when nation-states were at the peak of their power to direct, limit and influence both migratory movements and our thinking about them, as evidenced in the normalised view that the nation-state is the natural order of the social world and encompasses a more or less coherent social group, culture, polity and economy (Wimmer and Glick-Schiller 2002:307).

The (selective) sedentary bias

Particularly those working within the mobility paradigm have critiqued the sedentary bias of migration studies. Also Wimmer and Glick Schiller (2003:585) find that 'in the eyes of nation-state builders and social scientists alike, every move across national frontiers becomes an exception to the rule of sedentariness within the boundaries of the nation-state'. However, judging by the field's research foci, *some* border crossings have always been viewed as more anomalous and problematic than others. Bakewell (2008a) thus diagnoses a 'sedentary bias' specifically in research on African migrations, which he links back to colonial efforts to control labour mobility. Inasmuch as Euro-Americans themselves become positioned as immigrants, they are primarily located in the past, as an exemplary success story, or framed as skilled, often temporary, and relatively small segments of mobility that hardly upset the 'natural order' of spaces and bodies. Nineteenth-century European migration to the United States has become the 'paradigmatic case' informing theories of migrant incorporation (FitzGerald 2014) while contemporaneous migration flows in Africa and Asia, similarly significant in size and importance, are largely ignored (McKeown 2004). As McKeown (2004:155) writes, where historical African and Asian migrations enter Euro-American scholarship, they 'are usually described only as indentured migration subject to the needs of Europeans or as peasants fleeing overpopulation pressures, quite different from the free migrants that transformed the Atlantic world'. This historical oversight contin-ues in the scholarly disregard of present-day South-South migration which 'has only recently been "discovered"' despite being as large and consequential as South-North movements (Campillo-Carrete 2013:7; see also Anich et al. 2014). Instead, migration research focuses predominantly on migrations to Euro-America from the Global South or from its Eastern European peripheries. As Hayes

(2018:18) puts it, 'The distinctions between categories of migrants appear to demonstrate the coloniality of power, which mainstream migration scholarship inscribes in its analytical focus on people in the Global South moving to higher-income countries.' In these Northern 'host contexts', even the sedentary 'second' and 'third' generations become problematised as 'migrants' and discursively if not physically uprooted (Anderson 2013; Erel et al. 2016). Normalising Euro-America as host contexts helps reproduce their desirability and superiority, as discussed further below (Anich et al. 2014).

In sum, mainstream migration studies focuses disproportionately on a selection of global movements, and inadvertently normalises a migrant figure that moves from its 'Rest' to the 'West'. Because they do not centrally attend to the postcolonial context of migration studies' 'methodological nationalism', Wimmer and Glick Schiller (2003) arguably miss the fact that not border-crossing per se became an 'anomaly to be studied'. Migration scholarship has never problematised the movement of those labelled expatriates in the same way as the movement of those labelled migrants; indeed, for the most part, 'expatriate' movement was not recognised as something requiring study *as* migration at all. There was no 'sedentary bias' for expatriates; instead, a whole field of scholarship developed (largely unnoted my migration scholars) to examine how expatriate movement could be facilitated and best utilised. Expatriate mobility became framed as necessary, celebrated and thence not migration but its Other.

The ethnic lens of analysis

Another facet of 'methodological nationalism', as Wimmer and Glick Schiller (2003:584) discuss, is the equation of society, ethnicity and culture with the nation-state, 'which has induced generations of migration studies to measure and scrutinize the cultural differences between immigrants and nationals and to describe pathways of assimilation into the national group'. Scholarship of the 'ethnic lens' variety groups migrants first and foremost by (ascribed) ethnicity, and thus implicitly or explicitly frames migration as principally an ethnonational problem, also precluding research on e.g. class or political diversity within such groups, and shared experiences and solidarities across them. Accordingly, Glick Schiller (2009:19) suggests that 'the ethnic group has become the bedrock of studies of migrant settlement' and that 'casting the difference between native and foreigner in ethnic cultural terms has become so commonplace, it is hard to imagine this any other way' (Glick Schiller 2007:44; see also Wimmer 2009; Dahinden 2016; Runfors 2016). Such a framing of migration not only helps to sideline racism analytically – see Essed and Nimako (2006), Anderson (2013), and Lentin (2014) for a critique of the occlusion of racism in migration studies – but actually implicitly racialises migration. That is, rather than simply 'ignoring' race, the ethnic lens of analysis inadvertently reproduces racial thinking.

Wimmer and Glick Schiller (2003:591; see also Wimmer 2009) trace the 'ethnic lens of analysis' through different theories such as neo-assimilationism, immigrant integration and multiculturalism, all the way to migration studies' institutional and intellectual origins in the Chicago School of Sociology, which proposed

> a 'race-relations cycle' in which the process of acculturation and assimilation of immigrants occurred normally and naturally in the course of several generations (Park, 1950). Their casual use of the word race accepted the conflation of race and nation and placed together southern and eastern European immigrants, Jewish immigrants, and African Americans as all racially different from mainstream America, although with different degrees of distance that would affect their rates of assimilation. … The placing of African Americans with immigrants within the race-relations cycle, portrayed them as outside of the nation, although they had been part of the Americas since the period of conquest. This discursive move marked the nation as white and normalized the color line.

Absent from the Chicago School's medley of 'immigrants' are Northern and Western European newcomers, especially those who can claim the Anglo-Saxon whiteness ascribed to the US mainstream. Also absent are actual African and Afro-Caribbean newcomers, who are apparently subsumed within African American 'blackness' (Fields 2001). The Chicago School's incongruously assembled category immigrant, like much public discourse, conflates variously framed newcomers and long-established racialised minorities to position them as outside and Other to the nation: as 'immigrants'. Yet, what Wimmer and Glick Schiller (2003:591) describe as a casual 'conflation' of 'race' and 'nation' is precisely how 'race' is made – there is no 'race' other than imperfect concoctions of essentialised social categories. In other words, there can be no conflation because there is no independent 'race'. If ideas of 'nation' and 'race' have historically been co-constitutive, if different nations were once seen as different races, what does this imply for 'methodologically nationalist' migration studies? At the very least it means that it risks, if inadvertently, being also 'methodologically racialist': to partake in what Fields and Fields (2014) call 'racecraft'.

Indicatively, the work of the Chicago School was foundational also for the US sociology of race. The now largely separate academic fields studying 'race' and 'migration' thus trace a shared genealogy to the Chicago School and both remain significantly shaped by the School's 'ethnic paradigm' (Solomos 2003; Omi and Winant 2014). Led by the Chicago School, (some) US academics abandoned the then dominant biologistic notions of race and turned to ethnicity as a more progressive 'socially grounded, if not political, concept of race' (Omi and Winant 2014:6).[3] Ethnicity, with its appendage culture came to explain 'race' theoretically and reframe racialised subjects empirically (Fields and Fields 2014; Omi and Winant 2014). As Wimmer and Glick Schiller (2003:581) note, the study of ethnicity mirrored 'the nation-state project to define all those populations not thought to represent the "national culture" as racially and culturally different'. US ethnicity theory's main empirical case, and yardstick, was European immigrants' progression, via conflict and segregation, to eventual assimilation into the (white) mainstream (Omi and Winant 2014:26). This experience became generalised into the 'immigrant analogy' which proposed a 'natural' teleological assimilation of ethnically framed immigrant groups into a '"normalised" white society' (Omi and Winant 2014:43; see also Grosfoguel et al. 2014). This immigrant analogy was not only applied to later arrivals – as assimilation theory – but also became applied to African Americans who moved north within the US and whose struggle against discrimination was framed in the lexicon of integration (Omi and Winant 2014:34). In both cases, the ethnic framework obscured qualitatively different historical experiences and downplayed ongoing structural and state racism. Ethnicity theory and the immigrant analogy reframed racism in cultural terms and, at worst, reproduced racialisation in ethnic guise, explaining assimilatory 'failures' with 'pathological' group-internal factors, while leaving intact the assumed superiority of the (white) mainstream (Goldberg 1993; Omi and

Winant 2014). Thus, although ethnicity was meant to neutralise race thinking, the latter frequently came to inhabit it (Goldberg 1993; Gibel Mevorach 2007).

This (much abridged) critique of the ethnic paradigm is instructive for migration studies. In this analysis, migration scholarship of the ethnic lens variety arguably not so much ignores race as tacitly racialises migration. That is, it risks rendering racism invisible, while tacitly participating in the racialisation of migrants. Changed terminology does not necessarily imply changed analysis, and like 'race', ethnicity, culture or religion are frequently ascribed as pre-existing, static and unrelational characteristics of migrants, rather than studied as emerging from the migratory encounter (not least the research encounter) (Brubaker 2004; Wimmer 2009; Runfors 2016). The migrant emerges as an analytical category de facto marked by her ethnic – racial – Otherness. Inasmuch as this 'ethnic migrant' has traditionally been studied in and thus constructed against normatively white North American and Western European host contexts, the migrant remains coded as non-white.

And the critique of the ethnic paradigm also holds for ethnicity's often similarly homogenising and essentialising replacement culture (Barker 1981; Gilroy 1987; Stolcke 1995; Grosfoguel and Mielants 2006). As Lentin (2008:498) notes, much migration research risks 'anaesthetizing race and labelling it "ethnicity" or "culture"'. This construct of culture features heavily in IHRM, revealing important postcolonial parallels between migration studies and IHRM literature which, by way of ethnicity and culture, rely on the racialised framing and constitution of their subjects, in radically different ways yet with aligned power effects. Just like there is no 'sedentary bias' for expatriates, their lack of assimilation has hardly been problematised. While 'their' ethnically derived culture became an explanation for migrants' lack of social mobility, corporate and management culture became a central justification for expatriate privilege. Unlike migrants, expatriates were not expected to change culturally but to manage through 'cultural empathy' without 'going native' (read: assimilate). Expatriates became bearers of 'scientific management' techniques and 'cross-cultural competencies', expected to carry 'the corporate culture flag' into subsidiaries where it was 'locals' (potential-migrants-to-be) who remained bound by their culture, who had to 'integrate' into the corporate culture, whether as host country nationals (HCNs) or as inpatriates.

The marginal migrant

From the outset, research on expatriates saw itself as going against the migration studies mainstream that tended to prioritise the study of disadvantaged and exploited mobilities, often of South-North migrants. As Salt (1988:160–161) noted, most literature at the time, including that on highly skilled migration, focused on 'permanent moves from LDCs [least developed countries] to MDCs [more developed countries]' and their work thus faced 'the inadequacy of most existing migration models'. More recently, Anderson (2019:2) notes that 'migration studies continues to focus on the mobility of the poor and the subordinated'. In public as in much scholarly imagination, migrants 'do not voluntarily leave wealthy and power-ful countries for those that are less so, and they do not typically arrive at their destination possessing greater economic, cultural and political power than the majority of their hosts' (Croucher 2012:4; see also O'Reilly 2000; Fechter 2007; Anderson 2016). Both US and European scholarship have largely portrayed migration 'in terms of hardship, desperation and alienation' and placed emphasis on 'migrant marginality' (Croucher 2012:2). Silverstein (2005:365) notes a new 'savage slot' in Europe reserved for 'immigrants', functioning as states' new 'abject' and anthropology's preferred exotic 'Others'. Migration studies thus habitually assumes a disempowered migrant subject. Such assumptions often reveal themselves through seeming asides or casual examples. For instance, Salazar (2017:6) argues that 'We can identify many kinds of "movers": tourists and pilgrims; migrants and refugees; diplomats, businesspeople and those working for international organisations; missionaries, NGO-workers ....' Yet, what is the migrant here meant to signify, when the category can technically include all of these other movers as well? Salazar (2017:6) goes on to argue that 'movement generates positive "change", often conceived of as an improvement for oneself and one's kin (e.g. in the case of migrants) or for non-related others (e.g. in the case of NGO-workers)'. This casually equates 'migrants' with the poor or otherwise disadvantaged, seeking primarily self-interested social advancement, as opposed to altruistic middle-class 'NGO workers' – who in actual fact are often migrants too, who experience social mobility through their migration (Raghuram 2009; Hindman and Fechter 2010).

Some scholarship actively inscribes the figure of the migrant with notions of marginality. Accordingly, Nail (2015:3) intends to offer a 'philosophical history of the political subject we have become today: *the migrant*'. Beneath such generalising claims about an unspecified 'we', a marginal migrant reappears. Nail's (2015:2) key term associated with the migrant becomes 'expulsion', and when he distinguishes 'the "tourist" (the travelling academic, business professional, or vacationer) and the "vagabond" (migrant worker or refugee)', the migrant finds her familiar place among the marginal, excluded and exploited. Sara Ahmed (2000:81) warns against such 'fetishisation' of the migrant as 'granting the migrant the status as a figure (of speech) erases and conceals the historical determination of experiences of migration'. This is precisely what happens when Nail (2015:198) attempts to explain current Mexican immigration to the US with recourse to ancient Rome's 'barbarians':

> The second shared kinopolitical characteristic between the ancient and contemporary barbarian is that significant portions of the population of the United States believe that immigrants are naturally inferior, as they did in ancient empires. ... Thus, if it is true that many mobile subjects have also been treated as naturally inferior, it is precisely because this political idea was first invented and incarnated in the ancient barbarian and then redeployed historically.

This myth of origin does not explain but naturalises the subordination of the immigrant/barbarian as a historical constant dating back to (almost) time immemorial. The widespread belief in the 'inferiority' of immigrants (empirically unsupported) among the US population (from which immigrants are hereby excluded) is seen to spring from immigrants' mobility (i.e. originate with the mobile subject) rather than from a particular social context that systematically exploits and discriminates against *some* migrants, alongside some non-migrants.

Such a fetishised figure of the marginal immigrant a priori excludes *privileged* migrants from the category (im)migrant, an epistemic habit aided by the category expatriate. Many migrants of course do experience marginalisation and exploitation. But if these dimensions come to define the migrant as such, they create a homogenised and essentialised figure that risks naturalising socially constituted experiences with specific histories. That which becomes seen as a normal part of being a migrant easily goes unquestioned, even becomes unquestionable. Such a reified migrant also risks obscuring dimensions of marginalisation or subjugation that might have less to do with migrant status than with wider racialised, classed and gendered inequalities (Anderson 2013, 2016; Dahinden 2016). The migrant as already poor and exploited also renders invisible those migrants that in no way struggle, disrupt or transgress, and obscures how they benefit from and advance contemporary power formations through migration. These migrants instead become expatriates. Any deployment of the category migrant that *assumes* the migrants' subjugation therefore risks complicity with the postcolonial politics of the expatriate discussed throughout this book. At the very least, it allows some migrants, like a number of my interlocutors, to extract themselves from the category migrant while deploying it to engage in racialised and classed forms of Othering.

The postcolonial uses of methodological nationalism

Migration studies risks reproducing a reified figure of the migrant that is 'normally' poor and powerless, and moves from South to North or East to West. This analytical migrant is not accidental but reflects the postcolonial politics of knowledge production on migration. The critique of methodological nationalism in migration studies is well established but is less often articulated in explicitly post/ decolonial terms, which requires specification of *which* migrants become seen as problematic, in *which* nation-states, and *which* geographies old and new are rendered invisible by methodological nationalism. As Gilmartin (2017) notes, to understand what coloniality of power means in relation to migration requires understanding what gets construed as migration in the first place. Wimmer and Glick Schiller (2003) effectively trace migration studies' coming of age through the entangled rise of the social sciences and the nation-state. While they discuss the role of colonialism and racism in the pre-World War I era and note the transborder, often imperial context in which concepts such as a 'national population' were developed, they do not analytically centre the same racism and decolonisation in the post-World War II era, when empires fractured into supposedly separate nation-states and imperial populations were legally and socially reframed accordingly. Wimmer and Glick Schiller (2003:577) argue that 'the global forces of transnational capitalism and colonialism that reached their apogee precisely in the period when social sciences formed as independent disciplines left few traces in the basic paradigmatic assumptions of these disciplines and were hardly systematically reflected upon'. Yet, while maybe not systematically reflected upon, they did leave traces, not least in their very invisibility as topics of discussion.

The new imperial histories paradigm suggests that we need 'to recast the nation as an imperialized space' where the nation is not 'the sovereign ontological subject' but 'an unstable subject-in-the-making' (Burton 2003:4–5). The nation here appears a lot less secure than in many critiques of methodological nationalism. As outlined in Chapter 1, the emergence of nation-state control over movement was a historically fraught and contested process centrally bound up with transimperial projects of white supremacy. Following the mid-twentieth-century 'racial break' and reflecting ongoing imperial inequities, nation-state building became entwined not with the constitution of a more just new international order (Getachew 2019) but with racialised bordering and ordering: 'race is not neutral and not dissociable from nation building' (Lentin 2008:493). Mongia (2018:113) similarly notes that 'A blurring of the vocabularies of nationality and race is a founding strategy of the modern nation-state that makes it impossible to inquire into the modern state without attending to its creation in a global context of colonialism and racism.' Racialised nation-states were achieved also through the making of migration as a legal and sociocultural framework to govern populations. That is, migration was a productive material and discursive site and tool for the transformation of metropoles and colonies into nation-states, and of imperial space into an uneven nation-state system. These protracted processes of imperial disintegration made movers out of many people, while persistent imperial power relations rendered some of them migrants, and others expatriates. Because they do not centrally attend to this postcolonial context, Wimmer and Glick Schiller (2003) arguably miss the fact that not border-crossing per se became an 'anomaly to be studied', and there was no 'sedentary bias' for expatriates, whose (lack of) assimilation was hardly problematised.

Migration studies did not develop solely to understand or critique these matters. At least some knowledge production on migration was a complicit part of this racialised postcolonial governmentality. The institutionalisation of migration studies has to be situated in a postcolonial context, and if not analytically reflecting on the uneven postcolonial political economy underwriting knowledge production on migration, and the geopolitical uses this knowledge is put to, migration studies risks producing complicit knowledge – for instance by constructing and demarcating certain movements, often those of previously colonised subjects, as in need of inquiry, control or restriction (Grosfoguel et al. 2014). Hence, Grosfoguel and Mielants (2006:181) write:

> Since the 1980s,[4] the core zones of the world-economy have viewed immigration as a 'problem' and applied social science has become instrumental in creating an 'appropriate' apparatus to count, classify, and 'deal with' these strangers, the existing periphery within the core. Social sciences continue the colonial role inside the metropole by producing knowledge, complicit with the white-European/Euro-American state policies, of providing ever more models and theories to regulate and handle immigration.

Indeed, knowledge production on migration has a colonial genealogy, entangled with yet distinct from that of nation-state building. As Mongia (2018) shows, already in the very early twentieth century, white Canadians responded to the arrival of a 'relatively insignificant' number of Indians with an 'eruption' of 'mechanisms for generating, obtaining, and collecting knowledge' on this migration.

Many of the nation-states that became migration studies' prototypical host contexts developed out of imperial metropoles or white-ruled dominions. Former colonies and other peripheral countries, in turn, were positioned as sending states – ignoring the fact that they, too, received migrants including privileged ones and built nation-states through the racialised ordering of people. As Jaji (2019) similarly critiques, the classification of countries into sending or receiving countries largely reflects their position in hierarchies of geopolitical and economic power. This normative directionality of migration further inscribes powerful countries with desirability and modernity, rhetorically bolstering material inequalities. Migration scholarship never adopted the position of nation-states per se, as many critiques of 'methodological nationalism' have it, but has tended to adopt the position of powerful Northern states (Grosfoguel and Mielants 2006; Cervantes-Rodriguez et al. 2009; Grosfoguel et al. 2014). Different states hold widely varying power to control the movement of people, capital and goods – and to shape knowledge production on migration. Crucially, the rich countries of the Global North provide disproportionate research funding and host many of the universities and research centres where knowledge on migration is produced.

At the time when IHRM emerged to theorise the management practices of US corporate imperialism, migration studies thus became similarly entangled in the reorganisation of imperial political power. Migration scholarship participates in constituting migration as a material and discursive site for the translation of colonial into postcolonial power relations. As Raghuram (2009) has noted, methodological nationalism has postcolonial effects, not least the occlusion of past and present imperial geographies, connections and responsibilities (see also Mongia 2007; Bhambra 2017; Andrews 2020). As traced in Chapter 2, methodological nationalism was useful to many Euro-American states precisely because they were *imperial* states transforming themselves into nation-states, eager to hide their imperial constitution and shed their imperial responsibilities: to 'border the spoils of empire' (El-Enany 2020). Normalising the nation-state as a universal, equal and ahistorical social form and the individualised migrant as a neutral category, thus implies participating in imperial projects. Methodological nationalism also allowed the recuperation of racialised epistemologies and logics in a new categorical guise. Rather than radically transform ways of social categorisation crafted in the service of white supremacy, racism was translated into new language. Arguably, framing some mobilities as 'migration' was a strategy of imperial and colonial elites to deal with their disintegrating empires and reproduce – by other means – colonial power relations between colonially delimited groups of people. As the 'native', 'subject races' and 'the oriental Other' became the migrant in much political discourse and some scholarship, the former white settler became, to many, the 'expatriate'

– permanently temporary in their post-colonial 'host contexts' inasmuch as permanently defined by their, to many, superior national/racial origins.

Wimmer and Glick Schiller (2003:591) suggest that immigrants became seen 'as destroying the isomorphism between nation and people and thus a major challenge to the ongoing nation building project'. But maybe the idea of the migrant was not so much a major challenge as a major opportunity. Maybe, making migrants out of former colonial subjects was useful to deny them their material and political rights. Just like constructing the figure migrant as 'a major challenge' and quintessentially Other has been highly productive in creating the nation-state, and for governing not only migrant Others but society more generally. After all, the migrant is what allows an isomorphism of nation and people to be imagined – just like the 'fantasy citizenship of just rewards, decent work, and a social safety net' increasingly relies on 'migrant exceptions' (Anderson 2016:61). From this vantage point, methodological *nationalism* can be understood as a racialised technology of governance with an *imperial genealogy*. The disruption of these imperial projects is what is ultimately also at stake in the need to 'overcome the nation-state and ethnicity-centred epistemologies that continue to inform much of migration research' (Dahinden and Anderson 2021:9).

The imperial uses of methodological nationalism also lie in its obscuring of how corporations produce and profit from unequal migration, from mobilising labour differently – and from positioning some movements as not migration at all. Private actors ranging from major multinationals and the corporate cross-cultural training industry, to tax advisers and *InterNations* intervene in processes of migration and hasten the commercialisation of movement in the context of neoliberal globalisation. Multinational businesses, like international NGOs and institutions of international governance, are important makers and shapers of migration. Their HR policies and norms, routines and discourses produce deeply unequal mobilities and should be key concerns of migration studies. IHRM literature is squarely involved in this process, and like migration studies normalises particular geographies. IHRM normalises the imperial geographies of multinational business by reproducing a HQ-centred and, if one goes by its figure expatriate, a Euro-American-centred world managed by normative whiteness. This world is not primarily divided into nation-states. Nation-state borders are not central topics in IHRM. Indeed, reading IHRM, one might be forgiven for thinking that they mattered only tangentially in the present-day world, a nuisance but not a force. Much more relevant, it seems, are cultural boundaries that usually map onto the boundaries between headquarters and subsidiaries. In IHRM, a powerful corporate HQ thus becomes the centre, with its subsidiaries arranged around it according to their smaller or greater 'cultural distance'. Notions like globalising or internationalising evoke the teleological temporality of a HQ-driven modernity spreading outward, always bound up with access to and control over 'the global'. Here, belonging is defined in relation to the corporate HQ by notions like 'corporate citizenship' (Holland 1976), while integration might refer to the integration of the subsidiary into the global enterprise, or the integration of HCNs into the subsidiary management team hitherto dominated by PCN expatriates (Youssef 1973). IHRM's geography evidences the significant power of MNCs in the post-war international political economy, especially those headquartered in the Global North (although, reflecting shifting geopolitical and economic realities, growing research now also attends to Chinese-headquartered MNCs (Harvey 2014; Morgan 2018)). While the migrant in migration studies normalises an uneven system of nation-states, the expatriate of IHRM organises an imperial corporate form. Yet a methodologically nationalist migration studies does not recognise any of this as part of its scholarly remit.

Imperial and colonial racialised hierarchies were reworked, reformulated and recast, but not completely overcome in IHRM and migration studies' ordering of movement. Categories like expatriate and migrant are a technology 'through which the discussions are governed and its subjects produced' (Raghuram 2009:31). They allow some analytical connections to be made, while occluding others. While this is changing, differentiations between expatriates and migrants continue to enable the occlusion of inequalities and condone racialised silences and epistemic habits. As a category of *mobility* that ostensibly has little to do with *migration*, expatriate thus organises its own academic discipline concerned with supporting 'corporate assignees', with talented 'self-initiated expatriates', with 'global leaders' and 'borderless careers'.

Academic divisions of labour

IHRM can be read as simply another migration studies, and the fact that it is not recognised as such is revealing about the politics of migration. Scholarship creates borders, including through its organisation into disciplines, and these borders stand in a co-constitutive relationship with social and political ones. That is, bordering academic fields take part in the production of other borders, borders drawn around groups of people, within organisations or between territories, borders in our mind, and borders between migration as problem and mobility as potential. While the practice of bordering might be indispensable for making sense of and acting in the world, this also implies an ongoing imperative to reflect. As Mohanty (2003:2) argues, 'Feminism without borders is not the same as "border-less" feminism. It acknowledges the fault lines, conflicts, differences, fears, and containment that borders represent.' The bordering of these academic fields, as much as the bordering of their categories, constitutes a geography of power that reveals the coloniality of knowledge production on migration.

There is a potent division of labour between IHRM and migration studies in knowledge production on migration which depends on the fields' separation. The silent 'disciplinary borderland' of these adjoined fields is racialised and classed. Migration research largely ignores IHRM literature as a practice-oriented literature, and hence fails to critically interrogate it. Yet, IHRM literature, and the 'methodologically corporatist' world it helps construct, should be of great interest to migration scholars, given their substantial impact – possibly greater than migration studies' own – on producing migration and shaping public, corporate and political conceptions of migration. Moreover, migration studies could productively deploy such an engagement with IHRM to reflect on its own disciplinary habits and assumptions. Despite their many differences, the two fields reinforce each other in significant ways, also through their unalike research focus and framing, and their disciplinary disconnect. As discussed, the study of IHRM has been closely tied to its practice, and supporting 'expatriates' has become big business (Jack and Lorbiecki 2003; Hindman 2007, 2013; Cranston 2014, 2016). In this, IHRM spearheads a wider trend of converging universities and business as increasingly 'both are involved in translating knowledge into marketable products' (Mohanty 2003:182). Migration studies, in turn, has established its relevance primarily by speaking to Northern policymaking. As Anderson (2016:n.p.) notes, the very term migrant 'is a policy term that has become an analytical term'. One reason for migration studies' policy focus is its aim to speak back to the powerful, 'to nuance policy makers' and the general public's understandings of migration' (Anderson 2019:35). Another reason is the need for research funding, largely provided by rich and powerful states and supranational organisations via national funding bodies tasked with tackling 'issues of "national relevance"' (Wimmer and Glick Schiller 2003:579). As Bakewell (2008b:432; see also Anderson 2017) argues for forced migration studies, in particular,

> the search for policy relevance has encouraged researchers to take the categories, concepts and priorities of policy makers and practitioners as their initial frame of reference for identifying their areas of study and formulating research questions. This privileges the worldview of the policy makers in constructing the research, constraining the questions asked, the objects of study and the methodologies and analysis adopted. In particular, it leaves large groups of forced migrants invisible in both research and policy.

It does not help that the ongoing neoliberal restructuring of research practice and funding renders research funding increasingly project-based and tied to an impact agenda, with increasingly precarious academics tasked to justify their positions by proving 'impact', 'stakeholder engagement', 'policy-relevance' or by 'commercialising' their research. While there exist many reasons why migration studies has done so, one result of adopting the nation-state as a natural framework, its concerns as a key agenda and policymakers as prime conversation partners has been that migration studies participated not simply in nation-state building but in *racialised* nation-state building (Lake and Reynolds 2008; Mongia 2018). The academic division of labour discussed in this final chapter thus reflects a postcolonial political economy of knowledge production on migration.

Migration is a discursive and material site of governmentality, a key site for the negotiation of power and production of social inequality today. What and who we understand and study as migration and migrants – and who we excise from the category and framework – are critical questions here. The division of labour between IHRM and migration studies in knowledge production on migration contributes to the separation of the expatriate and migrant, their differential positioning and valuation. Put simply, the former became a (human) resource to be studied on behalf of corporations, while the latter became a problem to be studied from the vantage point of nation-states. Both needed to be 'managed' and 'moulded' but in radically different ways. Despite their mutual concern with migration, the two fields thus remain largely separate, a disconnect upheld from both sides and driven by diverging concerns as much as shared biases – where the former aims to support business practice, the latter largely answers to state concerns, yet both largely overlook the postcolonial and racialised power relations shaping their topic and the categories they work with. The border between migration studies and IHRM is racialised and classed and helps maintain both fields as racialised and classed formations. This division of labour and the academic border it creates need to be dismantled – but not through selectively stretching the category expatriate to include selected others, or by framing expatriates as skilled temporary migrants who are different from and possibly less problematic than other forms of migration.

Notes

1 Although most 'expatriates' (self-initiated and assigned) are (im)migrants according to the UN definition of long-term (im)migrants as those who move to a country other than that of their usual residence for at least one year (UN DESA 2002:11).
2 See for the European context in different time periods, for example Gilroy 1987; Wrench and Solomos 1993; Solomos 2003; Silverstein 2005; Anderson 2013, 2019; Dahinden 2016; Anderson and Blinder 2017.
3 This also reflects the systematic exclusion from academic institutions of African American scholars like W. E. B. DuBois who had long produced critical scholarship on 'race' and challenged the racism of mainstream social science (Omi and Winant 2014).
4 Although, according to Gilroy (1987) and Solomos (2003), this needs to be dated back to at least the 1940s or 1950s.

Conclusion

The current conjuncture is marked by increasingly bifurcated mobility regimes. Some movements are demonised while others are glorified. Some border crossers are greeted with violence, while others are impelled to mobilise. Especially in the rich countries of the Global North migration has become one of the most hotly debated topics and a key site for the development of new forms of governance and profit generation. States are devising new and intensifying old technologies of control and surveillance and increasingly, yet always selectively, securing and proliferating their borders – ostensibly all in response to migration. All over the world, right-wing groups and governments justify and popularise racist and xenophobic agendas by framing them as concerns about migrants, who are fast becoming quintessential social Others. Meanwhile, citizens of the Global North and to some extent wealthy Southern citizens are able to move around the globe ever faster and with fewer restrictions – and are increasingly doing so, whether for a visit, a season or a lifetime. New normativities are fast developing around 'travel' and 'international experience', with 'global' or 'cosmopolitan' tastes and habits constituting increasingly valuable forms of cultural capital. While 'invasions' of 'illegal immigrants' and 'bogus asylum seekers' supposedly require more (de)fences, 'highly skilled migrants' are a coveted 'resource' for 'knowledge economies' in the 'global race for talent'. As citizenship and residence become purchasable for 'investor migrants' and 'digital nomads', bordering becomes big business and migration is increasingly enunciated within a market logic, commodified according to the needs of capital and, supposedly, 'consumers'. Heated debates about belonging, citizenship and its associated rights result not only in new logics, apparatuses and economies to discern 'legitimate' insiders and aspirants; they transform social subjectivities and relations, hierarchies and exclusions. More recently, the Covid-19 pandemic has produced new logics of (im)mobilisation, and while what has been dubbed a global 'vaccine apartheid' implies immense profits for some, the cost of movement has risen for many. So far, the bordering of the pandemic seems to compound rather than obliterate historical geopolitical and economic fault lines.

At this political conjuncture, the need to study how inequality and power are (re)produced through the ordering of mobility is only growing in urgency. These complex, frequently incoherent and even self-contradictory processes are not best captured by neat narratives about the eradication of borders or the restriction of movement. They are better understood through detailed attention to the creeping differentiation, tense multiplicities and institutionalised inequalities of mobility regimes that often work by logics other than the meritocratic ones professed. Migration categories carry these tensions. They are not technical or neutral but historically produced by and productive of broader power formations. After all, fundamental to the differential treatment of people is their divisioning in such a way that their differential treatment can be justified. Historical inequalities are encapsulated in the potent if not uncontested conceptual disambiguation of the expatriate from its various local and migrant Others in public debate as much as some scholarly work. Migration studies is implicated in the governmentality of and through migration, not least through its role in constituting what counts as migration, who counts as a migrant, what aspects of migration need researching and what kind of migrant the expatriate might be. In parliaments, talk shows and academic journals, many conversations about 'migrants' are not at all about those migrants captured by official immigration statistics or law, while seemingly unrelated conversations about 'expats' are, by all definitions, about migrants. Such debates allocate value and worth rather than achieving neat and neutral classification. And sometimes they allocate value and worth under the cover of neat and neutral classification. Deliberations about technical definitions or classificatory matters, statistical number games or better facts about migration can only get us so far if they leave furtively racialised, classed and gendered categories intact. That is, we can ultimately neither fully understand, nor effectively address inequalities in migration if debates take place on the treacherous terrain laid out by categories like the expatriate and the migrant. An effective response to the politics of migration requires the deconstruction of its categories.

Migration categories are at the heart of the insidious ways that intersecting material and symbolic inequalities are enacted today, and any project for social justice thus needs to dissect and dismantle them. The work of this book has therefore been to attend to the category expatriate, to crack its veneer of neutrality, understand its historical formation and political operation, and make visible the multiple logics of power coursing through it. This book argues that it is crucial to move beyond debates about who *really* is an expatriate and what might be the *true* meaning of the term. Instead it has asked what the stakes are in such debates, what is achieved by positioning some movers as expatriates and others as not, how such positioning is achieved and what this allows us (not) to see. In short, the book has tried to reorient analytical habits from employing categories like expatriate towards studying them. Key to doing so is the recognition that the expatriate is a polysemic and malleable category. It is flexibly bordered and internally ordered according to changing logics, yet with consistently exclusionary outcomes. It comes with various meanings attached, and is invested with conflicting emotions; it is mobilised for varying personal and political projects in widely differing contexts. If polysemy arrests social history, then the expatriate's past transformations speak about social change and broader reconfigurations of power and privilege. An appreciation of the polysemy of the expatriate is also crucial to understanding its political sway. A pronounced multiplicity of meaning and the 'polysemic games' (Kunz 2020a) this enables are essential to how the expatriate operates today. Throughout, the book therefore locates the varying usage of the expatriate in the context of social, political and economic struggle, and explores the material and discursive work the expatriate performs in negotiating broader social inequalities and power relations.

Studying migration categories instead of studying migrants invites reflection on the questions we ask, methods we use and sources we consult. It also invites reflection on how the expatriate has (not) been used in studies of migration and what this says about the field and its participation in the postcolonial politics of migration. How we study migration is closely entangled with the politics of migration.

Methodology is theory inasmuch as it helps construct the very realities we research: methodologies centrally impact what is made (in)visible, who is (not) heard and on what terms. The methodological approach chosen here is also a choice against other approaches to studying migration. I have tried to study migration in a way that avoids methodological nationalism, its ethnicity-centred epistemology and the pronounced marginality bias which shapes not only migration studies but the empirical social sciences more generally; in a way that is historically attuned and analytically situates migration within broader social processes and power formations; that avoids reifying the distinction between movers and those that stay put, and shifts the focus from individualised migrants to the sociocultural making of migration. Doing so has surely relied on other generalisations and presuppositions. I also encountered various hurdles to 'studying up' (Nader 1972), including the (in)accessibility of corporate archives due to their privatised and scattered nature and the at times difficult access to elite category makers. Studying power and privilege often requires improvising and scrabbling, piecing together fragments and reading between the lines. A constant challenge is how to study the powerful without prioritising their voices and how to become aware of and abide by gaps that point to erasure and violence, even if one cannot fill them.

Conceptualising the expatriate as a social category opens up myriad analytical openings to inquire how it is discursively and materially realised. The expatriate directs bodies in space, shapes how bodies are presented, seen, felt, experienced, talked to and treated. It helps fashion subject positions, identities, groupness and social relations. It borders and connects, assembles and orders, shapes places and events, is read into and takes part in shaping urban space. The expatriate activates spatial imaginations and sets temporal horizons. It assembles literatures and archives, organises theories of migration and allocates value, expertise and purpose. It informs strategies of urban marketisation, justifies the need for special visas and the right to a family life, and allows differential treatment at borders or in municipal bureaucracies. Businesses use it to hail customers and mould employees, create needs, sell services and position themselves on the map of global (labour) markets. The expatriate suggests some should be moved and mobilised, while many others are grounded. The expatriate does all this and more as part of a growing consortium of migration and mobility categories, including everyday folk figures, cultural tropes and derogatory slurs, staff and analytical categories, statistical and legal terms. Understanding this genre of migration categories, and the relationships and tensions within it, is central to understanding the politics of migration.

I have thus argued for studying migration categories not solely as legal or statistical categories but more holistically as social categories. Accordingly, my focus has not primarily been on the nation-state, state practices and laws, or political debates. This is partly because the state is arguably overemphasised in research on migration (categorisation), to the detriment of our understanding of how other actors such as multinational corporations (MNCs), labour intermediaries and service providers shape migration and its categories. Also, the category expatriate is powerful despite (or maybe because of) *not* being a legally or statistically defined category in most contexts. However, if the state is not the key protagonist in making the category expatriate in the sites that this book visits, this does not imply that nation-states are not important. Rather, states' ostensible restraint when it comes to defining and governing the category expatriate is itself a finding to be considered.

One key arena where the expatriate *is* used today is the conjoined world of international business, development and governance, where 'expatriate' refers to often elite employees sent abroad in the service of organisations. Not only do the migrants thus designated regularly take part in building uneven economic and political relations, but the category expatriate itself plays a role in fashioning these relations. The expatriate as deployed in corporate practice and IHRM literature is not straightforward or neutral but productively entangled in the potent inequalities and power asymmetries shaping international business and the migrations it engenders. That IHRM's privileged labour migrants are still frequently white, male and from the Global North, or normatively imagined as such, attests to the imperial and colonial roots of today's global economy. And while these migrant demographics are to some extent changing in line with broader shifts in geopolitical and economic power, practices of imperial corporate governance have their own mobile trajectories worth tracing, as suggested for example by literatures on the management strategies of Japanese and Chinese businesses. This also shows the fruitfulness of studying the HR policies and categories of internationally active organisations as racialised and gendered mobility infrastructures, and as technologies that shape migration and our imagination of what migration *is*. Moreover, tracing the postcolonial genealogies of such infrastructures needs to cut across the profit/non-profit divide and trace shared genealogies of 'staff rotation' across development, business and governance. Corporations, not just nation-states, produce migrants and citizenship, belonging and borders, hierarchies and difference. HR policies of international organisations are migration policies too, that produce, allow, forbid, regulate, mould, discipline, channel, divide and (il)legalise movement.

In this context, the expatriate also reveals the varying temporalities of decolonisation. While political administrations have been formally decolonised in most contexts, though by no means all, decolonisation is arguably an unfinished project in international business. While the expatriate has been diversified, it has not been decolonised. Diversification has rather implied including 'contingent insiders' (Erel et al. 2016) while keeping undemocratic and unmeritocratic structures in place and reproducing whiteness as norm and normative. The white middle-class man has been reproduced as the prototype of the skilled migrant, knowledge migrant or global talent, which further helps create professional labour markets and privileged migration routes that are structurally easier to access for those with Western citizenship and credentials. Materially and discursively, the normativity of whiteness-as-management is reproduced (Roediger and Esch 2012). Corporate work and management hierarchies, HR policies and corporate discourses of culture remain key spaces for the reproduction of racialised and gendered social inequality today.

Yet whiteness is itself vague and varying in meaning and membership, and local racial regimes matter in making the category expatriate, which might be constructed against the 'African' and 'Asian' 'local' in Nairobi or the 'Moroccan youngster' in The Hague. The expatriate is thus articulated within shifting racial geographies, from the tripartite European-African-Asian to a white/non-white binary superimposed onto the world through the imagined 'West' and its 'Rest'. Following the expatriate allows us to witness these shifts in the category's racialised articulation and also to witness the translation of biologistic and cultural colonial racism into a postcolonial racism without race, encoded in the languages of culture as well as economics, business and management. Management itself – whether of corporations, human resources or diversity – has been called a 'racialised science' (Gordon 1995) and found to have transposed colonial into postcolonial modalities of control (Cooke 2003ab; Roediger and Esch 2012). These critiques seem relevant also for problematising today's discourses of 'managing migration', which further 'replace political communities with command and control, supplanting the messiness of democratic society with the efficiency of private authority' (Gordon 1995:21).

While the category expatriate has been historically associated with permanent emigration, especially in the US, it is now more often mobilised for temporary migrants, including the very privileged but sometimes also those less so. IHRM literature and some migration studies use expatriate interchangeably with 'global talent', 'transient professionals', 'highly skilled' or 'professional migrants': those who are seen to hold transnationally valid skills and knowledge and thus need to be enticed by states, cities and organisations alike in a 'global war for talent'. Especially in IHRM literature, these workers are often portrayed as driven, adaptable and restless, and hence by default temporary, not requiring integration let alone assimilation into imagined national communities. This figure is an ideological construct. For a start, not all those called expatriates are moving temporarily, and not all temporary migrants (skilled or unskilled) are categorised as expatriates. Moreover, shorter-term relocation and temporal flexibility mark many movements today, and those labelled expatriates are arguably no exception in often wanting to keep their options open, in keeping a return or onward move on the table. What perhaps better distinguishes many of them is their greater ability to do so on their own (privileged) terms. Neither does the category expatriate, in any period or context that this research has covered, map neatly onto 'skilled migration', whichever way skill is defined. Instead, the category expatriate was used for labour migrants with varying levels of skill, for those who moved for non-work reasons altogether and for some that did not work at all. Skill also did not figure in many interlocutors' own definitions of the expatriate, and hence also not in the assembly of 'expatriate communities'.

Even among those who are moving temporarily *and* are called expatriates, temporariness has widely varying causes and effects. For example, many of the self-identified 'expatriates' I met in Nairobi who intended to stay temporarily were not on generous compensation packages, with some working irregularly on visitor visas, for instance as yoga teachers. The widely differing experiences of temporariness are even more starkly exemplified by another group of migrants frequently labelled expatriates in public and political discourse. As Babar et al. (2019), Pagès-El Karoui (2016) and Le Renard (2021) discuss, a majority of the population of Gulf Cooperation Council countries are non-nationals; many are labour migrants who live with a legally prescribed temporary status, independent of how long they have lived in the Gulf. In the Gulf states, expatriate is a label associated with foreign workers, ranging from high-powered corporate managers and consultants to construction and domestic workers toiling under often exploitative and sometimes unfree conditions (Parween 2013; Al Mukrashi 2016). This attests to the fact that the term expatriate is used to position a socio-economically diverse set of people as temporary, in order to restrict their legal rights and claims to social belonging. This case also evidences the widely varying consequences of assigned temporariness, which can range from intensified exploitation to lush, tax-free salaries. Temporariness itself, whether assigned or chosen, cannot explain the very disparate social positions and experiences of 'temporary migrants', including those called expatriates.

While temporality and skill emerge as significant in making the expatriate, this is not simply as neutral definitional factors but as sites of struggle and tools of governance. Rather than classifying migrants by temporality or skill, we might thus inquire in grounded and contextual ways into who gets to imagine their own temporality and define their own skill, who gets to have options and which, as well as how temporality and skill get defined, for what purpose and with what effects (Kofman and Raghuram 2006; Liu-Farrer et al. 2021; Le Renard 2021). Alternatively, rather than using temporality or skill as criteria to define expatriates, we might trace the postcolonial genealogies of the skill and temporality of the expatriate. Accordingly, this book finds that expatriate temporal horizons have shifted in line with changing social, geopolitical and economic contexts – and were often adapted to serve organisations' and states' interests in response to these changing contexts. For example, what made the OSAS officer at the eve of Kenyan independence or the post-war Royal Dutch Shell manager expatriates was not that they moved temporarily. Rather, the temporality of the migration of a privileged group of employees – who became privileged employees partly because of their skill but largely because of ascribed and inherited characteristics of gender, racialisation, origin and class – was *shortened* so that they could continue to carry out their assigned roles, with the privileges they were accustomed to and which their roles required, in changed geopolitical contexts.

Not only does expatriate temporality have an instructive postcolonial genealogy, but temporality and skill remain tools of migration governance – for instance, to rhetorically justify and legally enact increasingly bifurcated migration policies that wed neoliberal capitalist logics with racist and ethnonationalist politics. In this context, categories and explanations centred on a decontextualised temporality or skill allow the historical power relations that shape temporalities of mobility and the construction of skill to be ignored. In their seemingly apolitical and technical innocuousness, temporality and skill are thus central to the political work of the expatriate. Such definitions eclipse but do not erase other less sanguine meanings and associations, which frequently taint or replace them. The interpretative space left open by vague and poorly operationalised designations is useful. Expatriate emerges as an unruly category: its often unacknowledged polysemy allows for a space of ambiguity, sheltered by official designations of the expatriate as 'temporary' or 'skilled' migration, in which differentiations are made by other logics to reproduce inherited inequalities.

Today, the category expatriate is regularly critiqued for obscuring the fact that white, Northern migrants are indeed migrants too, and unfairly privileged ones. Such critiques seem to have corresponded with a decline in the use of the terminology. Yet, too often expatriate is simply replaced with a shinier euphemism like the 'international'. This also highlights the limits of progressive politics that focus solely on language and labelling, without addressing the material inequalities that underwrite the unequal usage of categories. Rather than simply replacing migration categories, studying them allows an analysis of interconnected symbolic and material inequality. Articulating the expatriate through the international often involves positioning someone as casually mobile and not tied to any locality, as the perpetual embodiment of an elsewhere that frequently turns out to be a privilege-bestowing somewhere. This imagined international depends on rather more material ones, such as the unevenly bordered nation-state system or the internally differentiated MNC. The expatriate's associated international thus encodes neoliberal globalisation, inasmuch as it idealises flux and unhindered mobility across a space that remains intensely and unevenly bordered. The international expatriate is also realised at smaller, more intimate scales, through the unevenly valued labour that goes into making the international community, or the racialised and gendered orientation of bodies at *InterNations* events. The international is thus always contextually formed; it is ultimately a local event. The self-styled international person, who possibly even rejects the label expatriate, in their performance of a celebratory and 'border-blind' internationalism construed in progressive opposition to a supposedly parochial local and transcended nationalism, arguably has the markers of a tragic figure that is possibly well intentioned yet hubristic, invested in rereading structural privilege as individual achievement.

The category expatriate takes part in the ordering and interpretation of movement and belonging as a racialised and gendered technology of power in a postcolonial world. The system of categorisation of migration constitutes a form of symbolic violence inasmuch as it allocates symbolic worth based not solely on meritocratic measure or individual motivation but on ascribed and inherited social positions (also see Jaji 2019). Yet, despite the category expatriate's repeated enlistment in projects of white supremacy, it has never been only white migrants who have claimed the label or who have been labelled as such by others. This does not mean that the expatriate is racially undiscerning, but that categories like the expatriate are useful to racialised politics precisely through their conceptual multiplicity and malleability. Instead of assuming that expatriate status maps neatly onto the racial construct whiteness, the book has thus interrogated racialised struggles over who is an expatriate to uncover precise ways that 'race' is reproduced materially and discursively. It has shown how the category expatriate helps construct as *natural*, *normal* or *right* individual and systemic double standards, acts of discrimination, domination, exclusion and exploitation (Fields and Fields 2014); it forms part of mobility regimes that remain indebted to Euro-American imperial formations which have been challenged and destabilised, translated and adapted, but rarely fully dismantled.

Inquiring into the expatriate's historical uses, contestations and reformulations thus provides insight into broader social changes and political struggles that have contributed to today's political conjuncture. The sites in this book also suggest that the expatriate's subsumption within debates about migration is a more recent phenomenon than we might imagine. The expatriate was used, controversially discussed and studied separately from those called migrants for decades before this caused widespread indignation. The recent problematisation of the category expatriate might partly be a response to the increasing injustices and violence inflicted on those positioned as 'migrants'. More broadly, the more recent push to recognise expatriates as migrants might evince the increased politicisation of migration, the greater stakes and its growing political purchase. As Castles (2018) notes, it is only in the last few years that migration has become 'the bellwether theme, that decides elections and makes or breaks alliances' (cited in Jaji 2019:41). Thus, the very fact that the expatriate has become understood as a *migration* category evidences the increasing use of migration as a discursive, legal and everyday site of what Walters (2015) has called 'worldmaking': of articulating social subjects, producing social difference and inequality, and negotiating power relations.

As post/decolonial scholarship has shown, how we engage or evade the past affects whether we recognise or reproduce inequality today. The *necessity* for 'colonial aphasia' (Stoler 2016) is always found in present conditions. Not remembering or naming does not so much redeem the past, or enable 'moving on', but is more likely to open up space for its (intended or unintended) reproduction, including the resuscitation of scripts that already served as acts of active misrecognition in the past. If positioning the expatriate as the international, temporary or skilled migrant attempts to overwrite earlier uses, then their insufficiently redressed violent realities shine through, tainting and haunting today's expatriate. This book has thus argued that a historically and contextually grounded appreciation of migration categories like the expatriate is central to a careful and critical understanding of migration today. Multiply inflected and malleable, the expatriate, the migrant and other categories of mobility are entangled and complicit with old and new imperial projects. They allow racialised, classed and gendered inequality by folding such distinctions into seemingly innocuous labels, by cutting and arranging in specific ways, by directing attention and by suggesting sympathies and affinities. However, if this study has established a lineage between today's expatriate and Euro-American imperial and colonial projects, this is not a straightforward one. It has involved adaptation, rupture and translation. The moments of articulating and rearticulating the category expatriate discussed here involved contestation and resistance – nothing was automatic. Ultimately, postcolonial power relations work in and through categories in complex and open-ended ways. Terms like expatriate can serve divergent political projects, and can also be deconstructed and used to expose the injustices and double standards at the heart of today's mobility regimes.

References

Archives and records

ATRIA: Archive of the Institute on Gender Equality and Women's History, Amsterdam, Netherlands

EAC: Expatriate Archive Centre, The Hague, Netherlands

EAWL: East Africa Women's League Archives, Nairobi, Kenya

HC: The official report of all UK Parliamentary debates, House of Commons Hansard, available at https://hansard.parliament.uk/ [Accessed 22 June 2022]

HL: The official report of all UK Parliamentary debates, House of Lords Hansard, available at https://hansard.parliament.uk/ [Accessed 22 June 2022]

KNADS: Kenya National Archives and Documentation Service, Nairobi, Kenya

LegCo: The official record of the proceedings of the Legislative Council of the Colony and Protectorate of Kenya Hansard, available at https://books.google.co.uk/books?id=SVuz6fHl2pwC [Accessed 22 June 2022]

TNA: The National Archives, Kew, London, UK

Bibliography

Achiume, T. (2019). Migration as decolonization. *Stanford Law Review*, 71(6), 1509. Available at https://papers.ssrn.com/sol3/papers.cfm?abstract_id=3330353 [Accessed 1 July 2022].

Achiume, T. (2022). Racial borders. *Georgetown Law Journal*, 445, 21–33.

Adams, M. (1961). When tribesmen shift from jungle to jobs. *International Executive*, 3(2), 21–22.

Adu, A. (1965). *The Civil Service in New African States: Y. A. L. Adu*. Allen & Unwin.

References

261

Ahmed, S. (2000). *Strange Encounters: Embodied Others in Post-Coloniality*. Routledge.

Ahmed, S. (2007). A phenomenology of whiteness. *Feminist Theory*, 8(2), 149–168.

Ahmed, S. (2012). *On Being Included: Racism and Diversity in Institutional Life*. Duke University Press.

Ahmed, S., Castaneda, C., Fortier, A.-M. and Sheller, M. (eds) (2000). *Uprootings/Regroundings: Questions of Home and Migration*. Berg.

Ahmed, S. and Swan, E. (2006). Doing diversity. *Policy Futures in Education*, 4(2), 96–100.

Akbari, A. (2020). 'Follow the thing: Data'. *Antipode*, 52(2), 408–429.

Al Ariss, A. (2010). Modes of engagement: Migration, self-initiated expatriation, and career development. *Career Development International*, 15(4), 338–358.

Al Ariss, A. and Crowley-Henry, M. (2013). Self-initiated expatriation and migration in the management literature: Present theorizations and future research directions. *Career Development International*, 18(1), 78–96.

Al Ariss, A. and Özbilgin, M. (2010). Understanding self-initiated expatriates: Career experiences of Lebanese self-initiated expatriates in France. *Thunderbird International Business Review*, 52(4), 275–285.

Al Mukrashi, F. (2016). Absconding expatriate workers plead for amnesty in Oman. *GulfNews*, 10 December 2016. Available at http://gulfnews.com/news/gulf/oman/absconding-expatriate-workers-plead-for-amnesty-in-oman-1.1933517 [Accessed 7 February 2022].

Allard, L. A. C. (1996). Managing globe-trotting expats. *Management Review*, 85(5), 38–43.

Allen, M. (2005). 'Innocents abroad' and 'prohibited immigrants'; Australians in India and Indians in Australia 1890–1910. In A. Curthoys and M. Lake (eds), *Connected Worlds* (pp. 111–125). ANU Press.

Alpander, G. (1973). Foreign MBA: Potential managers for American international corporations. *Journal of International Business Studies*, 4(1), 1–13.

Alshahrani, S. and Morley, M. (2015). Accounting for variations in the patterns of mobility among conventional and self-initiated expatriates. *International Journal of Human Resource Management*, 26(15), 1936–1954.

Altman, Y. and Baruch, Y. (2012). Global self-initiated corporate expatriate careers: A new era in international assignments? *Personnel Review*, 41(2), 233–255.

American Women's Association Kenya (AWA) (n.d.). *Welcome to AWA Kenya*. Available at https://web.archive.org/web/20210612230154/http://awakenya.org/ [Accessed 1 July 2022].

Amersfoort, H. van and Niekerk, M. van (2006). Immigration as a colonial inheritance: Post-colonial immigrants in the Netherlands, 1945–2002. *Journal of Ethnic and Migration Studies*, 32(3), 323–346.

Anderson, B. (2013). *Us and Them?: The Dangerous Politics of Immigration Control.* Oxford University Press.

Anderson, B. (2016). Against fantasy citizenship: The politics of migration and austerity. *Renewal: A Journal of Labour Politics*, 24(1), 53–62.

Anderson, B. (2017). Towards a new politics of migration? *Ethnic and Racial Studies*, 40(9), 1527–1537.

Anderson, B. (2019). New directions in migration studies: Towards methodological de-nationalism. *Comparative Migration Studies*, 7(1), 1–13.

Anderson, B. and Blinder, S. (2017). Briefing: Who counts as a migrant? Definitions and their consequences. *Migration Observatory*, 11 January. Available at www.migrationobservatory.ox.ac.uk/resources/briefings/ who-counts-as-a-migrant-definitions-and-their-consequences/ [Accessed 25 November 2017].

Anderson, B. and Ruhs, M. (2010). Researching illegality and labour migration. *Population, Space and Place*, 16(3), 175–179.

Anderson-Levy, L. (2010). An (other) ethnographic dilemma: Subjectivity and the predicament of studying up. *Transforming Anthropology*, 18(2), 181–192.

Andresen, M., Bergdolt, F., Margenfeld, J. and Dickmann, M. (2014). Addressing international mobility confusion – developing definitions and differentiations for self-initiated and assigned expatriates as well as migrants. *International Journal of Human Resource Management*, 25(16), 2295–2318.

Andrews, K. (2020). Blackness, Empire and Migration: How black studies transforms the curriculum. *Area*, 52(4), 701–707.

Andrucki, M. (2010). The visa whiteness machine: Transnational motility in post-apartheid South Africa. *Ethnicities*, 10(3), 358–370.

Anich, R., Crush, J., Melde, S. and Oucho, J. O. (2014). *A New Perspective on Human Mobility in the South.* Springer.

Armbruster, H. (2010). 'Realising the self and developing the African': German immigrants in Namibia. *Journal of Ethnic and Migration Studies*, 36(8), 1229–1246.

Babar, Z., Ewers, M. and Khattab, N. (2019). Im/mobile highly skilled migrants in Qatar. *Journal of Ethnic and Migration Studies*, 45(9), 1553–1570.

Bakewell, O. (2008a). 'Keeping them in their place': The ambivalent relationship between development and migration in Africa. *Third World Quarterly*, 29(7), 1341–1358.

Bakewell, O. (2008b). Research beyond the categories: The importance of policy irrelevant research into forced migration. *Journal of Refugee Studies*, 21(4), 432–453.

Bakir, C. and Woods, J. (2018). Host state bargaining with multinationals. In A. Nölke and Christian May (eds), *Handbook of the International Political Economy of the Corporation* (pp. 279–294). Edward Elgar.

Bal, E. (2012). *Country Report: Indian Migration to the Netherlands*. CARIM-India Research Report 2012/07. Robert Schuman Centre for Advanced Studies, European University Institute.

Balibar, E. (2002). *Politics and the Other Scene*. Verso.

Bamberg, J. (2010). History of Royal Dutch Shell. *Business History Review*, 84(2), 363–367.

Barham, K. (1991). Developing the international manager. *Journal of European Industrial Training*, 15(1), 12–16.

Barker, M. (1981). *The New Racism: Conservatives and the Ideology of the Tribe*. Junction Books.

Baruch, Y., Dickmann, M., Altman, Y. and Bournois, F. (2013). Exploring international work: Types and dimensions of global careers. *International Journal of Human Resource Management*, 24(12), 2369–2393.

Bauder, H., Hannan, C.-A. and Lujan, O. (2017). International experience in the academic field: Knowledge production, symbolic capital, and mobility fetishism. *Population, Space and Place*, 23(6), 1–13.

Bauman, Z. (1998). *Globalization: The Human Consequences*. Polity Press.

Beaverstock, J. V. (2002). Transnational elites in global cities: British expatriates in Singapore's financial district. *Geoforum*, 33(4), 525–538.

Beaverstock, J. V. (2005). Transnational elites in the city: British highly-skilled inter-company transferees in New York City's financial district. *Journal of Ethnic and Migration Studies*, 31(2), 245–268. DOI: 10.1080/1369183042000339918.

Beaverstock, J. V. (2011). Servicing British expatriate 'talent' in Singapore. *Journal of Ethnic and Migration Studies*, 37(5), 709–728.

Beaverstock, J. (2018). New insights in reproducing transnational corporate elites. *Global Networks*, 18(3), 500–522.

Benjamin, W. (1968). Theses on the philosophy of history. In H. Arendt (ed.), *Illuminations* (pp. 253–264). Schocken Books.

Benjamin, W. (1999). *The Arcades Project*. Harvard University Press.

Bennell, P. (1982). The colonial legacy of salary structures in anglophone Africa. *Journal of Modern African Studies*, 20(1), 127–154.

Benson, M. and O'Reilly, K. (2016). From lifestyle migration to lifestyle in migration: Categories, concepts and ways of thinking. *Migration Studies*, 4(1), 20–37.

Berry, D. P. and Bell, M. P. (2012). 'Expatriates': Gender, race and class distinctions in international management. *Gender, Work & Organization*, 19(1), 10–28.

Bhambra, G. K. (2014). Postcolonial and decolonial dialogues. *Postcolonial Studies*, 17(2), 115–121. DOI: 10.1080/13688790.2014.966414.

Bhambra, G. K. (2017). Locating Brexit in the pragmatics of race, citizenship and empire. In W. Outhwaite (ed.), *Brexit: Sociological Responses*. Anthem Press.

Bhattacharyya, G. (2018). *Racial Capitalism*. Rowman & Littlefield.

Bickers, R. (2010). *Settlers and Expatriates: Britons Over the Seas*. Oxford University Press.

Bigo, D. (2002). Security and immigration: Toward a critique of the governmentality of unease. *Alternatives*, 27(1), 63–92.

Bijl, P. (2012). Colonial memory and forgetting in the Netherlands and Indonesia'. *Journal of Genocide Research*, 14(3–4), 441–461. DOI: 10.1080/14623528.2012.719375.

Bijl, P. (2015). *Emerging Memory: Photographs of Colonial Atrocity in Dutch Cultural Remembrance*. Amsterdam University Press.

Birkenkrahe, M. (2002). How large multi-nationals manage their knowledge. *Business Review*, 4(2), 2–12.

Bivand Erdal, M. (2017). Timespaces of return migration: The interplay of everyday practices and imaginaries of return in transnational social fields. In E. Mavroudi, A. Christou and B. Page (eds), *Timespace and International Migration* (pp. 104–118). Edward Elgar.

Blinder, S. (2015). Imagined immigration: The impact of different meanings of 'immigrants' in public opinion and policy debates in Britain. *Political Studies*, 63(1), 80–100.

Boatcă, M. (2016). Commodification of citizenship. Global inequalities and the modern transmission of property. In I. Wallerstein, C. Chase-Dunn and C. Suter (eds), *Overcoming Global Inequalities* (pp. 3–18). Routledge.

Bolognani, M. (2016). From myth of return to return fantasy: A psychosocial interpretation of migration imaginaries. *Identities*, 23(2), 193–209.

Bonache, J. and Zárraga-Oberty, C. (2017). The traditional approach to compensating global mobility: Criticisms and alternatives. *International Journal of Human Resource Management*, 28(1), 149–169.

Bonjour, S. and Block, L. (2016). Ethnicizing citizenship, questioning membership. Explaining the decreasing family migration rights of citizens in Europe. *Citizenship Studies*, 20(6–7), 779–794.

Bonjour, S. and Chauvin, S. (2018). Social class, migration policy and migrant strategies: An introduction. *International Migration*, 56(4), 5–18.

Bonjour, S. and Duyvendak, J. W. (2018). The 'migrant with poor prospects': Racialized intersections of class and culture in Dutch civic integration debates. *Ethnic and Racial Studies*, 41(5), 882–900.

Borrmann, W. A. (1968). The problem of expatriate personnel and their selection in international enterprises. *Management International Review*, 8(4/5), 37–48.

Bosma, U. (2012). *Post-Colonial Immigrants and Identity Formations in the Netherlands*. Amsterdam University Press.

Boussebaa, M. and Morgan, G. (2014). Pushing the frontiers of critical international business studies: The multinational as a neo-imperial space. *Critical Perspectives on International Business*, 10(1/2), 96–106.

Boussebaa, M., Morgan, G. and Sturdy, A. (2012). Constructing global firms? National, transnational and neocolonial effects in international management consultancies. *Organization Studies*, 33(4), 465–486. DOI: 10.1177/0170840612443454.

Brennand, T. (1988). *Petro-Canada International Assistance Corporation*. Shell China.

Brewster, C. and Suutari, V. (2005). Global HRM: Aspects of a research agenda. *Personnel Review*, 34(1), 5–21.

Bröckling, U. (2015). *The Entrepreneurial Self: Fabricating a New Type of Subject*. SAGE.

Brubaker, R. (2004). *Ethnicity Without Groups*. Harvard University Press.

Brubaker, R. and Cooper, F. (2000). Beyond 'identity'. *Theory and Society*, 29(1), 1–47.

Buettner, E. (2016). *Europe after Empire: Decolonization, Society, and Culture*. Cambridge University Press.

Burritt, B. (1988). Managing multinational staff in Saudi Arabia. *Journal of Management in Engineering*, 4(2), 108–112.

Burton, A. M. (ed.) (2003). *After the Imperial Turn: Thinking With and Through the Nation*. Duke University Press.

Burton, A. (ed.) (2005). *Archive Stories: Facts, Fictions, and the Writing of History*. Duke University Press.

Butler, J. (1990). *Gender Trouble: Feminism and the Subversion of Identity*. Routledge.

Cambridge Dictionary (n.d.). 'Expatriate'. Available at https://dictionary.cambridge.org/dictionary/english/expatriate [Accessed 24 February 2022].

Campbell, E. (2005). *Formalizing the Informal Economy: Somali Refugee and Migrant Trade Networks in Nairobi*. Global Migration Perspectives No. 47. Global Commission on International Migration. Available at www.iom.int/sites/g/files/tmzbdl486/files/jahia/webdav/site/myjahiasite/shared/shared/mainsite/policy_and_research/gcim/gmp/gmp47.pdf [Accessed 8 July 2022].

Campillo-Carrete, B. (2013). South–South migration. International Institute of Social Studies Working Paper Series, 570, 1–98. International Institute of Social Studies of Erasmus University (ISS).

Carens, J. (2013). *The Ethics of Immigration*. Oxford University Press.

Carmody, P. (2011). *The New Scramble for Africa*. Polity.

Castles, S. (1986). The guest-worker in Western Europe – an obituary. *International Migration Review*, 20(4), 761–778.

Castles, S. (2000). International migration at the beginning of the twenty-first century: Global trends and issues. *International Social Science Journal*, 52(165), 269–281. DOI: 10.1111/1468-2451.00258.

Castles, S. (2007). Twenty-first-century migration as a challenge to sociology. *Journal of Ethnic and Migration Studies*, 33(3), 351–371.

Cerdin, J.-L. and Brewster, C. (2014). Talent management and expatriation: Bridging two streams of research and practice. *Journal of World Business*, 49(2), 245–252. DOI: 10.1016/j.jwb.2013.11.008.

Cerdin, J.-L. and Pargneux, M. L. (2010). Career anchors: A comparison between organization-assigned and self-initiated expatriates. *Thunderbird International Business Review*, 52(4), 287–299.

Cerdin, J.-L. and Selmer, J. (2014). Who is a self-initiated expatriate? Towards conceptual clarity of a common notion. *International Journal of Human Resource Management*, 25(9), 1281–1301.

Cervantes-Rodriguez, M., Grosfoguel, R. and Mielants, E. H. (2009). *Caribbean Migration to Western Europe and the United States*. Temple University Press.

Charton-Bigot, H. and Rodriguez-Torres, D. (eds). (2010). *Nairobi Today: The Paradox of a Fragmented City*. Mkuki Na Nyota Publishers.

Chen, J., Wang, X., Beck, J., Wu, C. and Carroll, J. M. (2019). Beyond leaders and followers: Understanding participation dynamics in event-based social networks. *International Journal of Human–Computer Interaction*, 35(20), 1892–1905.

Chow, P., Huisman, M. and Bringhurst Familia, S. (2017). Expanding the boundaries of history: The Expatriate Archive Centre. In A. K. Levin (ed.), *Global Mobilities: Refugees, Exiles, and Immigrants in Museums and Archives* (pp. 311–328). Routledge.

Clausen, A. W. (1972). The internationalized corporation: An executive's view. *ANNALS of the American Academy of Political and Social Science*, 403(1), 12–21.

Clayton, A. and Savage, D. C. (1974). *Government and Labour in Kenya 1895–1963*. Routledge.

Cohen, E. (1977). Expatriate communities. *Current Sociology*, 24(3), 5–90.

Coles, A. and Fechter, A.-M. (eds). (2008). *Gender and Family Among Transnational Professionals*. Routledge.

Coles, A. and Walsh, K. (2010). From 'trucial state' to 'postcolonial' city? The imaginative geographies of British expatriates in Dubai. *Journal of Ethnic and Migration Studies*, 36(8), 1317–1333.

Collings, D. G. and Doherty, N. (2011). Understanding and supporting the career implications of international assignments. *Journal of Vocational Behavior*, 78(3), 361–371.

Collings, D. G., Scullion, H. and Morley, M. J. (2007). Changing patterns of global staffing in the multinational enterprise: Challenges to the conventional expatriate assignment and emerging alternatives. *Journal of World Business*, 42(2), 198–213.

Colpani, G., Mascat, J. M. H. and Smiet, K. (2022). Postcolonial responses to decolonial interventions. *Postcolonial Studies*, 25(1), 1–16. DOI: 10.1080/13688790.2022.2041695.

Cook, I. et al. (2004). Follow the thing: Papaya. *Antipode*, 36(4), 642–664.

Cooke, B. (2003a). The denial of slavery in management studies. *Journal of Management Studies*, 40(8), 1895–1918. DOI: 10.1046/j.1467-6486.2003.00405.x.

Cooke, B. (2003b). A new continuity with colonial administration: Participation in development management. *Third World Quarterly*, 24(1), 47–61. DOI: 10.1080/713701371.

Crang, P., Dwyer, C. and Jackson, P. (2003). Transnationalism and the spaces of commodity culture. *Progress in Human Geography*, 27(4), 438–456.

Cranston, S. (2014). Reflections on doing the expat show: Performing the global mobility industry. *Environment and Planning A: Economy and Space*, 46(5), 1124–1138.

Cranston, S. (2016). Producing migrant encounter: Learning to be a British expatriate in Singapore through the global mobility industry. *Environment and Planning D: Society and Space*, 34(4), 655–671.

Crenshaw, K. (1989). Demarginalizing the intersection of race and sex: A black feminist critique of antidiscrimination doctrine, feminist theory and antiracist politics. *University of Chicago Legal Forum*, 1989(1), 139–167.

Cresswell, T. (2010). Towards a politics of mobility. *Environment and Planning D: Society and Space*, 28(1), 17–31.

Croft, W. and Cruse, D. A. (2004). *Cognitive Linguistics*. Cambridge University Press.

Croucher, S. (2012). Privileged mobility in an age of globality. *Societies*, 2(1), 1–13.

Dabic, M., González-Loureiro, M. and Harvey, M. (2015). Evolving research on expatriates: What is 'known' after four decades (1970–2012). *International Journal of Human Resource Management*, 26(3), 316–337.

Dahinden, J. (2016). A plea for the 'de-migranticization' of research on migration and integration. *Ethnic and Racial Studies*, 39(13), 2207–2225.

Dahinden, J. and Anderson, B. (2021). Exploring new avenues for knowledge production in migration research: A debate between Bridget Anderson and Janine Dahinden pre and after the burst of the pandemic. *Swiss Journal of Sociology*, 47(1), 27–52. DOI: 10.2478/sjs-2021-0005.

Daniels, J. D. (1973). A profile of local subsidiary managers. *Academy of Management Journal*, 16(4), 695–700.

Daniels, J. D. (1974). The education and mobility of European executives in US subsidiaries: A comparative study. *Journal of International Business Studies*, 5(1), 9–24.

Darwin, J. (2010). Orphans of empire. In R. Bickers (ed.), *Settlers and Expatriates: Britons Over the Seas* (pp. 329–346). Oxford University Press.

de Araujo, B., Teixeira, M. L. M., da Cruz, P. B. and Malini, E. (2014). Understanding the adaptation of organisational and self-initiated expatriates in the context of Brazilian culture. *International Journal of Human Resource Management*, 25(18), 2489–2509.

De Cieri, H., Cox, J. W. and Fenwick, M. (2007). A review of international human resource management: Integration, interrogation, imitation. *International Journal of Management Reviews*, 9(4), 281–302.

De Genova, N. (2016). The European Question: Migration, race, and postcoloniality in Europe. *Social Text*, 34(3 (128)), 75–102.

de Haas, H. (2008). The myth of invasion: The inconvenient realities of African migration to Europe. *Third World Quarterly*, 29(7), 1305–1322.

de Haas, H., Natter, K. and Vezzoli, S. (2018). Growing restrictiveness or changing selection? The nature and evolution of migration policies. *International Migration Review*, 52(2), 324–367.

de Lange, T., Oomes, N., Gons, N. and Spanikova, V. (2019). *Labour Migration and Labour Market Integration of Migrants in the Netherlands: Barriers and Opportunities*. SEO Report No. 2019-24. SEO Amsterdam Economics.

Decker, S. (2008a). Dekolonisation der Wirtschaft? Wirtschaftsnationalismus in Afrika nach 1945. *Archiv Für Sozialgeschichte*, 48, 461–486.

Decker, S. (2008b). Building up goodwill: British business, development and economic nationalism in Ghana and Nigeria, 1945–1977. *Enterprise and Society*, 9(4), 602–613.

Diakite, P. (2021). How racism forced James Baldwin and other black figures to move abroad. *Travel Noire*, 12 May. Available at https://travelnoire.com/racism-forced-james-baldwin-others-move-abroad [Accessed 22 June 2022].

Dickinson, J. (2016). Chronicling Kenyan Asian diasporic histories: 'Newcomers', 'established' migrants, and the post-colonial practices of time-work. *Population, Space and Place*, 22(8), 736–749.

Dickover, G. (1965). Innocents abroad: The expatriates' lot. *Monthly Labor Review*, 88(2), 43–145.

Dickover, G. F. (1966). Compensating the American employee abroad. *International Executive*, 8(3), 9.

Dochuk, D. (2019). *Anointed with Oil: How Christianity and Crude Made Modern America* (Illustrated edition). Basic Books.

Doherty, N. (2013). Understanding the self-initiated expatriate: A review and directions for future research. *International Journal of Management Reviews*, 15(4), 447–469.

Doherty, N., Richardson, J. and Thorn, K. (2013). Self-initiated expatriation and self-initiated expatriates: Clarification of the research stream. *Career Development International*, 18(1), 97–112.

Doro, M. E. (ed.) (1979). 'Human souvenirs of another era': Europeans in post-Kenyatta Kenya. *Africa Today*, 26(3), 43–54.

Dragojlovic, A. (2016). *Beyond Bali: Subaltern Citizens and Post-Colonial Intimacy*. Amsterdam University Press.

Driessen, M. (2016). Pushed to Africa: Emigration and social change in China. *Journal of Ethnic and Migration Studies*, 42(15), 2491–2507. DOI: 10.1080/1369183X.2016.1174569.

Dzenovska, D. (2013). The Great Departure: Rethinking national(ist) common sense. *Journal of Ethnic and Migration Studies*, 39(2), 201–218.

EAC (2014). Save the date: New exhibition 'Expat History of The Hague'. *Archive News*, 28 October. Available at https://xpatarchive.com/save-the-date-new-exhibition-expat-history-of-the-hague/ [Accessed 1 March 2022].

EAC (2015a). Call for material for new exhibition 'Expat History of The Hague'. *Archive News*, 10 February. Available at https://xpatarchive.com/call-for-material-for-new-exhibition-expat-history-of-the-hague/ [Accessed 1 March 2022].

EAC (2015b). Come see The Hague through expat eyes! *Archive News*, 15 October. Available at https://xpatarchive.com/come-see-the-hague-through-expat-eyes/ [Accessed 1 March 2022].

EAC (2015c). Expatriate exhibition: Share your story. *Archive News*, 19 March. Available at https://xpatarchive.com/expatriate-exhibition-share-your-story-2/ [Accessed 1 March 2022].

EAC (2015d). Sponsorship opportunities at historical exhibition in City Hall. *Archive News*, 25 August. Available at https://xpatarchive.com/sponsorship-opportunities-at-historical-exhibition-in-city-hall/ [Accessed 1 March 2022].

EAC (2015e). Who is an expat? New exhibition opens today. *Archive News*, 26 October. Available at https://xpatarchive.com/who-is-an-expat-new-exhibition-opens-today/ [Accessed 1 March 2022].

EAC (2018) *Collection*. Available at https://web.archive.org/web/20180210111859/http://xpatarchive.com/collection/ [Accessed 1 July 2022].

EAC (2022a). *About Us*. Available at http://xpatarchive.com/about/ [Accessed 1 March 2022].

EAC (2022b). *Collecting Policy*. Available at https://xpatarchive.com/wp-content/uploads/2019/02/EAC-Collecting-Policy.pdf [Accessed 1 March 2022].

EAC (2022c). *Expatriate Archive Centre*. Available at http://xpatarchive.com/ [Accessed 1 March 2022].

Economist Intelligence Unit (EIU). (2009). *Global Diversity and Inclusion: Perceptions, Practices and Attitudes*. Society for Human Resource Management (SHRM).

Edström, A. and Galbraith, J. R. (1977). Transfer of managers as a coordination and control strategy in multinational organizations. *Administrative Science Quarterly*, 22(2), 248–263.

Egan, M. L. and Bendick, M. (2003). Workforce diversity initiatives of US multinational corporations in Europe. *Thunderbird International Business Review*, 45(6), 701–727.

Eldin, H. K. and Sadiq, S. (1971). Suggested criteria for selecting foreign management consultants in developing countries. *Management International Review*, 11(4/5), 123–132.

El-Enany, N. (2020). *(B)ordering Britain: Law, Race and Empire*. Manchester University Press.

Elrick, J. and Farah Schwartzman, L. (2015). From statistical category to social category: Organized politics and official categorizations of 'persons with a migration background' in Germany. *Ethnic and Racial Studies*, 38(9), 1539–1556.

Engbersen, G., van San, M. and Leerkes, A. (2006). A room with a view: Irregular immigrants in the legal capital of the world. *Ethnography*, 7(2), 209–242.

Erel, U., Murji, K. and Nahaboo, Z. (2016). Understanding the contemporary race–migration nexus. *Ethnic and Racial Studies*, 39(8), 1339–1360.

Essed, P. and Nimako, K. (2006). Designs and (co)incidents: Cultures of scholarship and public policy on immigrants/minorities in the Netherlands. *International Journal of Comparative Sociology*, 47(3–4), 281–312.

Este, J. (2013). Academic sleuthing uncovered British torture of Mau Mau fighters. The Conversation, 6 June. Available at https://theconversation.com/academic-sleuthing-uncovered-british-torture-of-mau-mau-fighters-15010 [Accessed 24 February 2022].

Evans, P. (1991). *Management Development as Glue Technology*. No. 91/59/0B. INSEAD. Available at https://flora.insead.edu/fichiersti_wp/Inseadwp1991/91-59.pdf [Accessed 7 July 2022].

Falkum, I. L. (2015). The how and why of polysemy: A pragmatic account. *Lingua*, 157, 83–99. DOI: https://doi.org/10.1016/j.lingua.2014.11.004.

Fanon, F. (1967). *The Wretched of the Earth* (C. Farrington, Trans.; New edition). Penguin.

Farndale, E., Pai, A., Sparrow, P. and Scullion, H. (2014). Balancing individual and organizational goals in global talent management: A mutual-benefits perspective. *Journal of World Business*, 49(2), 204–214.

Farndale, E., Scullion, H. and Sparrow, P. (2010). The role of the corporate HR function in global talent management. *Journal of World Business*, 45(2), 161–168.

Farrer, J. (2010). 'New Shanghailanders' or 'New Shanghainese': Western expatriates' narratives of emplacement in Shanghai. *Journal of Ethnic and Migration Studies*, 36(8), 1211–1228.

Favell, A. (2008). *Eurostars and Eurocities*. Wiley-Blackwell.

Favell, A. (2022). Immigration, integration and citizenship: Elements of a new political demography. *Journal of Ethnic and Migration Studies*, 48(1), 3–32.

Favell, A., Feldblum, M. and Smith, M. (2007). The human face of global mobility: A research agenda. *Society*, 44(2), 15–25.

Fayerweather, J. (1959). *The Executive Overseas: Administrative Attitudes and Relationships in a Foreign Culture*. Syracuse University Press.

Fayerweather, J. (1972). The internationalization of business. *Annals of the American Academy of Political and Social Science*, 403, 1–11.

Featherstone, M. (2006). Archive. *Theory Culture and Society*, 23(2), 591–597.

Fechter, A.-M. (2005). The 'Other' stares back: Experiencing whiteness in Jakarta. *Ethnography*, 6(1), 87–103.

Fechter, A.-M. (2007). *Transnational Lives: Expatriates in Indonesia*. Ashgate.

Fechter, A.-M. (2010). Gender, empire, global capitalism: Colonial and corporate expatriate wives. *Journal of Ethnic and Migration Studies*, 36(8), 1279–1297.

Fechter, A.-M. and Korpela, M. (2016). Interrogating child migrants or 'Third Culture kids' in Asia: An introduction. *Asian and Pacific Migration Journal*, 25(4), 422–428.

Fechter, A.-M. and Walsh, K. (2010). Examining 'expatriate' continuities: Postcolonial approaches to mobile professionals. *Journal of Ethnic and Migration Studies*, 36(8), 1197–1210.

Feely, A. J. and Harzing, A. (2003). Language management in multinational companies. *Cross Cultural Management: An International Journal*, 10(2), 37–52.

Fenton, M. and Spyra, D. (n.d.). *Transforming International Mobility Services*. Royal Dutch Shell.

Fieldhouse, D. K. (1978). *Unilever Overseas: The Anatomy of a Multinational, 1895–1965*. Croom Helm.

Fields, B. (2001). Whiteness, racism, and identity. *International Labor and Working Class History*, 60, 48–56.

Fields, B. and Fields, K. (2014). *Racecraft: The Soul of Inequality in American Life*. Verso Books.

Findlay, A. M. (1988). From settlers to skilled transients: The changing Structure of British international migration. *Geoforum*, 19(4), 401–410. DOI: 10.1016/S0016-7185(88)80012-5.

Findlay, A. and Cranston, S. (2015). What's in a research agenda? An evaluation of research developments in the arena of skilled international migration. *International Development Planning Review*, 37(1), 17–31.

Findlay, A. and Gould, W. T. S. (1989). Skilled international migration: A research agenda. *Area*, 21(1), 3–11.

Findlay, A., Li, F., Jowett, A. and Skeldon, R. (1996). Skilled international migration and the global city: A study of expatriates in Hong Kong. *Transactions of the Institute of British Geographers*, 21(1), 49–61.

Fisher, P. (1961). The economic role of unions in less-developed areas. *Monthly Labor Review*, 84(9), 951–956.

FitzGerald, D. S. (2014). The Sociology of International Migration. In C. B. Brettell and J. F. Hollifield (eds), *Migration Theory: Talking Across Disciplines* (pp. 115–147). Routledge.

FitzGerald, D. S. and Cook-Martín, D. (2014). *Culling the Masses: The Democratic Origins of Racist Immigration Policy in the Americas*. Harvard University Press.

FitzGerald, D. S., Cook-Martín, D., García, A. S. and Arar, R. (2018). Can you become one of us? A historical comparison of legal selection of 'assimilable' immigrants in Europe and the Americas. *Journal of Ethnic and Migration Studies*, 44(1), 27–47. DOI: 10.1080/1369183X.2017.1313106.

Fortier, A. (2006). The politics of scaling, timing and embodying: Rethinking the 'New Europe'. *Mobilities*, 1(3), 313–331.

Fortier, A.-M. (2013). The migration imaginary and the politics of person-hood. In M. Messer, R. Schroeder and R. Wodak (eds), *Migrations: Interdisciplinary Perspectives* (pp. 31–41). Springer.

Foucault, M. (2004). *Society Must Be Defended*. Penguin Books.

Frankenberg, R. (1993). *White Women, Race Matters: The Social Construction of Whiteness*. University of Minnesota Press.

Franko, L. (1973). Who manages multinational enterprises? *International Executive*, 15(3), 20–21.

Froese, F. (2012). Motivation and adjustment of self-initiated expatriates: The case of expatriate academics in South Korea. *International Journal of Human Resource Management*, 23(6), 1095–1112.

Furnée, J. H. (2012). *Plaatsen van Beschaafd Vertier: Standsbesef En Stedelijke Cultuur in Den Haag, 1850-1890*. Uitgeverij Bert Bakker.

Gaines, K. (2006). *American Africans in Ghana: Black Expatriates and the Civil Rights Era*. University of North Carolina Press.

Gammeltoft-Hansen, T. and Nyberg Sørensen, N. (eds) (2013). *The Migration Industry and the Commercialization of International Migration.* Routledge.

Garland, D. (2014). What is a 'history of the present'? On Foucault's genealogies and their critical preconditions. *Punishment & Society,* 16(4), 365–384.

Geiger, T. (1973). The fortunes of the West. *International Executive,* 15(2), 1–3.

Getachew, A. (2019). *Worldmaking after Empire.* Princeton University Press.

Ghezelbash, D. (2017). Legal transfers of restrictive immigration laws: A historical perspective. *International & Comparative Law Quarterly,* 66(1), 235–255.

Gibel Mevorach, K. (2007). Race, racism, and academic complicity. *American Ethnologist,* 34(2), 238–241.

Gilmartin, M. (2017). Political geography lecture: Decolonising migration, delivered 1 September, RGS-IBG Annual Meeting, London.

Gilroy, P. (1987). *There Ain't no Black in the Union Jack.* University of Chicago Press.

Glick Schiller, N. (2005). Transnational social fields and imperialism: bringing a theory of power to transnational studies. *Anthropological Theory,* 5(4), 439–461.

Glick Schiller, N. (2007). 'Beyond the nation state and its units of analysis: Towards a new research agenda for migration studies'. In K. Schnittenhelm et al. (eds), *Concepts and Methods in Migration Research: Conference Reader* (pp. 39–73). Available at http://sowi-serv2.sowi.uni-due.de/cultural-capital/reader/Concepts-and-Methods.pdf [Accessed 8 July 2022].

Glick Schiller, N. (2009). A global perspective on migration and development. *Social Analysis,* 53(3), 14–37. DOI: 10.3167/sa.2009.530302.

Glick Schiller, N. and Salazar, N. B. (2013). Regimes of mobility across the globe. *Journal of Ethnic and Migration Studies,* 39(2), 183–200. DOI: 10.1080/1369183X.2013.723253.

Gluck, C. and Tsing, A. (2009). *Words in Motion: Toward a Global Lexicon.* Duke University Press.

Goldberg, D. (1993). *Racist Culture: Philosophy and the Politics of Meaning.* Blackwell Publishing.

Gonzales, R. F. (1967). Expatriates. *MSU Business Topics,* 15(2), 69–73.

Gonzalez, R. and McMillan, C. Jr. (1961). The universality of American management philosophy. *Journal of the Academy of Management,* 4(1), 33–41.

Gonzales, R. and Negandhi, A. (1967). The United States overseas executive: His orientations and career patterns. *International Executive,* 9(3), 3–5.

Gopal, P. (2020). *Insurgent Empire: Anticolonial Resistance and British Dissent.* Verso Books.

Gordon, A. (1995). The work of corporate culture: Diversity management. *Social Text*, 44, 3–30.

Gordon, L. (2008). The Shell Ladies' Project: Making and remaking home. In A. Coles and A.-M. Fechter (eds), *Gender and Family Among Transnational Professionals* (pp. 21–39). Routledge.

Grant, R. (2008). Organizational restructuring within the Royal Dutch Shell Group. In *Contemporary Strategic Management* (6th edition, pp. 121–145). Wiley.

Green, N. (2009). Expatriation, expatriates, and expats: The American transformation of a concept. *American Historical Review*, 114(2), 307–328.

Griffiths, M., Rogers, A. and Anderson, B. (2013). *Migration, Time and Temporalities: Review and Prospect*. COMPAS Research Resources Paper.

Grosfoguel, R. and Mielants, E. (2006). Introduction: Minorities, racism and cultures of scholarship. *International Journal of Comparative Sociology*, 47(3–4), 179–189.

Grosfoguel, R., Oso, L. and Christou, A. (2014). 'Racism', intersectionality and migration studies: Framing some theoretical reflections. *Identities*, 22(6), 635–652. DOI: 10.1080/1070289X.2014.950974.

Grover, S. (2014). Labor relations with the 'Western expatriate': Domestic workers as ayahs, maids, and nannies in the globalizing economy of India. Paper presented at the 6th Next-Generation Global Workshop, 'Revising the Intimate and Public Spheres and the East–West Encounter', Kyoto University. Available at www.kuasu.cpier.kyoto-u.ac.jp/wp-content/uploads/2013/12/Postceedings-session-8.pdf [Accessed 8 July 2022].

Guha, R. and Spivak, G. C. (eds) (1988). *Selected Subaltern Studies*. Oxford University Press.

Gullestad, M. (2002). Invisible fences: Egalitarianism, nationalism and racism. *Journal of the Royal Anthropological Institute*, 8(1), 45–63.

Hacking, I. (2002). *Historical Ontology*. Harvard University Press.

Hall, C. (2004). Remembering Edward Said. *History Workshop Journal*, 57, 235–243.

Hall, E. (1960). The silent language in overseas business. *Harvard Business Review*, 38(3), 87–96.

Hall, E. T. and Whyte, W. F. (1960). Intercultural communication: A guide to men of action. *International Executive*, 2(4), 14–15. DOI: 10.1002/tie.5060020407.

Hall, S. (1993). The West and the rest: Discourse and power. In B. Gieben and S. Hall (eds), *The Formations of Modernity: Understanding Modern Societies, an Introduction, Book 1* (pp. 184–227). Polity.

Hall, S. (2001). Constituting an archive. *Third Text*, 15(54), 89–92.

Hannum, W. (1967). Profit maker by design, educator by circumstance. *Columbia Journal of World Business*, 2(5), 77–83.

Hansen, R. (1999). The Kenyan Asians, British politics, and the Commonwealth Immigrants Act, 1968. *Historical Journal*, 42(3), 809–834.

Harari, D. E. and Zeira, D. Y. (1974). Morale problems in non-American multinational corporations in the United States. *Management International Review*, 14(6), 43–53.

Harbison, F. (1963). High-level manpower development. *Monthly Labor Review*, 86(3), 65–267.

Harbison, F. and Myers, C. (1960). Management in the industrial world. *International Executive*, 2(2), 9–10.

Harrington, B. (2016). *Capital without Borders: Wealth Managers and the One Percent*. Harvard University Press.

Harvey, M. (1983). The multinational corporation's expatriate problem: An application of Murphy's Law. *Business Horizons*, 26(1), 71–78.

Harvey, M. (1993). Training 'inpatriate' managers to succeed in the domestic organization. In *Proceedings of the Fourth Symposium on Cross-Cultural Consumer Studies and Business Studies* (pp. 220–231).

Harvey, M. (1997). 'Inpatriation' training: The next challenge for international human resource management. *International Journal of Intercultural Relations*, 21(3), 393–428.

Harvey, M. G. and Buckley, M. R. (1997). Managing inpatriates: Building a global core competency. *Journal of World Business*, 32(1), 35–52.

Harvey, M. and Miceli, N. (1999). Exploring inpatriate manager issues: An exploratory empirical study. *International Journal of Intercultural Relations*, 23(3), 339–371.

Harvey, M., Myers, M. and Novicevic, M. M. (2002). The role of MNCs in balancing the human capital 'books' between African and developed countries. *International Journal of Human Resource Management*, 13(7), 1060–1076.

Harvey, M., Novicevic, M., Buckley, M. and Fung, H. (2005). Reducing inpatriate managers' 'liability of foreignness' by addressing stigmatization and stereotype threats. *Journal of World Business*, 40(3), 267–280.

Harvey, M., Novicevic, M. and Speier, C. (1999a). The role of inpatriates in a globalization strategy and challenges associated with the inpatriation process. *Human Resource Planning*, 22(1), 38–50.

Harvey, M., Ralston, D. and Napier, N. (2000). International relocation of inpatriate managers: Assessing and facilitating acceptance in the headquarters organization. *International Journal of Intercultural Relations*, 24(6), 825–846.

Harvey, M., Speier, C. and Novicevic, M. (1999b). The role of inpatriation in global staffing. *International Journal of Human Resource Management*, 10(3), 459–476.

Harvey, W. (2008). The social networks of British and Indian expatriate scientists in Boston. *Geoforum*, 39(5), 1756–1765.

Harvey, W. S. (2014). Winning the global talent war: A policy perspective. *Journal of Chinese Human Resource Management*, 5(1), 62–74. DOI: 10.1108/JCHRM-01-2014-0003.

Harzing, A.-W. K. (1995). The persistent myth of high expatriate failure rates. *International Journal of Human Resource Management*, 6(2), 457–474. DOI: 10.1080/09585199500000028.

Hayes, M. (2014). 'We gained a lot over what we would have had': The geographic arbitrage of North American lifestyle migrants to Cuenca, Ecuador. *Journal of Ethnic and Migration Studies*, 40(12), 1953–1971.

Hayes, M. (2018). *Gringolandia: Lifestyle Migration under Late Capitalism*. University of Minnesota Press.

Hays, R. (1974). Expatriate selection: Insuring success and avoiding failure. *Journal of International Business Studies*, 5(1), 25–37.

Heenan, D. (1970). The corporate expatriate: Assignment to ambiguity. *Columbia Journal of World Business*, 5(3), 49–54.

Hendriks, F. and van Niekerk, M. (2014). *City in Sight: Dutch Dealings with Urban Change*. Amsterdam University Press.

Henry, Z. (2015). Nairobi used to be a terrible place to do business. How did it transform into a tech hub? *Slate*, 18 August. Available at www.slate.com/blogs/moneybox/2015/08/18/nairobi_as_silicon_savannah_how_the_kenyan_capitol_grew_into_a_hub_for_digital.html [Accessed 22 February 2022].

Hindman, H. (2007). Outsourcing difference: How international organizations manufacture expatriates. In S. Sassen (ed.), *Deciphering the Global: Scales, Spaces and Subjects* (pp. 155–177). Routledge.

Hindman, H. (2009a). Cosmopolitan codifications: Elites, expatriates, and difference in Kathmandu, Nepal. *Identities*, 16(3), 249–270.

Hindman, H. (2009b). Shopping in the bazaar/bizarre shopping: Culture and the accidental elitism of expatriates in Kathmandu, Nepal. *Journal of Popular Culture*, 42(4), 663–679.

Hindman, H. (2013). *Mediating the Global: Expatria's Forms and Consequences in Kathmandu*. Stanford University Press.

Hindman, H. and Fechter, A.-M. (eds) (2010). *Inside the Everyday Lives of Development Workers: The Challenges and Futures of Aidland*. Kumarian Press.

Hodge, J. M. (2010). British colonial expertise, post-colonial careering and the early history of international development. *Journal of Modern European History*, 8(1), 24–46. DOI: 10.17104/1611-8944_2010_1_24.

Hodgson, F. (1963). The selection of overseas management. *MSU Business Topics*, 11(2), 49–54.

Holland, S. (1976). Exchange of people among international companies: Problems and benefits. *ANNALS of the American Academy of Political and Social Science*, 424(1), 52–66.

Holmes, Sir M. (1948). *Report of the Commission on the Civil Services of Kenya, Tanganyika, Uganda and Zanzibar 1947–48* (Holmes Report). HMSO. Available at http://kenyalaw.org/kl/fileadmin/CommissionReports/Report-of-the-Commission-on-the-Civil-Services-of-KENYA-TANGANYIKA,-UGANDA-&-ZANZIBAR-1947-1948.pdf [Accessed 6 July 2022].

hooks, bell. (1992). Eating the other: Desire and resistance. In *Black Looks: Race and Representation* (pp. 21–41). Turnaround.

Houston Chronicle (2002). Shell to give more senior level jobs to women. *Houston Chronicle*, 25 January. Available at www.chron.com/business/energy/article/Shell-to-give-more-senior-level-jobs-to-women-2062856.php [Accessed 22 February 2022].

Howard, C. (1970). International executives: A look into the 21st century. *Human Resource Management*, 9(1), 11–17.

Howard, C. (1974). The returning overseas executive: Cultural shock in reverse. *Human Resource Management*, 13(2), 22–26.

Howe-Walsh, L. and Schyns, B. (2010). Self-initiated expatriation: Implications for HRM. *International Journal of Human Resource Management*, 21(2), 260–273.

Hudson, P. (2017). *Bankers and Empire: How Wall Street Colonized the Caribbean*. University of Chicago Press.

Huete, R., Mantecón, A. and Estévez, J. (2013). Challenges in lifestyle migration research: Reflections and findings about the Spanish crisis. *Mobilities*, 8(3), 331–348. DOI: 10.1080/17450101.2013.814236.

HWWI (2007). *Focus-Migration: Country Profile Netherlands* (No. 11). Hamburg Institute of International Economics (HWWI).

Inkson, K., Arthur, M., Pringle, J. and Barry, S. (1997). Expatriate assignment versus overseas experience: Contrasting models of international human resource development. *Journal of World Business*, 32(4), 351–368.

Internal Revenue Service (IRS) (2022). Quarterly publication of individuals, who have chosen to expatriate. *Federal Register*, 26 January. Available at www.federalregister.gov/quarterly-publication-of-individuals-who-have-chosen-to-expatriate [Accessed 1 March 2022].

International Executive (1971). Compensating international executives. *International Executive*, 13(3), 9–11. DOI: 10.1002/tie.5060130307.

InterNations (2022a). *About InterNations: Our Mission*. Available at www.internations.org/about-internations/ [Accessed 1 March 2022].

InterNations (2022b). *About InterNations: The Albatross*. Available at www.internations.org/about-internations/albatross/ [Accessed 1 March 2022].

InterNations (2022c). *About InterNations: The Story*. Available at www.internations.org/about-internations/story/ [Accessed 1 March 2022].

InterNations (2022d). *Employment in Nairobi.* Available at www.internations. org/nairobi-expats/guide/working-short [Accessed 1 July 2022].

InterNations (2022e). *Why Become an InterNations Ambassador?* Available at www.internations.org/get-involved/internations-ambassador/ [Accessed 1 March 2022].

InterNations (2022f). *Why Become an InterNations Consul?* Available at www.internations.org/get-involved/internations-consul/ [Accessed 1 March 2022].

InterNations (2022g). *Your Expat Community in Nairobi.* Available at www.internations.org/nairobi-expats [Accessed 1 July 2022].

Ireton, B. (2013). *Britain's International Development Policies.* Palgrave Macmillan.

Ivancevich, J. M. (1969). Selection of American managers for overseas assignments. *Personnel Journal*, 48(3), 189–200.

Jack, G. and Lorbiecki, A. (2003). Asserting possibilities of resistance in the cross-cultural teaching machine: Re-viewing videos of others. In A. Prasad (ed.), *Postcolonial Theory and Organizational Analysis: A Critical Engagement* (pp. 213–231). Palgrave Macmillan.

Jackson, W. (2011). White man's country: Kenya colony and the making of a myth. *Journal of Eastern African Studies*, 5(2), 344–368.

Jaji, R. (2019). *Deviant Destinations: Zimbabwe and North to South Migration.* Lexington Books.

Jazeel, T. (2012). Postcolonialism: Orientalism and the geographical imagination. *Geography*, 97(1), 4–11.

Jazeel, T. (2014). Subaltern geographies: Geographical knowledge and postcolonial strategy. *Singapore Journal of Tropical Geography*, 35(1), 88–103.

Jazeel, T. (2019a). Singularity. A manifesto for incomparable geographies. *Singapore Journal of Tropical Geography*, 40(1), 5–21.

Jazeel, T. (2019b). *Postcolonialism.* Routledge.

Jokinen, T., Brewster, C. and Suutari, V. (2008). Career capital during international work experiences: Contrasting self-initiated expatriate experiences and assigned expatriation. *International Journal of Human Resource Management*, 19(6), 979–998.

Jones, A. (2008). A silent but mighty river: The costs of women's economic migration. *Signs: Journal of Women in Culture and Society*, 33(4), 761–769.

Jones, G. (2005). Multinationals from the 1930s to the 1980s. In A. Chandler and B. Mazlish (eds), *Leviathans* (pp. 81–104). Cambridge University Press.

Jones, T.-A. and Last, T. (2021). European immigrants in Johannesburg: Perceptions, privileges and their implications for migration experiences.

African Human Mobility Review, 7(2), 25–49. DOI: 10.14426/ahmr. v7i2.908.

Jonker, J. and van Zanden, J. (2007). *A History of Royal Dutch Shell. Vol.1: From Challenger to Joint Industry Leader, 1890–1939*. Oxford University Press.

Jonker, J., van Zanden, J., Howarth, S. and Sluyterman, K. (2007). *A History of Royal Dutch Shell*, vols 1–3. Oxford University Press.

K'Akumu, O. and Olima, W. (2007). The dynamics and implications of residential segregation in Nairobi. *Habitat International*, 31(1), 87–99.

Kaufman, B. (2008). The development of HRM in historical and international perspective. In P. M. Wright, J. Purcell and P. Boxall (eds), *The Oxford Handbook of Human Resource Management* (pp. 19–47). Oxford University Press.

Kennedy, D. K. (1987). *Islands of White: Settler Society and Culture in Kenya and Southern Rhodesia, 1890–1939*. Duke University Press.

Kirk, K. and Bal, E. (2020). Stimulating flexible citizenship: The impact of Dutch and Indian migration policies on the lives of highly skilled Indian migrants in the Netherlands. *Journal of Citizenship and Globalisation Studies*, 3(1), 1–13.

Kirk-Greene, A. (1999). *On Crown Service: A History of HM Colonial and Overseas Civil Services, 1837–1997*. I. B. Tauris.

Kirk-Greene, A. (2000). *Britain's Imperial Administrators, 1858–1966*. Springer.

Kittay, E. (1987). *Metaphor: Its Cognitive Force and Linguistic Structure*. Oxford University Press.

Klekowski von Koppenfels, A. (2014). *Migrants or Expatriates? Americans in Europe*. Palgrave Macmillan.

Knowles, C. (2014). *Flip-Flop: A Journey Through Globalisation's Backroads*. Pluto Press.

Knowles, C. and Harper, D. (2009). *Hong Kong: Migrant Lives, Landscapes, and Journeys*. University of Chicago Press.

Kobayashi, A. (2003). GPC ten years on: Is self-reflexivity enough? *Gender, Place & Culture*, 10(4), 345–349.

Koch, P.-P. (2014). Local elections 2014 – Political quirks. Quirksmode, March 20. Available at: www.quirksmode.org/politics/blog/archives/2014/03/ local_elections.html [Accessed 22 February 2022].

Kofman, E. and Raghuram, P. (2006). Gender and global labour migrations: Incorporating skilled workers. *Antipode*, 38(2), 282–303.

Kooperman, L. and Rosenberg, S. (1977). The British administrative legacy in Kenya and Ghana. *International Review of Administrative Sciences*, 43(3), 267–272.

Korpela, M. (2010). A postcolonial imagination? Westerners searching for authenticity in India. *Journal of Ethnic and Migration Studies*, 36(8), 1299–1315. DOI: 10.1080/13691831003687725.

Koser, K. and Salt, J. (1997). The geography of highly skilled international migration. *International Journal of Population Geography*, 3(4), 285–303. DOI: 10.1002/(SICI)1099-1220(199712)3:4<285::AID-IJPG72>3.0.CO;2-W.

Koskela, A. (2014). Shoes, boots and vertical polysemes: The dynamic construal and conventionality of word senses. *Review of Cognitive Linguistics*, 12(2), 259–287.

Kotef, H. (2015). *Movement and the Ordering of Freedom*. Duke University Press.

Kothari, U. (ed.) (2005). *A Radical History of Development Studies: Individuals, Institutions and Ideologies*. Zed Books.

Kothari, U. (2006). Spatial practices and imaginaries: Experiences of colonial officers and development professionals. *Singapore Journal of Tropical Geography*, 27(3), 235–253.

Koutonin, M. (2015). Why are white people expats when the rest of us are immigrants? *Guardian*, 13 March. Available at www.theguardian.com/global-development-professionals-network/2015/mar/13/white-people-expats-immigrants-migration [Accessed 22 February 2022].

Kunz, S. (2016). Privileged mobilities: Locating the expatriate in migration scholarship. *Geography Compass*, 10(3), 89–101.

Kunz, S. (2018). Post-colonial liminality: 'Expatriate' narratives in the East Africa Women's League. In P. Leonard and K. Walsh (eds), *British Migration* (pp. 75–94). Routledge.

Kunz, S. (2020a). Expatriate, migrant? The social life of migration categories and the polyvalent mobility of race. *Journal of Ethnic and Migration Studies*, 46(11), 2145–2162.

Kunz, S. (2020b). A business empire and its migrants: Royal Dutch Shell and the management of racial capitalism. *Transactions of the Institute of British Geographers*, 45(2), 377–391.

Ladwig, P., Roque, R., Tappe, O., Kohl, C. and Bastos, C. (2012). *Fieldwork Between Folders: Fragments, Traces, and the Ruins of Colonial Archives*. Max Planck Institute for Social Anthropology Working Papers No. 141.

Lake, M. (2005). From Mississippi to Melbourne via Natal: The invention of the literacy test as a technology of racial exclusion. In A. Curthoys and M. Lake (eds), *Connected Worlds* (pp. 209–230). ANU Press.

Lake, M. and Reynolds, H. (2008). *Drawing the Global Colour Line: White Men's Countries and the International Challenge of Racial Equality*. Cambridge University Press.

Lakoff, G. (1987). *Women, Fire and Dangerous Things: What Categories Reveal about the Mind*. University of Chicago Press.

Le Renard, A. (2021). *Western Privilege: Work, Intimacy, and Postcolonial Hierarchies in Dubai.* Stanford University Press.

Leggett, W. (2005). Terror and the colonial imagination at work in the transnational corporate spaces of Jakarta. *Identities*, 12(2), 271–302.

Leggett, W. (2010). Institutionalising the colonial imagination: Chinese middlemen and the transnational corporate office in Jakarta, Indonesia. *Journal of Ethnic and Migration Studies*, 36(8), 1265–1278.

Leinonen, J. (2012). Invisible immigrants, visible expats? Americans in Finnish discourses on immigration and internationalization. *Nordic Journal of Migration Research*, 2(3), 213–223.

Lentin, A. (2008). Europe and the silence about race. *European Journal of Social Theory*, 11(4), 487–503.

Lentin, A. (2014). Postracial silences: The othering of race in Europe. In W. Hund and A. Lentin (eds), *Racism and Sociology* (pp. 69–104). Lit Verlag.

Leonard, P. (2008). Migrating identities: Gender, whiteness and Britishness in post-colonial Hong Kong. *Gender, Place & Culture*, 15(1), 45–60. DOI: 10.1080/09663690701817519.

Leonard, P. (2010a). *Expatriate Identities in Postcolonial Organizations.* Ashgate.

Leonard, P. (2010b). Old colonial or new cosmopolitan? Changing white identities in the Hong Kong police. *Social Politics: International Studies in Gender, State & Society*, 17(4), 507–535.

Leonard, P. (2010c). Work, identity and change? Post/colonial encounters in Hong Kong. *Journal of Ethnic and Migration Studies*, 36(8), 1247–1263.

Leonard, P. and Walsh, K. (2018). *British Migration: Privilege, Diversity and Vulnerability.* Routledge.

Lesher, J. and Griffith, R. (1968). Structuring the international compensation program. Equitable pay for overseas executives. *Business Horizons*, 11(6), 53–62.

Lester, A. (2012). Foreword. In A.-M. Fechter and K. Walsh (eds), *The New Expatriates: Postcolonial Approaches to Mobile Professionals* (pp. 1–8). Routledge.

Lidbury, Sir D. (1954). *Report of the Commission on the Civil Services of the East African Territories and the East Africa High Commission, 1953–1954, under the chairmanship of Sir David Lidbury, 1954* (2 volumes). Available at http://kenyalaw.org/kl/fileadmin/CommissionReports/Report-of-the-Commission-on-the-Civil-Services-of-the-East-African-Territories-and-East-Africa-High-Commission,1953-1954-VOL-I.pdf and http://kenyalaw.org/kl/fileadmin/CommissionReports/Report-of-the-Commission-on-the-Civil-Services-of-the-East-African-Territories-and-the-East-Africa-High-Commission-1953-1954-VOL-II.pdf [Accessed 6 July 2022].

Lindeman, J. and Armstrong, D. (1961). Policies and practices of US subsidiaries in Canada. *International Executive*, 3(2), 5–6.

Liu-Farrer, G., Yeoh, B. S. and Baas, M. (2021). Social construction of skill: An analytical approach toward the question of skill in cross-border labour mobilities. *Journal of Ethnic and Migration Studies*, 47(10), 2237–2251. DOI: 10.1080/1369183X.2020.1731983.

Lloyd, C. (2006). *Eugene Bullard, Black Expatriate in Jazz-Age Paris*. University of Georgia Press.

Lonsdale, J. (2002). Town life in colonial Kenya. In A. Burton (ed.), *The Urban Experience in Eastern Africa, c.1750–2000* (pp. 207–222). British Institute in Eastern Africa.

Lonsdale, J. (2010). Kenya: Home county and African frontier. In R. Bickers (ed.), *Settlers and Expatriates: Britons Over the Seas* (pp. 75–111). Oxford University Press.

Lopez, A. (2005). *Postcolonial Whiteness: A Critical Reader on Race and Empire*. State University of New York Press.

Louis, W. M. R. and Robinson, R. (1994). The imperialism of decolonization. *Journal of Imperial and Commonwealth History*, 22(3), 462–511. DOI: 10.1080/03086539408582936.

Lowe, L. (1996). *Immigrant Acts: On Asian American Cultural Politics*. Duke University Press.

Lundström, C. (2014). *White Migrations: Gender, Whiteness and Privilege in Transnational Migration*. Palgrave Macmillan.

Luo, J. (2011). Imagining modernity: Memory, space and symbolism of The Hague. In P. Nas (ed.), *Cities Full of Symbols: A Theory of Urban Space and Culture*. Leiden University Press.

Lynch, M. (2000). Against reflexivity as an academic virtue and source of privileged knowledge. *Theory, Culture & Society*, 17(3), 26–54.

Madge, C., Raghuram, P. and Noxolo, P. (2015). Conceptualizing international education: From international student to international study. *Progress in Human Geography*, 39(6), 681–701.

Mahieu, C. (2001). Management development in Royal Dutch/Shell. *Journal of Management Development*, 20(2), 121–130.

Mains, S., Gilmartin, M., Cullen, D., Mohammad, R., Raghuram, P., Winders, J. and Kelly, D. T. (2013). Postcolonial migrations. *Social & Cultural Geography*, 14(2), 131–144.

Mamdani, M. (1996). *Citizen and Subject: Contemporary Africa and the Legacy of Late Colonialism*. Princeton University Press.

Mamdani, M. (2012). *Define and Rule: Native as Political Identity*. Harvard University Press.

Mandell, M. M. (1958). Selecting Americans for overseas assignments. *Personnel Administration*, 21(6), 25–30.

Mangone, G. J. (1958). New Americans in old societies. *Antioch Review*, 18(4), 395–410. DOI: 10.2307/4610095.

Marcus, G. (1995). Ethnography in/of the world system: The emergence of multi-sited ethnography. *Annual Review of Anthropology*, 24(1), 95–117.

Margolis, A. (2009). Expats. *In-House Perspective*, 5(3), 11–13.

Massey, D. B. (2005). *For Space*. SAGE Publications.

Matanle, P. (2011). Expatriate games. Mind your language. *Guardian*, 11 April. www.theguardian.com/media/mind-your-language/2011/apr/11/mind-your-language-expat-brits [Accessed 20 February 2022]

Matthews, G. (2019). *Talent on the Move: Time for a Rethink?* Corporate Research Forum.

Mau, S. (2010). Mobility citizenship, inequality, and the liberal state: The case of visa policies. *International Political Sociology*, 4(4), 339–361. DOI: 10.1111/j.1749-5687.2010.00110.x.

Mau, S., Gülzau, F., Laube, L. and Zaun, N. (2015). The global mobility divide: How visa policies have evolved over time. *Journal of Ethnic and Migration Studies*, 41(8), 1192–1213.

Mavroudi, E., Page, B. and Christou, A. (eds) (2017). *Timespace and International Migration*. Edward Elgar.

Maxon, R. M. (2011). *Britain and Kenya's Constitutions, 1950–1960*. Cambria Press.

Mays, L., Graham, J. and Vinnicombe, S. (2005). Shell Oil Company US: The 2004 Catalyst award winner for diversity initiatives. In R. Burke and M. Mattis (eds), *Supporting Women's Career Advancement: Challenges and Opportunities* (pp. 313–331). Edward Elgar.

Mboya, T. (1970). *The Challenge of Nationhood: A Collection of Speeches and Writings*. Praeger Publishers.

McCreary, E. A. (1965). The Americanization of Europe. *International Executive*, 7(1), 15–16.

McIntosh, J. (2016). *Unsettled: Denial and Belonging Among White Kenyans*. University of California Press.

McKeown, A. (2004). Global migration, 1846–1940. *Journal of World History*, 15(2), 155–189.

McNulty, Y. and Brewster, C. (2017). The concept of business expatriates. In Y. McNulty and J. Selmer (eds), *Research Handbook of Expatriates*. Edward Elgar.

McNulty, Y. and Selmer, J. (2017). Introduction: Overview of early expatriate studies, 1952 to 1979. In Y. McNulty and J. Selmer (eds), *Research Handbook of Expatriates* (pp. 3–20). Edward Elgar.

Meeteren, M., Van de Pol, S., Dekker, R., Engbersen, G. and Snel, E. (2013). Destination Netherlands. History of immigration and immigration policy in the Netherlands. In J. Ho (ed.), *Immigrants: Acculturation,*

Socioeconomic Challenges and Cultural Psychology (pp. 113–170). Nova Science Publishers.

Meier, L. (2016). Dwelling in different localities: Identity performances of a white transnational professional elite in the City of London and the Central Business District of Singapore. *Cultural Studies*, 30(3), 483–505.

Melamed, J. (2006). The spirit of neoliberalism from racial liberalism to neoliberal multiculturalism. *Social Text*, 24(4 (89)), 1–24.

Melamed, J. (2015). Racial capitalism. *Critical Ethnic Studies*, 1(1), 76–85.

Menon, S. (2016). Narrating Brunei: Travelling histories of Brunei indians. *Modern Asian Studies*, 50(2), 718–764.

Merriam-Webster Dictionary (2022). 'Expatriate'. Available at www.merriam-webster.com/dictionary/expatriate [Accessed 24 February 2022].

Michel, J.-B., Shen, Y. K., Aiden, A. P., Veres, A., Gray, M. K., Pickett, J. P. et al. (2011). Quantitative analysis of culture using millions of digitized books. *Science*, 331(6014), 176–182.

Mirvis, P. (2000). Transformation at Shell: Commerce and citizenship. *Business and Society Review*, 105(1), 63–84.

Moeller, M., Harvey, M. and Williams, W. (2010). Socialization of inpatriate managers to the headquarters of global organizations: A social learning perspective. *Human Resource Development Review*, 9(2), 169–193.

Mohanty, C. (2003). *Feminism without Borders: Decolonizing Theory, Practicing Solidarity*. Duke University Press.

Mongia, R. V. (2007). Historicizing state sovereignty: Inequality and the form of equivalence. *Comparative Studies in Society and History*, 49(2), 384–411.

Mongia, R. (2018). *Indian Migration and Empire: A Colonial Genealogy of the Modern State*. Duke University Press.

Moore, F. (2010). Tales from the archive: Methodological and ethical issues in historical geography research. *Area*, 42(3), 262–270.

Morgan, G. (2018). Power relations within multinational corporations. In A. Nölke and Christian May (eds), *Handbook of the International Political Economy of the Corporation* (pp. 262–78). Edgar Elgar.

Morokvasic, M. (2004). 'Settled in mobility': Engendering post-wall migration in Europe. *Feminist Review*, 77, 7–25.

Morrison, T. (1992). *Playing in the Dark: Whiteness and the Literary Imagination*. Harvard University Press.

Mosse, D. (ed.) (2011). *Adventures in Aidland: The Anthropology of Professionals in International Development*. Berghahn.

Mota, N. (2019). Álvaro Siza's negotiated code: Meaningful communication and citizens' participation in the urban renewal of The Hague (Netherlands) in the 1980s. *Urban Planning*, 4(3), 250–264. DOI: 10.17645/up.v4i3.2120.

Murray, F. (1975). Multinationals in a turbulent Third World: A prescription for survival. *Human Resource Management*, 14(4), 22–24.

Nader, L. (1972). Up the anthropologist: Perspectives gained from studying up. In D. Hymes (ed.), *Reinventing Anthropology* (pp. 284–311). Pantheon Books.

Nail, T. (2015). *The Figure of the Migrant*. Stanford University Press.

Ndlovu-Gatsheni, S. J. (2013). *Coloniality of Power in Postcolonial Africa: Myths of Decolonization*. CODESRIA.

Negandhi, A. (1966). Profile of the American overseas executive. *California Management Review*, 9(2), 57–64.

Nerlich, B. and Clarke, D. (2001). Ambiguities we live by: Towards a pragmatics of polysemy. *Journal of Pragmatics*, 33(1), 1–20.

Nerlich, B., Clarke, D., Vimala, H. and Todd, Z. (2011). *Polysemy: Flexible Patterns of Meaning in Mind and Language* (2nd edition). De Gruyter Mouton.

Nkrumah, K. (1965). *Neo-Colonialism: The Last Stage of Imperialism*. Panaf Books.

Noer, D. (1974). Integrating foreign service employees to home organization: The godfather approach. *Personnel Journal*, 53(1), 45–51.

O'Brien, R. (1974). Some problems in the consolidation of national independence in Africa. *African Affairs*, 73(290), 85–94.

Ogot, B. A. and Ochieng', W. R. (eds) (1995). *Decolonization and Independence in Kenya, 1940–93*. James Currey.

Omi, M. and Winant, H. (2014). *Racial Formation in the United States: From the 1960s to the 1990s*. Routledge.

Oostindie, G. (2011). *Postcolonial Netherlands: Sixty-Five Years of Forgetting, Commemorating, Silencing*. Amsterdam University Press.

O'Reilly, K. (2000). *The British on The Costa Del Sol*. Routledge.

Outpost Archive Centre (now EAC) (2008). *The Source Book, An Expatriate Social History, 1927–2007: Shell Lives Unshelved*. Summertime Publishing and Outpost Archive Centre.

Page, B., Christou, A. and Mavroudi, E. (2017). Introduction: From time to timespace and forward to time again in migration studies. In E. Mavroudi, A. Christou and B. Page (eds), *Timespace and International Migration* (pp. 1–16). Edward Elgar.

Pagès-El Karoui, D. (2016). Égyptiens expatriés aux Émirats arabes unis: ancrages, connexions transnationales et expériences cosmopolites. *Arabian Humanities: Revue internationale d'archéologie et de sciences sociales sur la péninsule Arabique*, 7 [online journal], https://doi.org/10.4000/cy.3151.

Paine, L. (1999a). Royal Dutch/Shell in transition (A): Case study 300039. *HBR Store*. Available at https://hbr.org/ [Accessed 1 July 2022].

Paine, L. (1999b). Royal Dutch/Shell in transition (B): Case study 300040. *HBR Store*. Available at https://hbr.org/ [Accessed 1 July 2022].

Park, Y. J. (2022). Forever foreign? Is there a future for Chinese people in Africa? *Journal of Ethnic and Migration Studies*, 48(4), 894–912. DOI: 10.1080/1369183X.2021.1983953.

Parker, B. and McEvoy, G. (1993). Initial examination of a model of intercultural adjustment. *International Journal of Intercultural Relations*, 17(3), 355–379.

Parutis, V. (2014). 'Economic migrants' or 'middling transnationals'? East European migrants' experiences of work in the UK. *International Migration*, 52(1), 36–55.

Parween, A. (2013). *'Invisible' White-Collar Indians in the Gulf*. Middle East Institute, 14 August. Available at www.mei.edu/content/%E2%80%9Cinvisible%E2%80%9D-white-collar-indians-gulf [Accessed 7 February 2022].

Peiperl, M., Levy, O. and Sorell, M. (2014). Cross-border mobility of self-initiated and organizational expatriates. *International Studies of Management & Organization*, 44(3), 44–65.

Peltonen, T. (2012). Critical approaches to international HRM human resource management. In G. Stahl, I. Björkman and S. Morris (eds), *Handbook of Research in International Human Resource Management* (pp. 532–548). Edward Elgar Publishing.

Perlmutter, H. (1969). The tortuous evolution of the multinational corporation. *Journal of World Business*, 4(1), 9–18.

Perlmutter, H. and Heenan, D. (1974). How multinational should your top-management be? *Harvard Business Review*, 52(6), 121–132.

Personnel Today (2005). Global group aims to strike right balance to keep talent. *Personnel Today*, 22 February. Available at www.personneltoday.com/hr/global-group-aims-to-strike-right-balance-to-keep-talent/ [Accessed 6 July 2022].

Peterson, R. B. (2003). The use of expatriates and inpatriates in central and eastern Europe since the wall came down. *Journal of World Business*, 38(1), 55–69.

Pierre-Louis, K. (2021). Understanding the fossil fuel industry's legacy of white supremacy. *DeSmog*, 29 March. Available at www.desmog.com/2021/03/29/understanding-the-fossil-fuel-industrys-legacy-of-white-supremacy/ [Accessed 7 February 2022].

Polson, E. (2011). Belonging to the network society: Social media and the production of a new global middle class. *Communication, Culture & Critique*, 4(2), 144–163.

Polson, E. (2015). A gateway to the global city: Mobile place-making practices by expats. *New Media & Society*, 17(4), 629–645. DOI: 10.1177/1461444813510135.

Polson, E. (2016). *Privileged Mobilities: Professional Migration, Geo-Social Media, and a New Global Middle Class.* Peter Lang Publishing.

Prasad, A. (2012). *Against the Grain: Advances in Postcolonial Organization Studies.* Copenhagen Business School Press.

Prasad, P., Mills, A., Elmes, M. and Prasad, A. (1997). *Managing the Organizational Melting Pot: Dilemmas of Workplace Diversity.* SAGE Publications.

Prasad, P. and Prasad, A. (2002). Casting the native subject: Ethnographic practice and the (re)production of difference. In B. Czarniawska and H. Hopfl (eds), *Casting the Other: The Production and Maintenance of Inequalities in Work Organizations* (pp. 185–204). Routledge.

Pratt, M. L. (2007). *Imperial Eyes: Travel Writing and Transculturation* (2nd edition). Routledge.

Pucik, V., Evans, P., Björkman, I. and Morris, S. (2016). *The Global Challenge: International Human Resource Management.* McGraw-Hill Education.

Pucik, V., Evans, P., Björkman, I. and Morris, S. (2017). *The Global Challenge: International Human Resource Management.* Chicago Business Press.

PwC (2015). *Into Africa: The Continent's Cities of Opportunity.* PwC. Available at www.pwc.com/gx/en/issues/strategy/emerging-markets/africa/assets/into-africa-report.pdf [Accessed 7 February 2022].

Raghuram, P. (2009). Caring about 'brain drain' migration in a postcolonial world. *Geoforum*, 40(1), 25–33.

Raghuram, P. (2021). Democratizing, stretching, entangling, transversing: Four moves for reshaping migration categories. *Journal of Immigrant & Refugee Studies*, 19(1), 9–24.

Raghuram, P., Madge, C. and Noxolo, P. (2009). Rethinking responsibility and care for a postcolonial world. *Geoforum*, 40(1), 5–13.

Rahbaran, S. and Herz, M. (2014). *Nairobi Kenya: Migration Shaping the City.* Lars Müller Publishers and ETH Studio Basel.

Redfield, P. (2012). The unbearable lightness of expats: Double binds of humanitarian mobility. *Cultural Anthropology*, 27(2), 358–382.

Reem, A. (2013). The oil town of Ahmadi since 1946: From colonial town to nostalgic city. *Comparative Studies of South Asia, Africa and the Middle East*, 33(1), 41–58.

Reiche, S. (2006). The inpatriate experience in multinational corporations: An exploratory case study in Germany. *International Journal of Human Resource Management*, 17(9), 1572–1590.

Reslow, N. (2018). Unfulfilled expectations: The contradictions of Dutch policy on temporary migration. In P. Pitkänen et al. (eds), *Characteristics of Temporary Migration in European-Asian Transnational Social Spaces* (pp. 193–211). Springer International Publishing.

Reynolds, C. (1997). Expatriate compensation in historical perspective. *Journal of World Business*, 32(2), 118–132.

Reynolds, C. (2004). *A Short History of IHRM in the US – A Personal Perspective*. Routledge Global Human Resource Management Series. Routledge. Available at https://routledgetextbooks.com/textbooks/_author/globalhrm/history.php [Accessed 1 July 2022].

Roach, B. (2005). A primer on multinational corporations. In A. D. Chandler and B. Mazlish (eds), *Leviathans: Multinational Corporations and the New Global History* (pp. 19–44). Cambridge University Press.

Robinson, C. J. (1983). *Black Marxism: The Making of the Black Radical Tradition*. University of North Carolina Press.

Robinson, C. (2000). *Black Marxism: The Making of the Black Radical Tradition*. University of North Carolina Press.

Roediger, D. and Esch, E. (2012). *The Production of Difference: Race and the Management of Labor in US History*. Oxford University Press.

Roggeband, C. and van der Haar, M. (2018). 'Moroccan youngsters': Category politics in the Netherlands. *International Migration*, 56(4), 79–95.

Rosch, E. (1973). Natural categories. *Cognitive Psychology*, 4(3), 328–350.

Rose, G. (1997). Situating knowledges: Positionality, reflexivities and other tactics. *Progress in Human Geography*, 21(3), 305–320.

Rosenberg, C. D. (2006). *Policing Paris: The Origins of Modern Immigration Control Between the Wars*. Cornell University Press.

Rothchild, D. (1970). Kenya's Africanization Program: Priorities of Development and Equity*. *American Political Science Review*, 64(3), 737–753.

Royal Dutch Shell (1999). *The Shell Report 1999: People, Planet & Profits: An Act of Commitment*.

Runfors, A. (2016). What an ethnic lens can conceal. *Journal of Ethnic and Migration Studies*, 42(11), 1846–1863.

Said, E. W. (1979). *Orientalism*. Vintage.

Said, E. (1993). *Culture and Imperialism*. Chatto & Windus.

Salazar, N. (2017). Key figures of mobility: An introduction. *Social Anthropology*, 25(1), 5–12.

Salles-Djelic, M.-L. (2019). The (geo-)politics of management ideas: Three moments in the trajectory of an instrument of power. In A. Sturdy et al. (eds), *The Oxford Handbook of Management Ideas* (pp. 392–410). Oxford University Press.

Salt, J. (1988). Highly-skilled international migrants, careers and internal labour markets. *Geoforum*, 19(4), 387–399.

Samaddar, R. (2020). *The Postcolonial Age of Migration*. Routledge.

Sanger, C. and Nottingham, J. (1964). The Kenya general election of 1963. *Journal of Modern African Studies*, 2(1), 1–40. DOI: 10.1017/S0022278X00003645.

Sassen, S. (1988). *The Mobility of Labor and Capital: A Study in International Investment and Labor Flow.* Cambridge University Press.

Sassen, S. (2001). *The Global City: New York, London, Tokyo.* Princeton University Press.

Sassen, S. (2006). Emergent global classes and what they mean for immigration politics. *Migration Information Source*, 1 November. Available at www.migrationpolicy.org/article/emergent-global-classes-and-what-they-mean-immigration-politics [Accessed 7 February 2022].

Schinkel, W. (2018). Against 'immigrant integration': For an end to neo-colonial knowledge production. *Comparative Migration Studies*, 6(1), 1–17. DOI: 10.1186/s40878-018-0095-1.

Schollhammer, H. (1969). The compensation of international executives. *MSU Business Topics*, 17, 19–30.

Schrover, M. (2013). Netherlands, migration 19th–20th century. In I. Ness (ed.), *The Encyclopedia of Global Human Migration* [online encyclopedia]. Blackwell Publishing.

Schwartz, J. and Cook, T. (2002). Archives, records, and power: From (postmodern) theory to (archival) performance. *Archival Science*, 2(1–2), 1–19.

Scott, S. (2006). The social morphology of skilled migration: The case of the British middle class in Paris. *Journal of Ethnic and Migration Studies*, 32(7), 1105–1129. DOI: 10.1080/13691830600821802.

Scullion, H. and Brewster, C. (2001). The management of expatriates: Messages from Europe? *Journal of World Business*, 36(4), 346–365.

Seccombe, I. (1986). 'A disgrace to American enterprise': Italian labour and the Arabian American oil company in Saudi Arabia, 1944–54. *Immigrants & Minorities*, 5(3), 233–257.

Seidler, V. (2018). Copying informal institutions: The role of British colonial officers during the decolonization of British Africa. *Journal of Institutional Economics*, 14(2), 289–312.

Sethi, S. and Swanson, C. (1979). Hiring alien executives in compliance with US civil rights laws. *Journal of International Business Studies*, 10(2), 37–50.

Shachar, A. (2006). The race for talent: Highly skilled migrants and competitive immigration regime. *New York University Law Review*, 81(1), 148–206.

Shachar, A. (2009). *The Birthright Lottery: Citizenship and Global Inequality.* Harvard University Press.

Shaffer, M., Harrison, D. and Gilley, K. (1999). Dimensions, determinants, and differences in the expatriate adjustment process. *Journal of International Business Studies*, 30(3), 557–581.

Shaffer, M. A., Harrison, D. A., Gregersen, H., Black, J. S. and Ferzandi, L. A. (2006). You can take it with you: Individual differences and expatriate effectiveness. *Journal of Applied Psychology*, 91(1), 109–125. DOI: 10.1037/0021-9010.91.1.109.

Shaffer, M., Kraimer, M., Chen, Y-P. and Bolino, M. (2012). Choices, challenges, and career consequences of global work experiences: A review and future agenda. *Journal of Management*, 38(4), 1282–1327.

Shearer, J. (1965). Exporting US standards to underdeveloped countries. *Monthly Labor Review*, 88(2), 145–147.

Shell (2008). *Royal Dutch Shell Sustainability Review 2008*. Royal Dutch Shell plc.

Shell HRP (Human Resource Planning) (1994). The status of expatriation. Project report of review of expatriation and proposed changes to policies. [unpublished].

Shell Ladies' Project (1993). *Life on the Move*. Shell Ladies' Project.

Shell Ladies' Project (1996). *Life Now*. Shell Ladies' Project.

Sheller, M. (2011). Mobility. *Sociopedia*, 1–12, DOI: 10.1177/205684601163.

Sheller, M. (2018). *Mobility Justice: The Politics of Movement in An Age of Extremes*. Verso.

Shetty, Y. (1971). International manager: A role profile. *Management International Review*, 11(4/5), 19–31.

Shilliam, R. (2014). Race and development. In H. Weber (ed.), *Politics of Development: A Survey* (pp. 31–48). Routledge.

Shohat, E. (1992). Notes on the 'post-colonial'. *Social Text*, 31/32, 99–113.

Shortland, S. M. (2012). Women's participation in expatriation: The contribution of organisational policy & practice. A case study of the oil & gas exploration & production sector. PhD thesis, University of Westminster.

Siddiqi, D. M. (2020). The 'gift' of freedom: Dissent, decolonisation and afterlives of empire. *Identities*, 27(6), 740–745. DOI: 10.1080/1070289X.2020.1816332.

Silverstein, P. A. (2005). Immigrant racialization and the new savage slot: Race, migration, and immigration in the new Europe. *Annual Review of Anthropology*, 34(1), 363–384. DOI: 10.1146/annurev.anthro.34.081804.120338.

Simmonds, K. (1967). Multinational? Well, not quite. *International Executive*, 9(1), 11–13.

Sims, L. J. (2017). 'A safeguard against oblivion': Memorializing French Algeria in the Centre de Documentation Des Français d'Algérie. In A. K. Levin (ed.), *Global Mobilities: Refugees, Exiles, and Immigrants in Museums and Archives* (pp. 122–143). Routledge.

Simson, R. (2020). The rise and fall of the bureaucratic bourgeoisie: Public sector employees and economic privilege in postcolonial Kenya and Tanzania. *Journal of International Development*, 32(5), 607–635.

Sirota, D. and Greenwood, J. (1971). Understand your overseas work force. *Harvard Business Review*, 49(1), 53–60.

Sluyterman, K. (2007). *A History of Royal Dutch Shell. Vol.3: Keeping Competitive in Turbulent Markets, 1973–2007*. Oxford University Press.

Sluyterman, K. (2009). Multinational companies and national business systems in the twentieth century: What we can learn from the Shell history. Paper for ESG seminar, 26 March 2009.

Sluyterman, K. (2020) Decolonisation and the organisation of the international workforce: Dutch multinationals in Indonesia, 1945–1967. *Business History*, 62(7), 1182–1201. DOI: 10.1080/00076791.2017.1350170.

Sluyterman, K. and Westerhuis, G. (2008). The flow of people: Globalisation and the organisation of the international workforce in multinational companies. Paper for the EBHA conference in Bergen, August 2008.

Sluyterman, K. and Wubs, B. (2010). Multinationals and the Dutch business system: The cases of Royal Dutch Shell and Sara Lee. *Business History Review*, 84(4), 799–822.

Smiley, S. (2010). 'Exclusionary space in Dar es Salaam: Fear and difference in expatriate communities'. *Africa Today*, 56(3), 24–40.

Smiley, S. (2013). Mental maps, segregation, and everyday life in Dar es Salaam, Tanzania. *Journal of Cultural Geography*, 30(2), 215–244.

Smith, J. (ed.) (1999). *Administering Empire: The British Colonial Service in Retrospect: Proceedings of a Conference Jointly Sponsored by the University of London and the Corona Club Held at the Senate House on 27th and 28th May 1999*. University of London Press.

Solomon, C. (1996). Expats say: help make us mobile. *Personnel Journal*, 75(7), 47.

Solomos, J. (2003). *Race and Racism in Britain* (3rd edition). Palgrave Macmillan.

Spiegel, A. and Mense-Petermann, U. (2016). Verflochtene Mobilitäten und ihr Management. Mobilitätspraktiken von Expatriate-Managern und ihren 'trailing spouses' im Auslandseinsatz. *Österreichische Zeitschrift für Soziologie*, 41(1), 15–31.

Spivak, G. (1988). Can the subaltern speak? In C. Nelson and L. Grossberg (eds), *Marxism and the Interpretation of Culture* (pp. 271–313). Macmillan Education.

Steinmetz, L. (1965). Selecting managers for international operations: The wife's role. *Human Resource Management*, 4(1), 26–29.

Stich, A. and Colyar, J. (2015). Thinking relationally about studying 'up'. *British Journal of Sociology of Education*, 36(5), 729–746.

Stolcke, V. (1995). Talking culture: New boundaries, new rhetorics of exclusion in Europe. *Current Anthropology*, 36(1), 1–24.

Stoler, A. L. (1995). *Race and the Education of Desire: Foucault's History of Sexuality and the Colonial Order of Things*. Duke University Press.

Stoler, A. L. (1997). Racial histories and their regimes of truth. In D. E. Davis (ed.), *Political Power and Social Theory*, Vol. 11 (pp. 183–206). JAI Press.

Stoler, A. L. (2002). Colonial archives and the arts of governance. *Archival Science*, 2(1–2), 87–109.

Stoler, A. L. (2010). *Along the Archival Grain: Epistemic Anxieties and Colonial Common Sense*. Princeton University Press.

Stoler, A. L. (2011). Colonial aphasia: Race and disabled histories in France. *Public Culture*, 23(1), 121–156. DOI: 10.1215/08992363-2010-018.

Stoler, A. L. (2016). *Duress: Imperial Durabilities in Our Times*. Duke University Press Books.

Stopford, J. M. (1976). Changing perspectives on investment by British manufacturing multinationals. *Journal of International Business Studies*, 7(2), 15–28.

Sucher, S. and Beyersdorfer, D. (2010). Global diversity and inclusion at Royal Dutch Shell (B): The impact of restructuring. *HBR Store*. Available at https://hbr.org/ [Accessed 1 July 2022].

Sucher, S. and Corsi, E. (2012). Global diversity and inclusion at Royal Dutch Shell (A) 613063. *HBR Store*. Available at https://hbr.org/ [Accessed 1 July 2022].

Sullivan, J. and Cheng, J. (2018). Contextualising Chinese migration to Africa. *Journal of Asian and African Studies*, 53(8), 1173–1187. DOI: 10.1177/0021909618776443.

Suutari, V. and Brewster, C. (2000). Making their own way: International experience through self-initiated foreign assignments. *Journal of World Business*, 35(4), 417–436.

Sylvester, C. (1999). Development studies and postcolonial studies: Disparate tales of the 'Third World'. *Third World Quarterly*, 20(4), 703–721.

Taylor, I. and Zajontz, T. (2020). In a fix: Africa's place in the Belt and Road Initiative and the reproduction of dependency. *South African Journal of International Affairs*, 27(3), 277–295. DOI: 10.1080/10220461.2020.1830165.

Theroux, P. (1967). Tarzan is an expatriate. *Transition*, 32, 12–19. https://doi.org/10.2307/2934617.

Thompson, D. M. (1959). Contracts for Americans working abroad. *International Executive*, 1(1), 19–20. DOI: 10.1002/tie.5060010110.

Tinker Salas, M. (2003). Races and cultures in the Venezuelan oil fields. In V. C. Peloso (ed.), *Work, Protest, and Identity in Twentieth-Century Latin America* (pp. 143–65). Scholarly Resources.

Tinker Salas, M. (2009). Oil, race, labor, and nationalism. In *The Enduring Legacy: Oil, Culture, and Society in Venezuela* (pp. 107–141). Duke University Press.

Tinker Salas, M. (2015). Life in a Venezuelan oil camp. *ReVista: Harvard Review of Latin America*, 15(1), 46–50.

Toh, S. M. and DeNisi, A. S. (2003). Host country national reactions to expatriate pay policies: A model and implications. *Academy of Management Review*, 28(4), 606–621. DOI: 10.5465/AMR.2003.10899387.

Torpey, J. (2000). *The Invention of the Passport: Surveillance, Citizenship and the State*. Cambridge University Press.

Tremayne, S. (1984). Shell wives in limbo. In H. Callan and S. Ardener (eds), *The Incorporated Wife* (pp. 120–134). Croom Helm.

Trimmer, J. G. (1980). The rewards and compensation for expatriates in the 1980s. *Management Decision*, 18(6), 342–347.

Tsurumi, Y. (1978). The best of times and the worst of times: Japanese management in America. *Columbia Journal of World Business*, 13(2), 56–61.

Tung, R. (1998). American expatriates abroad: From neophytes to cosmopolitans. *Journal of World Business*, 33(2), 125–144.

United Nations (2022). UN Careers. Available at https://careers.un.org/lbw/home.aspx?viewtype=SC [Accessed 1 March 2022].

United Nations, Department of Economic and Social Affairs (UN DESA) (2002). *International Migration Report 2002*. ST/ESA/SER.A/220. United Nations Department of Economic and Social Affairs.

United Nations, Department of Economic and Social Affairs, Population Division (UN DESA) (2019). *International Migrant Stock 2019: Country Profile United Arab Emirates*. Available at www.un.org/en/development/desa/population/migration/data/estimates2/countryprofiles.asp [Accessed 7 July 2022].

Urry, J. (1999). *Sociology Beyond Societies: Mobilities for the Twenty-First Century* (1st edition). Routledge.

Uusihakala, K. (1999). From impulsive adventure to postcolonial commitment: Making white identity in contemporary Kenya. *European Journal of Cultural Studies*, 2(1), 27–45.

Vaiman, V., Haslberger, A. and Vance, C. (2015). Recognizing the important role of self-initiated expatriates in effective global talent management. *Human Resource Management Review*, 25(3), 280–286.

Valentine, D. (2007). *Imagining Transgender: An Ethnography of a Category*. Duke University Press.

van Bochove, M. and Engbersen, G. (2013). Beyond cosmopolitanism and expat bubbles: Challenging dominant representations of knowledge workers and trailing spouses. *Population, Space and Place*, 21(4), 295–309.

van Bochove, M., Rusinovic, K. and Engbersen, G. (2011). *On the Red Carpet: Expats in Rotterdam and The Hague*. Erasmus University Rotterdam. Available at https://repub.eur.nl/pub/33097/metis_176261.pdf [Accessed 8 July 2022].

van den Bergh, R. and Du Plessis, Y. (2012). Highly skilled migrant women: A career development framework. *Journal of Management Development*, 31(2), 142–158.

Van Overstraten Kruysse, M. P. C. (1985). Graduate manpower requirements for a large multinational group of companies. *European Journal of Engineering Education*, 10(1), 7–9. DOI: 10.1080/03043798508939204.

Vinnai, V. (1974). The creation of an African civil service in Kenya. *Verfassung in Recht Und Übersee*, 7(2), 175–188.

Virdee, S. (2019). Racialized capitalism: An account of its contested origins and consolidation. *Sociological Review*, 67(1), 3–27.

Vitalis, R. (2009). *America's Kingdom: Mythmaking on the Saudi Oil Frontier*. Verso.

Vivian, J. (1968). Expatriate executives – overpaid but undercompensated. *Columbia Journal of World Business*, 3(1), 29–40.

wa Thiong'o, N. (1986). *Decolonising the Mind: The Politics of Language in African Literature*. East African Educational Publishers.

wa Thiong'o, N. (2012). *Globalectics*. Columbia University Press.

Wald, P. M. and Lang, R. (2012). Reorganization of HRM – past, present, and future. In W. J. Rothwell and G. M. (Bud) Benscoter (eds), *The Encyclopedia of Human Resource Management: Thematic Essays, Vol. 3* (pp. 173–180). Pfeiffer (Wiley).

Wallace, W. J. (1959). How to maintain productive working relationships with overseas managers. *International Executive*, 1(2), 17–18. DOI: 10.1002/tie.5060010209.

Walsh, K. (2006). 'Dad says I'm tied to a shooting star!' Grounding (research on) British expatriate belonging. *Area*, 38(3), 268–278.

Walsh, K. (2010). Negotiating migrant status in the emerging global city: Britons in Dubai. *Encounters*, 2, 235–255.

Walsh, K. (2011). Migrant masculinities and domestic space: British home-making practices in Dubai. *Transactions of the Institute of British Geographers*, 36(4), 516–529.

Walsh, K. (2012). Emotion and migration: British transnationals in Dubai. *Environment and Planning D: Society and Space*, 30(1), 43–59.

Walters, W. (2015). Reflections on migration and governmentality. *Movements: Journal Für Kritische Migrations- Und Grenzregimeforschung*, 1(1), 1–25.

Wasserman, G. (1974). European settlers and Kenya colony thoughts on a conflicted affair. *African Studies Review*, 17(2), 425–434. DOI: 10.2307/523642.

Waterfield, B. (2013). Rotterdam and The Hague rebel against EU immigrant influx. *Telegraph*, 9 December. Available at www.telegraph.co.uk/news/worldnews/europe/eu/10506248/Rotterdam-and-The-Hague-rebel-against-EU-immigrant-influx.html [Accessed 7 November 2022].

Weiss, A. (2005). The transnationalization of social inequality: Conceptualizing social positions on a world scale. *Current Sociology*, 53(4), 707–728.

Wekker, G. (2016). *White Innocence: Paradoxes of Colonialism and Race.* Duke University Press.

Werlin, H. H. (1973). Review of 'Development Administration: The Kenyan Experience'. *American Political Science Review*, 67(1), 253–255.

White, S. (2002). Thinking race, thinking development. *Third World Quarterly*, 23(3), 407–419. DOI: 10.1080/01436590220138358.

White, W. and McGowan, J. (1977). Expatriate compensation at the crossroads. *Advanced Management Journal*, 42(4), 14–23.

Whyte, W. (2013 [1956]). *The Organization Man.* University of Pennsylvania Press.

Wilkins, M. (1966). The businessman abroad. *Annals of the American Academy of Political and Social Science*, 368, 83–94.

Williams, P. (1964). *British Aid – 4 Technical Assistance: A Factual Survey of Britain's Aid to Overseas Development through Technical Assistance* (2nd edition). The Overseas Development Institute Ltd (ODI). Available at https://odi.org/en/publications/technical-assistance-a-factual-survey-of-britains-aid-to-overseas-development-through-technical-assistance/ [Accessed 8 July 2022].

Williams, W., Moeller, M. and Harvey, M. (2010). Inpatriates' adjustment to home country headquarters: A social/cultural conundrum. *Leadership & Organization Development Journal*, 31(1), 71–93.

Wilson, K. (2012). *Race, Racism and Development: Interrogating History, Discourse and Practice.* Zed Books.

Wimmer, A. (2009). Herder's heritage and the boundary-making approach: Studying ethnicity in immigrant societies. *Sociological Theory*, 27(3), 244–270.

Wimmer, A. and Glick Schiller, N. (2002). Methodological nationalism and beyond: Nation–state building, migration and the social sciences. *Global Networks*, 2(4), 301–334. DOI: 10.1111/1471-0374.00043.

Wimmer, A. and Glick Schiller, N. (2003). Methodological nationalism, the social sciences, and the study of migration: An essay in historical epistemology. *International Migration Review*, 37(3), 576–610.

Winant, H. (2001). *The World is a Ghetto: Race and Democracy since World War II.* Basic Books.

Wittgenstein, L. (1953). *Philosophical Investigations.* Macmillan.

Woodhams, F. (2013). Expat stereotypes – Jack the Kenya cowboy. *Telegraph*, 27 August. Available at www.telegraph.co.uk/expat/expatlife/10252226/

Expat-stereotypes-Jack-the-Kenya-cowboy.html [Accessed 7 February 2022].

Wrench, J. and Solomos, J. (1993). *Racism and Migration in Western Europe.* Berg.

Yan, H., Sautman, B. and Lu, Y. (2019). Chinese and 'Self-Segregation' in Africa. *Asian Ethnicity*, 20(1), 40–66. DOI: 10.1080/14631369.2018.1511370.

Yanow, D. and van der Haar, M. (2013). People out of place: Allochthony and autochthony in the Netherlands' identity discourse – metaphors and categories in action. *Journal of International Relations and Development*, 16(2), 227–261.

Yeoh, B. (2006). Bifurcated labour: The unequal incorporation of transmigrants in Singapore. *Tijdschrift Voor Economische En Sociale Geografie*, 97(1), 26–37.

Yeoh, B. and Khoo, L. (1998). Home, work and community: Skilled international migration and expatriate women in Singapore. *International Migration*, 36(2), 159–186.

Yeoh, B. and Willis, K. (2005). Singaporeans in China: Transnational women elites and the negotiation of gendered identities. *Geoforum*, 36(2), 211–222.

Yeung, H. W. (1998). Capital, state and space: Contesting the borderless world. *Transactions of the Institute of British Geographers*, 23(3), 291–309. DOI: 10.1111/j.0020-2754.1998.00291.x.

Yijälä, A., Jasinskaja-Lahti, I., Likki, T. and Stein, D. (2012). Pre-migration adaptation of highly skilled self-initiated foreign employees: The case of an EU agency. *International Journal of Human Resource Management*, 23(4), 759–778.

Yoshi, T. (1978). The best of times and the worst of times: Japanese management in America. *Columbia Journal of World Business*, 13(2), 56–61.

Young, D. (1973). Fair compensation for expatriates. *Harvard Business Review*, 51(4), 117–126.

Youssef, S. M. (1973). The integration of local nationals into the managerial hierarchy of American overseas subsidiaries. *International Executive*, 15(2), 18–20. DOI: 10.1002/tie.5060150211.

Zeira, Y. (1976). Rotation of expatriates in MNCs. *Management International Review*, 16(3), 37–46.

Zeira, Y., Harari, E. and Nundi, D. I. (1975). Some structural and cultural factors in ethnocentric multinational corporations and employee morale. *Journal of Management Studies*, 12(1–2), 66–82.

Index

EU authorised representative for GPSR:
Easy Access System Europe, Mustamäe tee 50,
10621 Tallinn, Estonia
gpsr.requests@easproject.com

www.ingramcontent.com/pod-product-compliance
Lightning Source LLC
Chambersburg PA
CBHW071015280326
41935CB00011B/1358